GENTLE MEASURES

By

JACOB ABBOTT

CHAPTER I.

THE THREE MODES OF MANAGEMENT.

It is not impossible that in the minds of some persons the idea of employing gentle measures in the management and training of children may seem to imply the abandonment of the principle of *authority*, as the basis of the parental government, and the substitution of some weak and inefficient system of artifice and manoeuvring in its place. To suppose that the object of this work is to aid in effecting such a substitution as that, is entirely to mistake its nature and design. The only government of the parent over the child that is worthy of the name is one of authority—complete, absolute, unquestioned *authority*. The object of this work is, accordingly, not to show how the gentle methods which will be brought to view can be employed as a substitute for such authority, but how they can be made to aid in establishing and maintaining it.

Three Methods.

There are three different modes of management customarily employed by parents as means of inducing their children to comply with their requirements. They are,

1. Government by Manoeuvring and Artifice.

2. By Reason and Affection.

3. By Authority.

Manoeuvring and Artifice.

1. Many mothers manage their children by means of tricks and contrivances, more or less adroit, designed to avoid direct issues with them, and to beguile them, as it were, into compliance with their wishes. As, for example, where a mother, recovering from sickness, is going out to take the air with her husband for the first time, and—as she is still feeble—wishes for a very quiet drive, and so concludes not to take little Mary with her, as she usually does on such occasions; but knowing that if Mary sees the chaise at the door, and discovers that her father and mother are going in it, she will be very eager to go too, she adopts a system of manoeuvres to conceal her design. She brings down her bonnet and shawl by stealth, and before the chaise comes to the door she sends Mary out into the garden with her sister, under pretense of showing her a bird's nest which is not there, trusting to her sister's skill in diverting the child's mind, and amusing her with something else in the garden, until the chaise has gone. And if, either from hearing the sound of the wheels, or from any other cause, Mary's suspicions are awakened—and children habitually managed on these principles soon learn to be extremely distrustful and suspicious—and she insists on going into the house, and thus discovers the stratagem, then, perhaps, her mother tells her that they are only going to the doctor's, and that if Mary goes with them, the doctor will give her some dreadful medicine, and compel her to take it, thinking thus to deter her from insisting on going with them to ride.

As the chaise drives away, Mary stands bewildered and perplexed on the door-step, her mind in a tumult of excitement, in which hatred of the doctor, distrust and suspicion of her mother, disappointment, vexation, and ill humor, surge and swell among those delicate organizations on which the structure and development of the soul so closely depend—doing perhaps an irreparable injury. The mother, as soon as the chaise is so far turned that Mary can no longer watch the expression of her countenance, goes away from the door with a smile of complacency and satisfaction upon her face at the ingenuity and success of her little artifice.

In respect to her statement that she was going to the doctor's, it may, or may not, have been true. Most likely not; for mothers who manage their children on this system find the line of demarkation between deceit and falsehood so vague and ill defined that they soon fall into the habit of disregarding it altogether, and of saying, without hesitation, any thing which will serve the purpose in view.

Governing by Reason and Affection.

2. The theory of many mothers is that they must govern their children by the influence of reason and affection. Their method may be exemplified by supposing that, under circumstances similar to those described under the preceding head, the mother calls Mary to her side, and, smoothing her hair caressingly with her hand while she speaks, says to her,

"Mary, your father and I are going out to ride this afternoon, and I am going to explain it all to you why you can not go too. You see, I have been sick, and am getting well, and I am going out to ride, so that I may get well faster. You love mamma, I am sure, and wish to have her get well soon. So you will be a good girl, I know, and not make any trouble, but will stay at home contentedly—won't you? Then I shall love you, and your papa will love you, and after I get well we will take you to ride with us some day."

The mother, in managing the case in this way, relies partly on convincing the reason of the child, and partly on an appeal to her affection.

Governing by Authority.

3. By the third method the mother secures the compliance of the child by a direct exercise of authority. She says to her—the circumstances of the case being still supposed to be the same—

"Mary, your father and I are going out to ride this afternoon, and I am sorry, for your sake, that we can not take you with us."

"Why can't you take me?" asks Mary.

"I can not tell you why, now," replies the mother, "but perhaps I will explain it to you after I come home. I think there *is* a good reason, and, at any rate, I have decided that you are not to go. If you are a good girl, and do not make any difficulty, you can have your little chair out upon the front door-step, and can see the chaise come to the door, and see your father and me get in and drive away; and you can wave your handkerchief to us for a good-bye."

Then, if she observes any expression of discontent or insubmission in Mary's countenance, the mother would add,

"If you should *not* be a good girl, but should show signs of making us any trouble, I shall have to send you out somewhere to the back part of the house until we are gone."

But this last supposition is almost always unnecessary; for if Mary has been habitually managed on this principle she will *not* make any trouble. She will perceive at once that the question is settled—settled irrevocably—and especially that it is entirely beyond the power of any demonstrations of insubmission or rebellion that she can make to change it. She will acquiesce at once.[A] She may be sorry that she can not go, but she will make no resistance. Those children only attempt to carry their points by noisy and violent demonstrations who find, by experience, that such measures are usually successful. A child, even, who has become once accustomed to them, will soon drop them if she finds, owing to a change in the system of management, that they now never succeed. And a child who never, from the beginning, finds any efficiency in them, never learns to employ them at all.

Conclusion.

Of the three methods of managing children exemplified in this chapter, the last is the only one which can be followed either with comfort to the parent or safety to the child; and to show how this method can be brought effectually into operation by gentle measures is the object of this book. It is, indeed, true that the importance of tact and skill in the training of the young, and of cultivating their reason, and securing their affection, can not be overrated. But the influences secured by these means form, at the best, but a sandy foundation for filial obedience to rest upon. The child is not to be made to comply with the requirements of his parents by being artfully inveigled into compliance, nor is his obedience to rest on his love for father and mother, and his unwillingness to displease them, nor on his conviction of the rightfulness and reasonableness of their commands, but on simple *submission to authority*—that absolute and almost unlimited authority which all parents are commissioned by God and nature to exercise over their offspring during the period while the offspring remain dependent upon their care.

CHAPTER II.

WHAT ARE GENTLE MEASURES?

It being thus distinctly understood that the gentle measures in the training of children herein recommended are not to be resorted to as a *substitute* for parental authority, but as the easiest and most effectual means of establishing and maintaining that authority in its most absolute form, we have now to consider what the nature of these gentle measures is, and by what characteristics they are distinguished, in their action and influence, from such as may be considered more or less violent and harsh.

Gentle measures are those which tend to exert a calming, quieting, and soothing influence on the mind, or to produce only such excitements as are pleasurable in their character, as means of repressing wrong and encouraging right action. Ungentle measures are those which tend to inflame and irritate the mind, or to agitate it with *painful* excitements.

Three Degrees of Violence.

There seem to be three grades or forms of violence to which a mother may resort in controlling her children, or, perhaps, rather three classes of measures which are more or less violent in their effects. To illustrate these we will take an example.

Case supposed.

One day Louisa, four years old, asked her mother for an apple. "Have you had any already?" asked her mother.

"Only one," replied Louisa. "Then Bridget may give you another," said the mother.

What Louisa said was not true. She had already eaten two apples. Bridget heard the falsehood, but she did not consider it her duty to betray the child, so she said nothing. The mother, however, afterwards, in the course of the day, accidentally ascertained the truth.

Now, as we have said, there are three grades in the kind and character of the measures which may be considered violent that a mother may resort to in a case like this.

Bodily Punishment.

1. First, there is the infliction of bodily pain. The child may be whipped, or tied to the bed-post, and kept in a constrained and uncomfortable position for a long time, or shut up in solitude and darkness, or punished by the infliction of bodily suffering in other ways.

And there is no doubt that there is a tendency in such treatment to correct or cure the fault. But measures like these, whether successful or not, are certainly violent measures. They shock the whole nervous system, sometimes with the excitement of pain and terror, and always, probably, with that of resentment and anger. In some cases this excitement is extreme. The excessively delicate organization of the brain, through which such agitations reach the sensorium, and which, in children of an early age, is in its most tender and sensitive state of development, is subjected to a most intense and violent agitation.

Evil Effects of Violence in this Form.

The evil effects of this excessive cerebral action may *perhaps* entirely pass away in a few hours, and leave no trace of injury behind; but then, on the other hand, there is certainly reason to fear that such commotions, especially if often repeated, tend to impede the regular and healthful development of the organs, and that they may become the origin of derangements, or of actual disorganizations, resulting very seriously in future years. It is impossible, perhaps, to know with certainty whether permanent ill effects follow in such cases or not. At any rate, such a remedy is a violent one.

The Frightening System.

2. There is a second grade of violence in the treatment of such a case, which consists in exciting pain or terror, or other painful or disagreeable emotions, through the imagination, by presenting to the fancy of the child images of phantoms, hobgoblins, and other frightful monsters, whose ire, it is pretended, is greatly excited by the misdeeds of children, and who come in the night-time to take them away, or otherwise visit them with terrible retribution. Domestic servants are very prone to adopt this mode of discipline. Being forbidden to resort to personal violence as a means of exciting pain and terror, they attempt to accomplish the same end by other means, which, however, in many respects, are still more injurious in their action.

Management of Nurses and Servants.

Nurses and attendants upon children from certain nationalities in Europe are peculiarly disposed to employ this method of governing children placed under their care. One reason is that they are accustomed to this mode of management at home; and another is that many of them are brought up under an idea, which prevails extensively in some of those countries, that it is right to tell falsehoods where the honest object is to accomplish a charitable or useful end. Accordingly, inasmuch as the restraining of the children from wrong is a good and useful object, they can declare the existence of giants and hobgoblins, to carry away and devour bad girls and boys, with an air of positiveness and seeming honesty, and with a calm and persistent assurance, which aids them very much in producing on the minds of the children a conviction of the truth of what they say; while, on the other hand, those who, in theory at least, occupy the position that the direct falsifying of one's word is *never* justifiable, act at a disadvantage in attempting this method. For although, in practice, they are often inclined to make an exception to their principles in regard to truth in the case of what is said to young children, they can not, after all, tell children what they know to be not true with that bold and confident air necessary to carry full conviction to the children's minds. They are embarrassed by a kind of half guilty feeling, which, partially at least, betrays them, and the children do not really and fully believe what they say. They can not suppose that their mother would really tell them what she knew was false, and yet they can not help perceiving that she does not speak and look as if what she was saying was actually true.

Monsieur and Madame Croquemitaine.

In all countries there are many, among even the most refined and highly cultivated classes, who are not at all embarrassed by any moral delicacy of this kind. This is especially the case in those countries in Europe, particularly on the Continent, where the idea above referred to, of the allowableness of falsehood in certain cases as a means for the attainment of a good end, is generally entertained. The French have two terrible bugbears, under the names of Monsieur and Madame Croquemitaine, who are as familiar to the imaginations of French children as Santa Claus is, in a much more agreeable way, to the juvenile fancy at our firesides. Monsieur and Madame Croquemitaine are frightful monsters, who come down the chimney, or through the roof, at night, and carry off bad children. They learn from their *little fingers*—which whisper in their ears when they hold them near—who the bad children are, where they live, and what they have done. The instinctive faith of young children in their mother's truthfulness is so strong that no absurdity seems gross enough to overcome it.

The Black Man and the Policeman.

There are many mothers among us who—though not quite prepared to call in the aid of ghosts, giants, and hobgoblins, or of Monsieur and Madame Croquemitaine, in managing their children—still, sometimes, try to eke out their failing authority by threatening them with the "black man," or the "policeman," or some other less, supernatural terror. They seem to imagine that inasmuch as, while there is no such thing in existence as a hobgoblin, there really are policemen and prisons, they only half tell an untruth by saying to the recalcitrant little one that a policeman is coming to carry him off to jail.

Injurious Effects.

Although, by these various modes of exciting imaginary fears, there is no direct and outward infliction of bodily suffering, the effect produced on the delicate organization of the brain by such excitements is violent in the extreme. The paroxysms of agitation and terror which they sometimes excite, and which are often spontaneously renewed by darkness and solitude, and by other exciting causes, are of the nature of temporary insanity. Indeed, the extreme nervous excitability which they produce sometimes becomes a real insanity, which, though it may, in many cases, be finally outgrown, may probably in many others lead to lasting and most deplorable results.

Harsh Reproofs and Threatenings.

3. There is a third mode of treatment, more common, perhaps, among *us* than either of the preceding, which, though much milder in its character than they, we still class among the violent measures, on account of its operation and effects. It consists of stern and harsh rebukes, denunciations of the heinousness of the sin of falsehood, with solemn premonitions of the awful consequences of it, in this life and in that to come, intended to awaken feelings of alarm and distress in the mind of the child, as a means of promoting repentance and reformation. These are not violent measures, it is true, so far as outward physical action is concerned; but the effects which they produce are sometimes of quite a violent nature, in their operation on the delicate nervous and mental susceptibilities which are excited and agitated by them. If the mother is successful in making the impression which such a mode of treatment is designed to produce, the child, especially if a girl, is agitated and distressed. Her nervous system is greatly disturbed. If calmed for a

time, the paroxysm is very liable to return. She wakes in the night, perhaps, with an indefinable feeling of anxiety and terror, and comes to her mother's bedside, to seek, in her presence, and in the sense of protection which it affords, a relief from her distress.

The conscientious mother, supremely anxious to secure the best interests of her child, may say that, after all, it is better that she should endure this temporary suffering than not be saved from the sin. This is true. But if she can be saved just as effectually without it, it is better still.

The Gentle Method of Treatment.

4. We now come to the gentle measures which may be adopted in a case of discipline like this. They are endlessly varied in form, but, to illustrate the nature and operation of them, and the spirit and temper of mind with which they should be enforced, with a view of communicating; to the mind of the reader some general idea of the characteristics of that gentleness of treatment which it is the object of this work to commend, we will describe an actual case, substantially as it really occurred, where a child, whom we will still call Louisa, told her mother a falsehood about the apple, as already related.

Choosing the Right Time.

Her mother—though Louisa's manner, at the time of giving her answer, led her to feel somewhat suspicious—did not express her suspicions, but gave her the additional apple. Nor did she afterwards, when she ascertained the facts, say any thing on the subject. The day passed away as if nothing unusual had occurred. When bed-time came she undressed the child and laid her in her bed, playing with her, and talking with her in an amusing manner all the time, so as to bring her into a contented and happy frame of mind, and to establish as close a connection as possible of affection and sympathy between them. Then, finally, when the child's prayer had been said, and she was about to be left for the night, her mother, sitting in a chair at the head of her little bed, and putting her hand lovingly upon her, said:

The Story.

"But first I must tell you one more little story.

"Once there was a boy, and his name was Ernest. He was a pretty large boy, for he was five years old."

Louisa, it must be recollected, was only four.

"He was a very pretty boy. He had bright blue eyes and curling hair. He was a very good boy, too. He did not like to do any thing wrong. He always found that it made him feel uncomfortable and unhappy afterwards when he did any thing wrong. A good many children, especially good children, find that it makes them feel uncomfortable and unhappy when they do wrong. Perhaps you do."

"Yes, mamma, I do," said Louisa.

"I am glad of that," replied her mother; "that is a good sign."

"Ernest went one day," added the mother, continuing her story, "with his little cousin Anna to their uncle's, in hopes that he would give them some apples. Their uncle had a beautiful garden, and in it there was an apple-tree which bore most excellent apples. They were large, and rosy, and mellow, and sweet. The children liked the apples from that tree very much, and Ernest and Anna went that day in hopes that their uncle would give them some of them. He said he would. He would give them three apiece. He told them to go into the garden and wait there until he came. They must not take any apples off the tree, he said, but if they found any *under* the tree they might take them, provided that there were not more than three apiece; and when he came he would take enough off the tree, he said, to make up the number to three.

"So the children went into the garden and looked under the tree. They found *two* apples there, and they took them up and ate them—one apiece. Then they sat down and began to wait for their uncle to come. While they were waiting Anna proposed that they should not tell their uncle that they had found the two apples, and so he would give them three more, which he would take from the tree; whereas, if he knew that they had already had one apiece, then he would only give them two more. Ernest said that his uncle would ask them about it. Anna said, 'No matter, we can tell him that we did not find any.'

"Ernest seemed to be thinking about it for a moment, and then, shaking his head, said, 'No, I think we had better not tell him a lie!'

"So when he saw their uncle coming he said, 'Come, Anna, let us go and tell him about it, just how it was. So they ran together to meet their uncle, and told him that they had found two apples under the tree, one apiece, and had eaten them. Then he gave them two more apiece, according to his promise, and they went home feeling contented and happy.

"They might have had one more apple apiece, probably, by combining together to tell a falsehood; but in that case they would have gone home feeling guilty and unhappy."

The Effect.

Louisa's mother paused a moment, after finishing her story, to give Louisa time to think about it a little.

"I think," she added at length, after a suitable pause, "that it was a great deal better for them to tell the truth, as they did."

"I think so too, mamma," said Louisa, at the same time casting down her eyes and looking a little confused.

"But you know," added her mother, speaking in a very kind and gentle tone, "that you did not tell me the truth to-day about the apple that Bridget gave you."

Louisa paused a moment, looked in her mother's face, and then, reaching up to put her arms around her mother's neck, she said,

"Mamma, I am determined never to tell you another wrong story as long as I live."

Only a Single Lesson, after all.

Now it is not at all probable that if the case had ended here, Louisa would have kept her promise. This was one good lesson, it is true, but it was only *one*. And the lesson was given by a method so gentle, that no nervous, cerebral, or mental function was in any degree irritated or morbidly excited by it. Moreover, no one who knows any thing of the workings of the infantile mind can doubt that the impulse in the right direction given by this conversation was not only better in character, but was greater in amount, than could have been effected by either of the other methods of management previously described.

How Gentle Measures operate.

By the gentle measures, then, which are to be here discussed and recommended, are meant such as do not react in a violent and irritating manner, in any way, upon the extremely delicate, and almost embryonic condition of the cerebral and nervous organization, in which the gradual development of the mental and moral faculties are so intimately involved. They do not imply any, the least, relaxation of the force of parental authority, or any lowering whatever of the standards of moral obligation, but are, on the contrary, the most effectual, the surest and the safest way of establishing the one and of enforcing the other.

CHAPTER III.

THERE MUST BE AUTHORITY.

The first duty which devolves upon the mother in the training of her child is the establishment of her *authority* over him—that is, the forming in him the habit of immediate, implicit, and unquestioning obedience to all her commands. And the first step to be taken, or, rather, perhaps the first essential condition required for the performance of this duty, is the fixing of the conviction in her own mind that it *is* a duty.

Unfortunately, however, there are not only vast numbers of mothers who do not in any degree perform this duty, but a large proportion of them have not even a theoretical idea of the obligation of it.

An Objection.

"I wish my child to be governed by reason and reflection," says one. "I wish him to see the *necessity* and *propriety* of what I require of him, so that he may render a ready and willing compliance with my wishes, instead of being obliged blindly to submit to arbitrary and despotic power."

She forgets that the faculties of reason and reflection, and the power of appreciating "the necessity and propriety of things," and of bringing considerations of future, remote, and perhaps contingent good and evil to restrain and subdue the impetuousness of appetites and passions eager for present pleasure, are qualities that appear late, and are very slowly developed, in the infantile mind; that no real reliance whatever can be placed upon them in the early years of life; and that, moreover, one of the chief and expressly intended objects of the establishment of the parental relation is to provide, in the mature reason and reflection of the father and mother, the means of guidance which the embryo reason and reflection of the child could not afford during the period of his immaturity.

The two great Elements of Parental Obligation.

Indeed, the chief end and aim of the parental relation, as designed by the Author of nature, may be considered as comprised, it would seem, in these two objects, namely: first, the *support* of the child by the *strength* of his parents during the period necessary for the development of *his* strength, and, secondly, his guidance and direction by their *reason* during the development of his reason. The second of these obligations is no less imperious than the first. To expect him to provide the means of his support from the resources of his own embryo strength, would imply no greater misapprehension on the part of his father and mother than to look for the exercise of any really controlling influence over his conduct by his embryo reason. The expectation in the two cases would be equally vain. The only difference would be that, in the failure which would inevitably result from the trial, it would be in the one case the body that would suffer, and in the other the soul.

The Judgment more slowly developed than the Strength.

Indeed, the necessity that the conduct of the child should be controlled by the reason of the parents is in one point of view greater, or at least more protracted, than that his wants should be supplied by their power; for the development of the thinking and reasoning powers is late and slow in comparison with the advancement toward maturity of the physical powers. It is considered that a boy attains, in this country, to a sufficient degree of strength at the age of from *seven to ten* years to earn his living; but his reason is not sufficiently mature to make it safe to intrust him with the care of himself and of his affairs, in the judgment of the law, till he is of more than twice that age. The parents can actually thus sooner look to the *strength* of the child for his support than they can to his *reason* for his guidance.

What Parents have to do in Respect to the Reasoning Powers of Children.

To aid in the development and cultivation of the thinking and reasoning powers is doubtless a very important part of a parent's duty. But to cultivate these faculties is one thing, while to make any control which may be procured for them over the mind of the child the basis of government, is another. To explain the reasons of our commands is excellent, if it is done in the right time and manner. The wrong time is when the question of obedience is pending, and the wrong manner is when they are offered as inducements to obey. We may offer reasons for *recommendations*, when we leave the child to judge of their force, and to act according to our recommendations or not, as his judgment shall dictate. But reasons should never be given as inducements to obey a command. The more completely the obedience to a command rests on the principle of simple submission to authority, the easier and better it will be both for parent and child.

Manner of exercising Authority.

Let no reader fall into the error of supposing that the mother's making her authority the basis of her government renders it necessary for her to assume a stern and severe aspect towards her children, in her intercourse with them; or to issue her commands in a harsh, abrupt, and imperious manner; or always to refrain from explaining, at the time, the reasons for a command or a prohibition. The more gentle the manner, and the more kind and courteous the tones in which the mother's wishes are expressed, the better, provided only that the wishes, however expressed, are really the mandates of an authority which is to be yielded to at once without question or delay. She may say, "Mary, will you please to leave your doll and take this letter for me into the library to your father?" or, "Johnny, in five minutes it will be time for you to put your blocks away to go to bed; I will tell you when the time is out;" or, "James, look at the clock"—to call his attention to the fact that the time is arrived for him to go to school. No matter, in a word, under how mild and gentle a form the mother's commands are given, provided only that the children are trained to understand that they are at once to be obeyed.

A second Objection.

Another large class of mothers are deterred from making any efficient effort to establish their authority over their children for fear of thereby alienating their affections. "I wish my child to love me," says a mother of this class. "That is the supreme and never-ceasing wish of my heart; and if I am continually thwarting and constraining her by my authority, she will soon learn to consider me an obstacle to her happiness, and I shall become an object of her aversion and dislike."

There is some truth, no doubt, in this statement thus expressed, but it is not applicable to the case, for the reason that there is no need whatever for a mother's "continually thwarting and constraining" her children in her efforts to establish her authority over them. The love which they will feel for her will depend in a great measure upon the degree in which she sympathizes and takes part with them in their occupations, their enjoyments, their disappointments, and their sorrows, and in which she indulges their child-like desires. The love, however, awakened by these means will be not weakened nor endangered, but immensely strengthened and confirmed, by the exercise on her part of a just and equable, but firm and absolute, authority. This must always be true so long as a feeling of respect for the object of affection tends to strengthen, and not to weaken, the sentiment of love. The mother who does not govern her children is bringing them up not to love her, but to despise her.

Effect of Authority.

If, besides being their playmate, their companion, and friend, indulgent in respect to all their harmless fancies, and patient and forbearing with their childish faults and foolishness, she also exercises in cases requiring it an authority over them which, though just and gentle, is yet absolute and supreme, she rises to a very exalted position in their view. Their affection for her has infused into it an element which greatly aggrandizes and ennobles it—an element somewhat analogous to that sentiment of lofty devotion which a loyal subject feels for his queen.

Effect of the Want of Authority.

On the other hand, if she is inconsiderate enough to attempt to win a place in her children's hearts by the sacrifice of her maternal authority, she will never succeed in securing a place there that is worth possessing. The children will all, girls and boys alike, see and understand her weakness, and they will soon learn to look down upon her, instead of looking up to her, as they ought. As they grow older they will all become more and more unmanageable. The insubordination of the girls must generally be endured, but that of the boys will in time grow to be intolerable, and it will become necessary to send them away to school, or to adopt some other plan for ridding the house of their turbulence, and relieving the poor mother's heart of the insupportable burden she has to bear in finding herself contemned and trampled upon by her own children. In the earlier years of life the feeling entertained for their mother in such a case by the children is simply that of contempt; for the sentiment of gratitude which will modify it in time is very late to be developed, and has not yet begun to act. In later years, however, when the boys have become young men, this sentiment of gratitude begins to come in, but it only changes the contempt into pity. And when years have passed away, and the mother is perhaps in her grave, her sons think of her with a mingled feeling excited by the conjoined remembrance of her helpless imbecility and of her true maternal love, and say to each other, with a smile, "Poor dear mother! what a time she had of it trying to govern us boys!"

If a mother is willing to have her children thus regard her with contempt pure and simple while they are children, and with contempt transformed into pity by the infusion of a tardy sentiment of gratitude, when they are grown, she may try the plan of endeavoring to secure their love by *indulging* them without *governing* them. But if she sets her heart on being the object through life of their respectful love, she may indulge them as much as she pleases; but she *must govern* them.

Indulgence.

A great deal is said sometimes about the evils of indulgence in the management of children; and so far as the condemnation refers only to indulgence in what is injurious or evil, it is doubtless very just. But the harm is not in the indulgence itself—that is, in the act of affording gratification to the child—but in the injurious or dangerous nature of the things indulged in. It seems to me that children are not generally indulged enough. They are thwarted and restrained in respect to the gratification of their harmless wishes a great deal too much. Indeed, as a general rule, the more that children are gratified in respect to their childish fancies and impulses, and even their caprices, when no evil or danger is to be apprehended, the better.

When, therefore, a child asks, "May I do this?" or, "May I do that?" the question for the mother to consider is not whether the thing proposed is a wise or a foolish thing to do—that is, whether it would be wise or foolish for *her*, if she, with her ideas and feelings, were in the place of the child—but only whether there is any harm or danger in it; and if not, she should give her ready and cordial consent.

Antagonism between Free Indulgence and Absolute Control.

There is no necessary antagonism, nor even any inconsistency, between the freest indulgence of children and the maintenance of the most absolute authority over them. Indeed, the authority can be most easily established in connection with great liberality of indulgence. At any rate, it will be very evident, on reflection, that the two principles do not stand at all in opposition to each other, as is often vaguely supposed. Children may be greatly indulged, and yet perfectly governed. On the other hand, they may be continually checked and thwarted, and their lives made miserable by a continued succession of vexations, restrictions, and refusals, and yet not be governed at all. An example will, however, best illustrate this.

Mode of Management with Louisa.

A mother, going to the village by a path across the fields, proposed to her little daughter Louisa to go with her for a walk.

Louisa asked if she might invite her Cousin Mary to go too. "Yes," said her mother; "I *think* she is not at home; but you can go and see, if you like."

Louisa went to see, and returned in a few minutes, saying that Mary was *not* at home.

"Never mind," replied her mother; "it was polite in you to wish to invite her."

They set out upon the walk. Louisa runs hither and thither over the grass, returning continually to her mother to bring her flowers and curiosities. Her mother looks at them all, seems to approve of, and to sympathize in, Louisa's wonder and delight, and even points out new charms in the objects which she brings to her, that Louisa had not observed.

At length Louisa spied a butterfly.

"Mother," said she, "here's a butterfly. May I run and catch him?"

"You may try," said her mother.

Louisa ran till she was tired, and then came back to her mother, looking a little disappointed.

"I could not catch him, mother."

"Never mind," said her mother, "you had a good time trying, at any rate. Perhaps you will see another by-and-by. You may possibly see a bird, and you can try and see if you can catch *him*."

So Louisa ran off to play again, satisfied and happy.

A little farther on a pretty tree was growing, not far from the path on one side. A short, half-decayed log lay at the foot of the tree, overtopped and nearly concealed by a growth of raspberry-bushes, grass, and wild flowers.

"Louisa," said the mother, "do you see that tree with the pretty flowers at the foot of it?"

"Yes, mother."

"I would rather not have you go near that tree. Come over to this side of the path, and keep on this side till you get by."

Louisa began immediately to obey, but as she was crossing the path she looked up to her mother and asked why she must not go near the tree.

"I am glad you would like to know why," replied her mother, "and I will tell you the reason as soon as we get past."

Louisa kept on the other side of the path until the tree was left well behind, and then came back to her mother to ask for the promised reason.

"It was because I heard that there was a wasp's nest under that tree," said her mother.

"A wasp's nest!" repeated Louisa, with a look of alarm.

"Yes," rejoined her mother, "and I was afraid that the wasps might sting you."

Louisa paused a moment, and then, looking back towards the tree, said,

"I am glad I did not go near it."

"And I am glad that you obeyed me so readily," said her mother. "I knew you would obey me at once, without my giving any reason. I did not wish to tell you the reason, for fear of frightening you while you were passing by the tree. But I knew that you would obey me without any reason. You always do, and that is why I always like to have you go with me when I take a walk."

Louisa is much gratified by this commendation, and the effect of it, and of the whole incident, in confirming and strengthening the principle of obedience in her heart, is very much greater than rebukes or punishments for any overt act of disobedience could possibly be.

"But, mother," asked Louisa, "how did you know that there was a wasp's nest under that tree?"

"One of the boys told me so," replied her mother.

"And do you really think there is one there?" asked Louisa.

"No," replied her mother, "I do not really think there is. Boys are very apt to imagine such things."

"Then why would you not let me go there?" asked Louisa.

"Because there *might be* one there, and so I thought it safer for you not to go near."

Louisa now left her mother's side and resumed her excursions, running this way and that, in every direction, over the fields, until at length, her strength beginning to fail, she came back to her mother, out of breath, and with a languid air, saying that she was too tired to go any farther.

"I am tired, too," said her mother; "we had better find a place to sit down to rest."

"Where shall we find one?" asked Louisa.

"I see a large stone out there before us a little way," said her mother. "How will that do?"

"I mean to go and try it," said Louisa; and, having seemingly recovered her breath, she ran forward to try the stone. By the time that her mother reached the spot she was ready to go on.

These and similar incidents marked the whole progress of the walk.

We see that in such a case as this firm government and free indulgence are conjoined; and that, far from there being any antagonism between them, they may work together in perfect harmony.

Mode of Management with Hannah.

On the other hand, there may be an extreme limitation in respect to a mother's indulgence of her children, while yet she has no government over them at all. We shall see how this might be by the case of little Hannah.

Hannah was asked by her mother to go with her across the fields to the village under circumstances similar to those of Louisa's invitation, except that the real motive of Hannah's mother, in proposing that Hannah should accompany her, was to have the child's help in bringing home her parcels.

"Yes, mother," said Hannah, in reply to her mother's invitation, "I should like to go; and I will go and ask Cousin Sarah to go too."

"Oh no," rejoined her mother, "why do you wish Sarah to go? She will only be a trouble to us."

"She won't be any trouble at all, mother, and I mean to go and ask her," said Hannah; and, putting on her bonnet, she set off towards the gate.

"No, Hannah," insisted her mother, "you *must not* go. I don't wish to have
Sarah go with us to-day."

Hannah paid no attention to this prohibition, but ran off to find Sarah. After a few minutes she returned, saying that Sarah was not at home.

"I am glad of it," said her mother; "I told you not to go to ask her, and you did very wrong to disobey me. I have a great mind not to let you go yourself."

Hannah ran off in the direction of the path, not caring for the censure or for the threat, knowing well that they would result in nothing.

Her mother followed. When they reached the pastures Hannah began running here and there over the grass.

"Hannah!" said her mother, speaking in a stern and reproachful tone; "what do you keep running about so for all the time, Hannah? You'll get tired out before we get to the village, and then you'll be teasing me to let you stop and rest. Come and walk along quietly with me."

But Hannah paid no attention whatever to this injunction. She ran to and fro among the rocks and clumps of bushes, and once or twice she brought to her mother flowers or other curious things that she found.

"Those things are not good for any thing, child," said her mother. "They are nothing but common weeds and trash. Besides, I told you not to run about so much. Why can't you come and walk quietly along the path, like a sensible person?"

Hannah paid no attention to this reiteration of her mother's command, but continued to run about as before.

"Hannah," repeated her mother, "come back into the path. I have told you again and again that you must come and walk with me, and you don't pay the least heed to what I say. By-and-by you will fall into some hole, or tear your clothes against the bushes, or get pricked with the briers. You must not, at any rate, go a step farther from the path than you are now."

Hannah walked on, looking for flowers and curiosities, and receding farther and farther from the path, for a time, and then returning towards it again, according to her own fancy or caprice, without paying any regard to her mother's directions.

"Hannah," said her mother, "you *must not* go so far away from the path. Then, besides, you are coming to a tree where there is a wasps' nest. You must not go near that tree; if you do, you will get stung."

Hannah went on, looking for flowers, and gradually drawing nearer to the tree.

"Hannah!" exclaimed her mother, "I tell you that you must not go near that tree. You will *certainly* get stung."

Hannah went on—somewhat hesitatingly and cautiously, it is true—towards the foot of the tree, and, seeing no signs of wasps there, she began gathering the flowers that grew at the foot of it.

"Hannah! Hannah!" exclaimed her mother; "I told you not to go near that tree! Get your flowers quick, if you must get them, and come away."

Hannah went on gathering the flowers at her leisure.

"You will *certainly* get stung," said her mother.

"I don't believe there is any hornets' nest here," replied Hannah.

"Wasps' nest," said her mother; "it was a wasps' nest."

"Or wasps' nest either," said Hannah.

"Yes," rejoined her mother, "the boys said there was."

"That's nothing," said Hannah; "the boys think there are wasps' nests in a great many places where there are not any."

After a time Hannah, having gathered all the flowers she wished for, came back at her leisure towards her mother.

"I told you not to go to that tree," said her mother, reproachfully.

"You told me I should certainly get stung if I went there," rejoined Hannah, "and I didn't."

"Well, you *might* have got stung," said her mother, and so walked on.

Pretty soon after this Hannah said that she was tired of walking so far, and wished to stop and rest.

"No," replied her mother, "I told you that you would get tired if you ran about so much; but you would do it, and so now I shall not stop for you at all."

Hannah said that *she* should stop, at any rate; so she sat down upon a log by the way-side. Her mother said that *she* should go on and leave her. So her mother walked on, looking back now and then, and calling Hannah to come. But finding that Hannah did not come, she finally found a place to sit down herself and wait for her.

The Principle illustrated by this Case.

Many a mother will see the image of her own management of her children reflected without exaggeration or distortion in this glass; and, as the former story shows how the freest indulgence is compatible with the maintenance of the most absolute authority, this enables us to see how a perpetual resistance to the impulses and desires of children may co-exist with no government over them at all.

Let no mother fear, then, that the measures necessary to establish for her the most absolute authority over her children will at all curtail her power to promote their happiness. The maintenance of the best possible government over them will not in any way prevent her yielding to them all the harmless gratifications they may desire. She may indulge them in all their childish impulses, fancies, and even caprices, to their heart's content, without at all weakening her authority over them. Indeed, she may make these very indulgences the means of strengthening her authority. But without the authority she can never develop in the hearts of her children the only kind of love that is worth possessing—namely, that in which the feeling of affection is dignified and ennobled by the sentiment of respect.

One more Consideration.

There is one consideration which, if properly appreciated, would have an overpowering influence on the mind of every mother in inducing her to establish and maintain a firm authority over her child during the early years of his life, and that is the possibility that he may not live to reach maturity. Should the terrible calamity befall her of being compelled to follow her boy, yet young, to his grave, the character of her grief, and the degree of distress and anguish which it will occasion her, will depend very much upon the memories which his life and his relations to her have left in her soul. When she returns to her home, bowed down by the terrible burden of her bereavement, and wanders over the now desolated rooms which were the scenes of his infantile occupations and joys, and sees the now useless playthings and books, and the various objects of curiosity and interest with which he was so often and so busily engaged, there can, of course, be nothing which can really assuage her overwhelming grief; but it will make a vital difference in the character of this grief, whether the image of her boy, as it takes its fixed and final position in her memory and in her heart, is associated with recollections of docility, respectful regard for his mother's wishes, and of ready and unquestioning submission to her authority and obedience to her commands; or whether, on the other hand, the picture of his past life, which is to remain forever in her heart, is to be distorted and marred by memories of outbreaks, acts of ungovernable impulse and insubordination, habitual disregard of all authority, and disrespectful, if not contemptuous, treatment of his mother.

There is a sweetness as well as a bitterness of grief; and something like a feeling of joy and gladness will spring up in the mother's heart, and mingle with and soothe her sorrow, if she can think of her boy, when he is gone, as always docile, tractable, submissive to her authority, and obedient to her commands. Such recollections, it is true, can not avail to remove her grief—perhaps not even to diminish its intensity; but they will greatly assuage the bitterness of it, and wholly take away its *sting*.

CHAPTER IV.

GENTLE PUNISHMENT OF DISOBEDIENCE.

Children have no natural instinct of obedience to their parents, though they have other instincts by means of which the habit of obedience, as an acquisition, can easily be formed.

The true state of the case is well illustrated by what we observe among the lower animals. The hen can call her chickens when she has food for them, or when any danger threatens, and they come to her. They come, however, simply under the impulse of a desire for food or fear of danger, not from any instinctive desire to conform their action to their mother's will; or, in other words, with no idea of submission to parental authority. It is so, substantially, with many other animals whose habits in respect to the relation between parents and offspring come under human observation. The colt and the calf follow and keep near the mother, not from any instinct of desire to conform their conduct to her will, but solely from love of food, or fear of danger. These last are strictly instinctive. They act spontaneously, and require no training of any sort to establish or to maintain them.

The case is substantially the same with children. They run to their mother by instinct, when want, fear, or pain impels them. They require no teaching or training for this. But for them to come simply because their mother wishes them to come—to be controlled, in other words, by her will, instead of by their own impulses, is a different thing altogether. They have no instinct for that. They have only a *capacity for its development*.

Instincts and Capacities.

It may, perhaps, be maintained that there is no real difference between instincts and capacities, and it certainly is possible that they may pass into each other by insensible gradations. Still, practically, and in reference to our treatment of any intelligent nature which is in course of gradual development under our influence, the difference is wide. The dog has an instinct impelling him to attach himself to and follow his master;

but he has no instinct leading him to draw his master's cart. He requires no teaching for the one. It comes, of course, from the connate impulses of his nature. For the other he requires a skillful and careful training. If we find a dog who evinces no disposition to seek the society of man, but roams off into woods and solitudes alone, he is useless, and we attribute the fault to his own wolfish nature. But if he will not fetch and carry at command, or bring home a basket in his mouth from market, the fault, if there be any fault, is in his master, in not having taken the proper time and pains to train him, or in not knowing how to do it. He has an instinct leading him to attach himself to a human master, and to follow his master wherever he goes. But he has no instinct leading him to fetch and carry, or to draw carts for any body. If he shows no affection for man, it is his own fault—that is, the fault of his nature. But if he does not fetch and carry well, or go out of the room when he is ordered out, or draw steadily in a cart, it is his teacher's fault. He has not been properly trained.

Who is Responsible?

So with the child. If he does not seem to know how to take his food, or shows no disposition to run to his mother when he is hurt or when he is frightened, we have reason to suspect something wrong, or, at least, something abnormal, in his mental or physical constitution. But if he does not obey his mother's commands—no matter how insubordinate or unmanageable he may be—the fault does not, certainly, indicate any thing at all wrong in *him*. The fault is in his training. In witnessing his disobedience, our reflection should be, not "What a bad boy!" but "What an unfaithful or incompetent mother!"

I have dwelt the longer on this point because it is fundamental As long as a mother imagines, as so many mothers seem to do, that obedience on the part of the child is, or ought to be, a matter of course, she will never properly undertake the work of training him. But when she thoroughly understands and feels that her children are not to be expected to submit their will to hers, *except so far as she forms in them the habit of doing this by special training*, the battle is half won.

Actual Instincts of Children.

The natural instinct which impels her children to come at once to her for refuge and protection in all their troubles and fears, is a great source of happiness to every mother. This instinct shows itself in a thousand ways. "A mother, one morning"—I quote the anecdote from a newspaper[B] which came to hand while I was writing this chapter—"gave her two little ones books and toys to amuse them, while she went to attend to some work in an upper room. Half an hour passed quietly, and then a timid voice at the foot of the stairs called out:

"'Mamma, are you there?'

"'Yes, darling.'

"'All right, then!' and the child went back to its play.

"By-and-by the little voice was heard again, repeating,

"'Mamma, are you there?'

"'Yes.'

"'All right, then;' and the little ones returned again, satisfied and reassured, to their toys."

The sense of their mother's presence, or at least the certainty of her being near at hand, was necessary to their security and contentment in their plays. But this feeling was not the result of any teachings that they had received from their mother, or upon her having inculcated upon their minds in any way the necessity of their keeping always within reach of maternal protection; nor had it been acquired by their own observation or experience of dangers or difficulties which had befallen them when too far away. It was a native instinct of the soul—the same that leads the lamb and the calf to keep close to their mother's side, and causes the unweaned babe to cling to its mother's bosom, and to shrink from being put away into the crib or cradle alone.

The Responsibility rests upon the Mother.

The mother is thus to understand that the principle of obedience is not to be expected to come by nature into the heart of her child, but to be implanted by education. She must understand this so fully as to feel that if she finds that her children are disobedient to her commands—leaving out of view cases of peculiar and extraordinary temptation—it is *her* fault, not theirs. Perhaps I ought not to say her *fault* exactly, for she may have done as well as she knows how; but, at any rate, her failure. Instead, therefore, of being angry with them, or fretting and complaining about the trouble they give her, she should leave them, as it were, out of the case, and turn her thoughts to herself, and to her own management, with a view to the discovery and the correcting of her own derelictions and errors. In a word, she must set regularly and systematically about the work of *teaching* her children to subject their will to hers.

Three Methods.

I shall give three principles of management, or rather three different classes of measures, by means of which children may certainly be made obedient. The most perfect success will be attained by employing them all. But they require very different degrees of skill and tact on the part of the mother. The first requires very little skill. It demands only steadiness, calmness, and perseverance. The second draws much more upon the mother's mental resources, and the last, most of all. Indeed, as will presently be seen, there is no limit to the amount of tact and ingenuity, not to say genius, which may be advantageously exercised in the last method. The first is the most essential; and it will alone, if faithfully carried out, accomplish the end. The second, if the mother has the tact and skill to carry it into effect, will aid very much in accomplishing the result, and in a manner altogether more agreeable to both parties. The third will make the work of forming the habit of obedience on the part of the mother, and of acquiring it on the part of the child, a source of the highest enjoyment to both. But then, unfortunately, it requires more skill and dexterity, more gentleness of touch, so to speak, and a more delicate constitution of soul, than most mothers can be expected to possess.

But let us see what the three methods are.

First Method.

1. The first principle is that the mother should so regulate her management of her child, that he should *never* gain any desired end by any act of insubmission, but *always* incur some small trouble, inconvenience, or privation, by disobeying or neglecting to obey his mother's command. The important words in this statement of the principle are *never* and *always*. It is the absolute certainty that disobedience will hurt him, and not help him, in which the whole efficacy of the rule consists.

It is very surprising how small a punishment will prove efficacious if it is only *certain* to follow the transgression. You may set apart a certain place for a prison—a corner of the sofa, a certain ottoman, a chair, a stool, any thing will answer; and the more entirely every thing like an air of displeasure or severity is excluded, in the manner of making the preliminary arrangements, the better. A mother without any tact, or any proper understanding of the way in which the hearts and minds of young children are influenced, will begin, very likely, with a scolding.

"Children, you are getting very disobedient. I have to speak three or four times before you move to do what I say. Now, I am going to have a prison. The prison is to be that dark closet, and I am going to shut you up in it for half an hour every time you disobey. Now, remember! The very next time!"

Empty Threatening.

Mothers who govern by threatening seldom do any thing but threaten. Accordingly, the first time the children disobey her, after such an announcement, she says nothing, if the case happens to be one in which the disobedience occasions her no particular trouble. The next time, when the transgression is a little more serious, she thinks, very rightly perhaps, that to be shut up half an hour in a dark closet would be a disproportionate punishment. Then, when at length some very willful and grave act of insubordination occurs, she happens to be in particularly good-humor, for some reason, and has not the heart to shut "the poor thing" in the closet; or, perhaps, there is company present, and she does not wish to make a scene. So the penalty announced with so much emphasis turns out to be a dead letter, as the children knew it would from the beginning.

How Discipline may be both Gentle and Efficient.

With a little dexterity and tact on the mother's part, the case may be managed very differently, and with a very different result. Let us suppose that some day, while she is engaged with her sewing or her other household duties, and her children are playing around her, she tells them that in some great schools in Europe, when the boys are disobedient, or violate the rules, they are shut up for punishment in a kind of prison; and perhaps she entertains them with invented examples of boys that would not go to prison, and had to be taken there by force, and kept there longer on account of their contumacy; and also of other noble boys, tall and handsome, and the best players on the grounds, who went readily when they had done wrong and were ordered into confinement, and bore their punishment like men, and who were accordingly set free all the sooner on that account. Then she proposes to them the idea of adopting that plan herself, and asks them to look all about the room and find a good seat which they can have for their prison—one end of the sofa, perhaps, a stool in a corner, or a box used as a house for a kitten. I once knew an instance where a step before a door leading to a staircase served as penitentiary, and sitting upon it for a minute or less was the severest punishment required to maintain most perfect discipline in a family of young children for a long time.

When any one of the children violated any rule or direction which had been enjoined upon them—as, for example, when they left the door open in coming in or going out, in the winter; or interrupted their mother when she was reading, instead of standing quietly by her side and waiting until she looked up from her book and gave them leave to speak to her; or used any violence towards each other, by pushing, or pulling, or struggling for a plaything or a place; or did not come promptly to her when called; or did not obey at once the first command in any case, the mother would say simply, "Mary!" or "James! Prison!" She would pronounce this sentence without any appearance of displeasure, and often with a smile, as if they were only playing prison, and then, in a very few minutes after they had taken the penitential seat, she would say *Free*! which word set them at liberty again.

Must begin at the Beginning.

I have no doubt that some mothers, in reading this, will say that such management as this is mere trifling and play; and that real and actual children, with all their natural turbulence, insubordination, and obstinacy, can never be really governed by any such means. I answer that whether it proves on trial to be merely trifling and play or not depends upon the firmness, steadiness, and decision with which the mother carries it into execution. Every method of management requires firmness, perseverance, and decision on the part of the mother to make it successful, but, with these qualities duly exercised, it is astonishing what slight and gentle penalties will suffice for the most complete establishment of her authority. I knew a mother whose children were trained to habits of almost perfect obedience, and whose only method of punishment, so far as I know, was to require the offender to stand on one foot and count five, ten, or twenty, according to the nature and aggravation of the offense. Such a mother, of course, begins early with her children. She trains them from their earliest years to this constant subjection of their will to hers. Such penalties, moreover, owe their efficiency not to the degree of pain or inconvenience that they impose upon the offender, but mainly upon their *calling his attention, distinctly*, after every offense, to the fact that he has done wrong. Slight as this is, it will prove to be sufficient if it *always* comes—if no case of disobedience or of willful wrong-doing of any kind is allowed to pass unnoticed, or is not followed by the infliction of the proper penalty. It is in all cases the certainty, and not the severity, of punishment which constitutes its power.

Suppose one is not at the Beginning.

What has been said thus far relates obviously to cases where the mother is at the commencement of her work of training. This is the way to *begin*; but you can not begin unless you are at the beginning. If your children are partly grown, and you find that they are not under your command, the difficulty is much greater. The principles which should govern the management are the same, but they can not be applied by means so gentle. The prison, it may be, must now be somewhat more real, the terms of imprisonment somewhat longer, and there may be cases of insubordination so decided as to require the offender to be carried to it by force, on account of his refusal to go of his own accord, and perhaps to be held there, or even to be tied. Cases requiring treatment so decisive as this must be very rare with children under ten years of age; and when they occur, the mother has reason to feel great self-condemnation—or at least great self-abasement—at finding that she has failed so entirely in the first great moral duty of the mother, which is to train her children to complete submission to her authority from the beginning.

Children coming under New Control.

Sometimes, however, it happens that children are transferred from one charge to another, so that the one upon whom the duty of government devolves, perhaps only for a time, finds that the child or children put under his or her charge have been trained by previous mismanagement to habits of utter insubordination. I say, trained to such habits, for the practice of allowing children to gain their ends by any particular means is really training them to the use of those means. Thus multitudes of children are taught to disobey, and trained to habits of insubmission and insubordination, by the means most effectually adapted to that end.

Difficulties.

When under these circumstances the children come under a new charge, whether permanently or temporarily, the task of re-form in or their characters is more delicate and difficult than where one can begin at the beginning; but the principles are the same, and the success is equally certain. The difficulty is somewhat increased by the fact that the person thus provisionally in charge has often no natural authority over the child, and the circumstances may moreover be such as to make it necessary to abstain carefully from any measures that would lead to difficulty or collision, to cries, complaints to the mother, or any of those other forms of commotion or annoyance, which ungoverned children know so well how to employ in gaining their ends. The mother may be one of those weak-minded women who can never see any thing unreasonable in the crying complaints made by their children against other people. Or she may be sick, and it may be very important to avoid every thing that could agitate or disturb her.

George and Egbert.

This last was the case of George, a young man of seventeen, who came to spend some time at home after an absence of two years in the city. He found his mother sick, and his little brother, Egbert, utterly insubordinate and unmanageable.

"The first thing I have to do," said George to himself, when he observed how things were, "is to get command of Egbert;" and as the first lesson which he gave his little brother illustrates well the principle of gentle but efficient punishment, I will give it here.

Egbert was ten years of age. He was very fond of going a-fishing, but he was not allowed to go alone. His mother, very weak and vacillating about some things, was extremely decided about this. So Egbert had learned to submit to this restriction, as he would have done to all others if his mother had been equally decided in respect to all.

The first thing that Egbert thought of the next morning after his brother's return was that George might go a-fishing with him.

"I don't know," replied George, in a hesitating and doubtful tone. "I don't know whether it will do for me to go a-fishing with you. I don't know whether I can depend upon your always obeying me and doing as I say."

Egbert made very positive promises, and so it was decided to go. George took great interest in helping Egbert about his fishing-tackle, and did all in his power in other ways to establish friendly relations with him, and at length they set out. They walked a little distance down what was in the winter a wood road, and then came to a place where two paths led into a wood. Either of them led to the river. But there was a brook to cross, and for one of these paths there was a bridge. There was none for the other. George said that they would take the former. Egbert, however, paid no regard to this direction, but saying simply "No, I'd rather go this way," walked off in the other path.

"I was afraid you would not obey me," said George, and then turned and followed Egbert into the forbidden path, without making any further objection. Egbert concluded at once that he should find George as easily to be managed as he had found other people.

The Disobedience.

When they came in sight of the brook, George saw that there was a narrow log across it, in guise of a bridge. He called out to Egbert, who had gone on before him, not to go over the log until *he* came. But Egbert called back in reply that there was no danger, that he could go across alone, and so went boldly over. George, on arriving at the brook, and finding that the log was firm and strong, followed Egbert over it. "I told you I could go across it," said Egbert. "Yes," replied George, "and you were right in that. You did cross it. The log is very steady. I think it makes quite a good bridge."

Egbert said he could hop across it on one foot, and George gave him leave to try, while he, George, held his fishing-pole for him. George followed him over the log, and then told him that he was very sorry to say it, but that he found that they could not go a-fishing that day. Egbert wished to know the reason. George said it was a private reason and he could not tell him then, but that he would tell him that evening after he had gone to bed. There was a story about it, too, he said, that he would tell him at the same time.

Egbert was curious to know what the reason could be for changing the plan, and also to hear the story. Still he was extremely disappointed in having to lose his fishing, and very much disposed to be angry with George for not going on. It was, however, difficult to get very angry without knowing George's reason, and George, though he said that the reason was a good one—that it was a serious difficulty in the way of going a-fishing that day, which had only come to his knowledge since they left home, steadily persisted in declining to explain what the difficulty was until the evening, and began slowly to walk back toward the house.

Egbert becomes Sullen.

Egbert then declared that, at any rate, he would not go home. If he could not go a-fishing he would stay there in the woods. George readily fell in with this idea. "Here is a nice place for me to sit down on this flat rock under the trees," said he, "and I have got a book in my pocket. You can play about in the woods as long as you please. Perhaps you will see a squirrel; if you do, tell me, and I will come and help you catch him." So saying, he took out his book and sat down under the trees and began to read. Egbert, after loitering about sullenly a few minutes, began to walk up the path, and said that he was going home.

George, however, soon succeeded in putting him in good-humor again by talking with him in a friendly manner, and without manifesting any signs of displeasure, and also by playing with him on the way. He took care to keep on friendly terms with him all the afternoon, aiding him in his various undertakings, and contributing to his amusement in every way as much as he could, while he made no complaint, and expressed no dissatisfaction with him in any way whatever.

Final Disposition of the Case.

After Egbert had gone to bed, and before he went to sleep, George made him a visit at his bedside, and, after a little playful frolic with him, to put him in special good-humor, said he would make his explanation.

"The reason why I had to give up the fishing expedition," he said, "was, I found that I could not depend upon your obeying me."

Egbert, after a moment's pause, said that he did not disobey him; and when George reminded him of his taking the path that he was forbidden to take, and of his crossing the log bridge against orders, he said that that path led to the river by the shortest way, and that he knew that the log was firm and steady, and that he could go over it without falling in. "And so you thought you had good reasons for disobeying me," rejoined George. "Yes," said Egbert, triumphantly. "That is just it," said George. "You are willing to obey, except when you think you have good reasons for disobeying, and then you disobey. That's the way a great many boys do, and that reminds me of the story I was going to tell you. It is about some soldiers."

George then told Egbert a long story about a colonel who sent a captain with a company of men on a secret expedition with specific orders, and the captain disobeyed the orders and crossed a stream with his force, when he had been directed to remain on the hither side of it, thinking himself that it would be better to cross, and in consequence of it he and all his force were captured by the enemy, who were lying in ambush near by, as the colonel knew, though the captain did not know it. George concluded his story with some very forcible remarks, showing, in a manner adapted to Egbert's state of mental development, how essential it was to the character of a good soldier that he should obey implicitly all the commands of his superior, without ever presuming to disregard them on the ground of his seeing good reason for doing so.

He then went on to relate another story of an officer on whom the general could rely for implicit and unhesitating obedience to all his commands, and who was sent on an important expedition with orders, the reasons for which he did not understand, but all of which he promptly obeyed, and thus brought the expedition to a successful conclusion. He made the story interesting to Egbert by narrating many details of a character adapted to Egbert's comprehension, and at the end drew a moral from it for his instruction.

The Moral.

This moral was not, as some readers might perhaps anticipate, and as, indeed, many persons of less tact might have made it, that Egbert ought himself, as a boy, to obey those in authority over him. Instead of this he closed by saying: "And I advise you, if you grow up to be a man and ever become the general of an army, never to trust any captain or colonel with the charge of an important enterprise, unless they are men that know how to obey." Egbert answered very gravely that he was "determined that he wouldn't."

Soon after this George bade him good-night and went away. The next day he told Egbert not to be discouraged at his not having yet learned to obey. "There are a great many boys older than you," he said, "who have not learned this lesson; but you will learn in time. I can't go a-fishing with you, or undertake any other great expeditions, till I find I can trust you entirely to do exactly as I say in cases where I have a right to decide; but you will learn before long, and then we can do a great many things together which we can not do now."

The Principles Illustrated.

Any one who has any proper understanding of the workings of the juvenile mind will see that George, by managing Egbert on these principles, would in a short time acquire complete ascendency over him, while the boy would very probably remain, in relation to his mother, as disobedient and insubordinate as ever. If the penalty annexed to the transgression is made as much as possible the necessary and natural consequence of it, and is insisted upon calmly, deliberately, and with inflexible decision, but without irritation, without reproaches, almost without any indications even of displeasure, but is, on the contrary, lightened as much as possible by sympathy and kindness, and by taking the most indulgent views, and admitting the most palliating considerations in respect to the nature of the offense, the result will certainly be the establishment of the authority of the parent or guardian on a firm and permanent basis.

There are a great many cases of this kind, where a child with confirmed habits of insubordination comes under the charge of a person who is not responsible for the formation of these habits. Even the mother herself sometimes finds herself in substantially this position with her own children; as, for example, when after some years of lax and inefficient government she becomes convinced that her management has been wrong, and that it threatens to bring forth bitter fruits unless it is reformed. In these cases, although the work is somewhat more difficult, the principles on which success depends are the same. Slight penalties, firmly, decisively, and invariably enforced—without violence, without scolding, without any manifestation of resentment or anger, and, except in extreme cases, without even expressions of displeasure—constitute a system which, if carried out calmly, but with firmness and decision, will assuredly succeed.

The real Difficulty.

The case would thus seem to be very simple, and success very easy. But, alas! this is far from being the case. Nothing is required, it is true, but firmness, steadiness, and decision; but, unfortunately, these are the very requisites which, of all others, it seems most difficult for mothers to command. They can not govern their children because they can not govern themselves.

Still, if the mother possess these qualities in any tolerable degree, or is able to acquire them, this method of training her children to the habit of submitting implicitly to her authority, by calmly and good-naturedly, but firmly and invariably, affixing some slight privation or penalty to every act of resistance to her will, is the easiest to practice, and will certainly be successful. It requires no ingenuity, no skill, no contrivance, no thought—nothing but steady persistence in a simple routine. This was the first of the three modes of action enumerated at the commencement of this discussion. There were two others named, which, though requiring higher qualities in the mother than simple steadiness of purpose, will make the work far more easy and agreeable, where these qualities are possessed.

Some further consideration of the subject of punishment, with special reference to the light in which it is to be regarded in respect to its nature and its true mode of action, will occupy the next chapter.

CHAPTER V.

THE PHILOSOPHY OF PUNISHMENT.

It is very desirable that every parent and teacher should have a distinct and clear conception of the true nature of punishment, and of the precise manner in which it is designed to act in repressing offenses. This is necessary in order that the punitive measures which he may employ may accomplish the desired good, and avoid the evils which so often follow in their train.

Nature and Design of Punishment.

The first question which is to be considered in determining upon the principles to be adopted and the course to be pursued with children in respect to punishment, is, which of the two views in respect to the nature and design of punishment which prevail in the minds of men we will adopt in shaping our system. For,

1. Punishment may be considered in the light of a vindictive retribution for sin—a penalty demanded by the eternal principles of justice as the natural and proper sequel and complement of the past act of transgression, with or without regard to any salutary effects that may result from it in respect to future acts. Or,

2. It may be considered as a remedial measure, adopted solely with reference to its influence as a means of deterring the subject of it, or others, from transgression in time to come.

According to the first view, punishment is a *penalty* which *justice* demands as a satisfaction for the past. According to the other it is a *remedy* which *goodness* devises for the benefit of the future.

Theologians have lost themselves in endless speculations on the question how far, in the government of God, punishment is to be considered as possessing one or the other of these two characters, or both combined. There seems to be also some uncertainty in the minds of men in relation to the precise light in which the penalties of violated law are to be regarded by civil governments, and the spirit in which they are to be administered—they being apparently, as prescribed and employed by most governments, in some respects, and to some extent, retributive and vindictive, and in other respects remedial and curative.

It would seem, however, that in respect to school and family government there could be no question on this point. The punishment of a child by a parent, or of a pupil by a teacher, ought certainly, one would think, to exclude the element of vindictive retribution altogether, and to be employed solely with reference to the salutary influences that may be expected from it in time to come. If the injunction "Vengeance is mine, I will repay it, saith the Lord" is to be recognized at all, it certainly ought to be acknowledged here.

This principle, once fully and cordially admitted, simplifies the subject of punishment, as administered by parents and teachers, very much. One extremely important and very striking result of it will appear from a moment's reflection. It is this, namely:

It excludes completely and effectually all manifestations of irritation or excitement in the infliction of punishment—all harsh tones of voice, all scowling or angry looks, all violent or threatening gesticulations, and every other mode, in fact, of expressing indignation or passion. Such indications as these are wholly out of place in punishment considered as the *application of a remedy* devised beneficently with the sole view of accomplishing a future good. They comport only with punishment considered as vengeance, or a vindictive retribution for the past sin.

This idea is fundamental. The mother who is made angry by the misconduct of her children, and punishes them in a passion, acts under the influence of a brute instinct. Her family government is in principle the same as that of the lower animals over their young. It is, however, at any rate, a *government*; and such government is certainly better than none. But human parents, in the training of their human offspring, ought surely to aim at something higher and nobler. They who do so, who possess themselves fully with the idea that punishment, as they are to administer it, is wholly remedial in its character—that is to say, is to be considered solely with reference to the future good to be attained by it, will have established in their minds a principle that will surely guide them into right ways, and bring them out successfully in the end. They will soon acquire the habit of never threatening, of never punishing in anger, and of calmly considering, in the case of the faults which they observe in their children, what course of procedure will be most effectual in correcting them.

Parents seem sometimes to have an idea that a manifestation of something like anger—or, at least, very serious displeasure on their part —is necessary in order to make a proper impression in respect to its fault on the mind of the child. This, however, I think, is a mistake. The impression is made by what we *do*, and not by the indications of irritation or displeasure which we manifest in doing it. To illustrate this, I will state a case, narrating all its essential points just as it occurred. The case is very analogous, in many particulars, to that of Egbert and George related in the last chapter.

Mary's Walk.

"Mary," said Mary's aunt, Jane, who had come to make a visit at Mary's mother's in the country, "I am going to the village this afternoon, and if you would like you may go with me."

Mary was, of course, much pleased with this invitation.

"A part of the way," continued her aunt, "is by a path across the fields. While we are there you must keep in the path all the time, for it rained a little this morning, and I am afraid that the grass may not be quite dry."

"Yes, Aunt Jane; I'll keep in the path," said Mary.

So they set out on the walk together. When they came to the gate which led to the path across the fields, Aunt Jane said, "Remember, Mary, you must keep in the path."

Mary said nothing, but ran forward. Pretty soon she began to walk a little on the margin of the grass, and, before long, observing a place where the grass was short and where the sun shone, she ran out boldly upon it, and then, looking down at her shoes, she observed that they were not wet. She held up one of her feet to her aunt as she came opposite to the place, saying,

"See, aunt, the grass is not wet at all."

"I see it is not," said her aunt. "I *thought* it would not be wet; though I was not sure but that it might be. But come," she added, holding out her hand, "I have concluded not to go to the village, after all. We are going back home."

"Oh, Aunt Jane!" said Mary, following her aunt as she began retracing her steps along the path. "What is that for?"

"I have altered my mind," said her aunt.

"What makes you alter your mind?"

By this time Aunt Jane had taken hold of Mary's hand, and they were walking together along the path towards home.

"Because you don't obey me," she said.

"Why, auntie," said Mary, "the grass was not wet at all where I went."

"No," said her aunt, "it was perfectly dry."

"And it did not do any harm at all for me to walk upon it," said Mary.

"Not a bit of harm," said her aunt.

"Then why are you going home?" asked Mary.

"Because you don't obey me," replied her aunt.

"You see," said her aunt, "there is one thing about this that you don't understand, because you are such a little girl. You will understand it by-and-by, when you grow older; and I don't blame you for not knowing it now, because you are so young."

"What is it that I don't know?" asked Mary.

"I am afraid you would not understand it very well if I were to explain it," replied her aunt.

"Try me," said Mary.

"Well, you see," replied her aunt, "I don't feel safe with any child that does not obey me. This time no harm was done, because the grass happened to be dry; but farther on there was a brook. I might have told you not to go near the brink of the brook for fear of your falling in. Then you might have gone, notwithstanding, if you thought there was no danger, just as you went out upon the grass because you thought it was not wet, notwithstanding my saying that you must keep in the path. So you see I never feel safe in taking walks in places where there is any danger with children that I can not always depend upon to do exactly what I say."

Mary was, of course, now ready to make profuse promises that she would obey her aunt in future on all occasions and began to beg that she would continue her walk to the village.

"No," said her aunt, "I don't think it would be quite safe for me to trust to your promises, though I have no doubt you honestly mean to keep them. But you remember you promised me that you would keep in the path when we planned this walk; and yet when the time of temptation came you could not keep the promise; but you will learn. When I am going on some perfectly safe walk I will take you with me again; and if I stay here some time you will learn to obey me so perfectly that I can take you with me to any place, no matter how dangerous it may be."

Aunt Jane thus gently, but firmly, persisted in abandoning the walk to the village, and returning home; but she immediately turned the conversation away from the subject of Mary's fault, and amused her with stories and aided her in gathering flowers, just as if nothing had happened; and when she arrived at home she said nothing to any one of Mary's disobedience. Here now was punishment calculated to make a very strong impression —but still without scolding, without anger, almost, in fact, without even any manifestations of displeasure. And yet how long can any reasonable person suppose it would be before Mary would learn, if her aunt acted invariably on the same principles, to submit implicitly to her will?

A Different Management.

Compare the probable result of this mode of management with the scolding and threatening policy. Suppose Aunt Jane had called to Mary angrily,

"Mary! Mary! come directly back into the path. I told you not to go out of the path, and you are a very naughty child to disobey me. The next time you disobey me in that way I will send you directly home."

Mary would have been vexed and irritated, perhaps, and would have said to herself, "How cross Aunt Jane is to-day!" but the "next time" she would have been as disobedient as ever.

If mothers, instead of scowling, scolding, and threatening now, and putting off doing the thing that ought to be done to the "next time," would do that thing at once, and give up the scowling, scolding, and threatening altogether, they would find all parties immensely benefited by the change.

It is evident, moreover, that by this mode of management the punishment is employed not in the way of retribution, but as a remedy. Mary loses her walk not on the ground that she deserved to lose it, but because it was not safe to continue it.

An Objection.

Some mother may perhaps say, in reference to the case of Mary and her aunt, that it may be all very well in theory, but that practically mothers have not the leisure and the means for adopting such moderate measures. We can not stop, she may say, every time we are going to the village, on important business perhaps, and turn back and lose the afternoon on account of the waywardness of a disobedient child.

My answer is that it will not have to be done *every time*, but only very seldom. The effect of acting once or twice on this principle, with the certainty on the part of the child that the mother or the aunt will always act so when the occasion calls for it, very soon puts an end to all necessity for such action. Indeed, if Mary, in the instance above given, had been managed in this way from infancy, she would not have thought of leaving the path when forbidden to do so. It is only in some such case as that of an aunt who knows how to manage right, coming as a visitor into the family of a mother who manages wrong, that such an incident as this could occur.

Still it must be admitted that the gentle methods of discipline, which reason and common sense indicate as the true ones for permanently influencing the minds of children and forming their characters, do, in each individual case, require more time and care than the cuffs and slaps dictated by passion. A box on the ear, such as a cat gives to a rebellious kitten, is certainly the *quickest* application that can be made. The measures that are calculated to reach and affect the heart can not vie with blows and scoldings in respect to the promptness of their action. Still, the parent or the teacher who will begin to act on the principles here recommended with children while they are young will find that such methods are far more prompt in their action and more effectual in immediate results than they would suppose, and that they will be the means of establishing the only kind of authority that is really worthy of the name more rapidly than any other.

The special point, however, with a view to which these illustrations are introduced, is, as has been already remarked, that penalties of this nature, and imposed in this spirit, are not vindictive, but simply remedial and reformatory. They are not intended to satisfy the sense of justice for what is past, but only to secure greater safety and happiness in time to come.

The Element of Invariableness.

Punishments may be very light and gentle in their character, provided they are certain to follow the offense. It is in their *certainty*, and not in their *severity*, that the efficiency of them lies. Very few children are ever severely burnt by putting their fingers into the flame of a candle. They are effectually taught not to put them in by very slight burnings, on account of the *absolute invariableness* of the result produced by the contact.

Mothers often do not understand this. They attempt to cure some habitual fault by scoldings and threats, and declarations of what they will certainly do "next time," and perhaps by occasional acts of real severity in cases of peculiar aggravation, instead of a quiet, gentle, and comparatively trifling infliction in *every instance* of the fault, which would be altogether more effectual.

A child, for example, has acquired the habit of leaving the door open. Now occasionally scolding him, when it is specially cold, and now and then shutting him up in a closet for half an hour, will never cure him of the fault. But if there were an automaton figure standing by the side of the door, to say to him *every time* that he came through without shutting it, *Door*! which call should be a signal to him to go back and shut the door, and then sit down in a chair near by and count ten; and if this slight penalty was *invariably* enforced, he would be most effectually cured of the fault in a very short time.

Now, the mother can not be exactly this automaton, for she can not always be there; but she can recognize the principle, and carry it into effect as far as possible—that is, *invariably, when she is there*. And though she will not thus cure the boy of the fault so soon as the automaton would do it, she will still do it very soon.

Irritation and Anger.

Avoid, as much as possible, every thing of an irritating character in the punishments inflicted, for to irritate frequently the mind of a child tends, of course, to form within him an irritable and unamiable temper. It is true, perhaps, that it is not possible absolutely to avoid this effect of punishment in all cases; but a great deal may be done to diminish the evil by the exercise of a little tact and ingenuity on the part of the mother whose attention is once particularly directed to the subject.

The first and most important measure of precaution on this point is the absolute exclusion of every thing like angry looks and words as accompaniments of punishment. If you find that any wrong which your child commits awakens irritation or anger in your mind, suspend your judgment of the case and postpone all action until the irritation and anger have subsided, and you can consider calmly and deliberately what to do, with a view, not of satisfying your own resentment, but of doing good to the child. Then, when you have decided what to do, carry your decision into effect in a good-natured manner—firmly and inflexibly—but still without any violence, or even harshness, of manner.

Co-operation of the Offender.

There are many cases in which, by the exercise of a little tact and ingenuity, the parent can actually secure the *co-operation* of the child in the infliction of the punishment prescribed for the curing of a fault. There are many advantages in this, when it can be done. It gives the child an interest in curing himself of the fault; it makes the punishment more effectual; and it removes almost all possibility of its producing any irritation or resentment in his mind. To illustrate this we will give a case. It is of no consequence, for the purpose of this article, whether it is a real or an imaginary one.

Little Egbert, seven years old, had formed the habit so common among children of wasting a great deal of time in dressing himself, so as not to be ready for breakfast when the second bell rang. His mother offered him a reward if he would himself devise any plan that would cure him of the fault.

"I don't know what to do, exactly, to cure you," she said; "but if you will think of any plan that will really succeed, I will give you an excursion in a carriage."

"How far?" asked Egbert.

"Ten miles," said his mother. "I will take you in a carriage on an excursion anywhere you say, for ten miles, if you will find out some way to cure yourself of this fault."

"I think you ought to punish me," said Egbert, speaking in rather a timid tone.

"That's just it," said his mother, "It is for you to think of some kind of punishment that won't be too disagreeable for me to inflict, and which will yet be successful in curing you of the fault. I will allow you a fortnight to get cured. If you are not cured in a fortnight I shall think the punishment is not enough, or that it is not of a good kind; but if it works so well as to cure you in a fortnight, then you shall have the ride."

Egbert wished to know whether he must think of the punishment himself, or whether his sister Mary might help him. His mother gave him leave to ask any body to help him that he pleased. Mary, after some reflection, recommended that, whenever he was not dressed in time, he was to have only one lump of sugar, instead of four, in his tumbler of water for breakfast.

His usual drink at breakfast was a tumbler of water, with four lumps of sugar in it. The first bell was rung at half-past six, and breakfast was at half-past seven. His sister recommended that, as half an hour was ample time for the work of dressing, Egbert should go down every morning and report himself ready before the clock struck seven. If he failed of this, he was to have only one lump of sugar, instead of four, in his glass of water.

There was some question about the necessity of requiring him to be ready before seven; Egbert being inclined to argue that if he was ready by breakfast-time, that would be enough. But Mary said no. "To allow you a full hour to dress," she said, "when half an hour is enough, may answer very well in respect to having you ready for breakfast, but it is no way to cure you of the fault. That would enable you to play half of the time while you are dressing, without incurring the punishment; but the way to cure you is to make it sure that you will have the punishment to bear if you play at all."

So it was decided to allow only half an hour for the dressing-time.

Egbert's mother said she was a little afraid about the one lump of sugar that was left to him when he failed.

"The plan *may* succeed," she said; "I am very willing that you should try it; but I am afraid that when you are tempted to stop and play in the midst of your dressing, you will say, I shall have *one* lump of sugar, at any rate, and so will yield to the temptation. So perhaps it would be safer for you to make the rule that you are not to have any sugar at all when you fail. Still, *perhaps* your plan will succeed. You can try it and see. I should wish myself to have the punishment as slight as possible to produce the effect."

By such management as this, it is plain that Egbert is brought into actual co-operation with his mother in the infliction of a punishment to cure him of a fault. It is true, that making such an arrangement as this, and then leaving it to its own working, would lead to no result. As in the case of all other plans and methods, it must be strictly, firmly, and perseveringly followed up by the watchful efficiency of the mother. We can not *substitute* the action of the child for that of the parent in the work of early training, but we can often derive very great advantage by securing his cooperation.

Playful Punishments.

So true is it that the efficacy of any mode of punishment consists in the *certainty of its infliction*, that even playful punishments are in many cases sufficient to accomplish the cure of a fault. George, for example, was in the habit of continually getting into disputes and mild quarrels with his sister Amelia, a year or two younger than himself. "I know it is very foolish," he said to his mother, when she was talking with him on the subject one evening after he had gone to bed, and she had been telling him a story, and his mind was in a calm and tranquil state. "It is very foolish, but somehow I can't help it. I forget."

"Then you must have some punishment to make you remember," said his mother.

"But sometimes *she* is the one to blame," said George, "and then she must have the punishment."

"No," replied his mother. "When a lady and a gentleman become involved in a dispute in polite society, it is always the gentleman that must be considered to be to blame."

"But Amelia and I are not polite society," said George.

"You ought to be," said his mother. "At any rate, when you, an older brother, get into disputes with your sister, it is because you have not sense enough to manage so as to avoid them. If you were a little older and wiser you would have sense enough."

"Well, mother, what shall the punishment be?" said George.

"Would you really like to have a punishment, so as to cure yourself of the fault?" asked his mother.

George said that he *would* like one.

"Then," said his mother, "I propose that every time you get into a dispute with Amelia, you turn your jacket wrong side out, and wear it so a little while as a symbol of folly."

George laughed heartily at this idea, and said he should like such a punishment as that very much. It would only be fun, he said. His mother explained to him that it would be fun, perhaps, two or three times, but after that it would only be a trouble; but still, if they decided upon that as a punishment, he must submit to it in every case. Every time he found himself getting into any dispute or difficulty with his sister, he must stop at once and turn his jacket inside out; and if he did not himself think to do this, she herself, if she was within hearing, would simply say, "Jacket!" and then he must do it.

"No matter which of us is most to blame?" asked George.

"You will always be the one that is most to blame," replied his mother, "or, at least, almost always. When a boy is playing with a sister younger than himself, *he* is the one that is most to blame for the quarrelling. His sister may be to blame by doing something wrong in the first instance; but he is the one to blame for allowing it to lead to a quarrel. If it is a little thing, he ought to yield to her, and not to mind it; and if it is a great thing, he ought to go away and leave her, rather than to stop and quarrel about it. So you see you will be the one to blame for the quarrel in almost all cases. There may possibly be some cases where you will not be to blame at all, and then you will have to be punished when you don't deserve it, and you must bear it like a man. This is a liability that happens under all systems."

"We will try the plan for one fortnight," she continued. "So now remember, every single time that I hear you disputing or quarrelling with Amelia, you must take off your jacket and put it on again wrong side out —no matter whether you think you were to blame or not—and wear it so a few minutes. You can wear it so for a longer or shorter time, just as you think is best to make the punishment effectual in curing you of the fault. By the end of the fortnight we shall be able to see whether the plan is working well and doing any good."

"So now," continued his mother, "shut up your eyes and go to sleep. You are a good boy to wish to cure yourself of such faults, and to be willing to help me in contriving ways to do it. And I have no doubt that you will submit to this punishment good-naturedly every time, and not make me any trouble about it."

Let it be remembered, now, that the efficacy of such management as this consists not in the devising of it, nor in holding such a conversation as the above with the boy—salutary as this might be—but in the *faithfulness and strictness with which it is followed up* during the fortnight of trial.

In the case in question, the progress which George made in diminishing his tendency to get into disputes with his sister was so great that his mother told him, at the end of the first fortnight, that their plan had succeeded "admirably"—so much so, she said, that she thought the punishment of taking off his jacket and turning it inside out would be for the future unnecessarily severe, and she proposed to substitute for it taking off his cap, and putting it on wrong side before.

The reader will, of course, understand that the object of such an illustration as this is not to recommend the particular measure here described for adoption in other cases, but to illustrate the spirit and temper of mind in which all measures adopted by the mother in the training of her children should be carried into effect. Measures that involve no threats, no scolding, no angry manifestations of displeasure, but are even playful in their character, may be very efficient in action if they are firmly and perseveringly maintained.

Punishments that are the Natural Consequence of the Offense.

There is great advantage in adapting the character of the punishment to that of the fault—making it, as far as possible, the natural and proper consequence of it. For instance, if the boys of a school do not come in promptly at the close of the twenty minutes' recess, but waste five minutes by their dilatoriness in obeying the summons of the bell, and the teacher keeps them for *five minutes beyond the usual hour of dismissal*, to make up for the lost time, the punishment may be felt by them to be deserved, and it may have a good effect in diminishing the evil it is intended to remedy; but it will probably excite a considerable degree of mental irritation, if not of resentment, on the part of the children, which will diminish the good effect, or is, at any rate, an evil which is to be avoided if possible.

If now, on the other hand, he assigns precisely the same penalty in another form, the whole of the good effect may be secured without the evil. Suppose he addresses the boys just before they are to go out at the next recess, as follows:

"I think, boys, that twenty minutes is about the right length of time for the recess, all told—that is, from the time you go out to the time when you are *all* back in your seats again, quiet and ready to resume your studies. I found yesterday that it took five minutes for you all to come in —that is, that it was five minutes from the time the bell was rung before all were in their seats; and to-day I shall ring the bell after *fifteen* minutes, so as to give you time to come in. If I find to-day that it takes ten minutes, then I will give you more time to come in to-morrow, by ringing the bell after you have been out *ten* minutes."

"I am sorry to have you lose so much of your recess, and if you can make the time for coming in shorter, then, of course, your recess can be longer. I should not wonder if, after a few trials, you should find that you could all come in and get into your places in *one* minute; and if so, I shall be very glad, for then you can have an uninterrupted recess of *nineteen* minutes, which will be a great gain."

Every one who has had any considerable experience in the management of boys will readily understand how different the effect of this measure will be from that of the other, while yet the penalty is in both cases precisely the same—namely, the loss, for the boys, of five minutes of their play.

The Little Runaway.

In the same manner, where a child three or four years old was in the habit, when allowed to go out by himself in the yard to play, of running off into the street, a very appropriate punishment would be to require him, for the remainder of the day, to stay in the house and keep in sight of his mother, on the ground that it was not safe to trust him by himself in the yard. This would be much better than sending him to bed an hour earlier, or subjecting him to any other inconvenience or privation having no obvious connection with the fault. For it is of the greatest importance to avoid, by every means, the exciting of feelings of irritation and resentment in the mind of the child, so far as it is possible to do this without impairing the efficiency of the punishment. It is not always possible to do this. The efficiency of the punishment is, of course, the essential thing; but parents and teachers who turn their attention to the point will find that it is much less difficult than one would suppose to secure this end completely without producing the too frequent accompaniments of punishment—anger, ill-temper, and ill-will.

In the case, for example, of the child not allowed to go out into the yard, but required to remain in the house in sight of his mother, the mother should not try to make the punishment *more heavy* by speaking again and again of his fault, and evincing her displeasure by trying to make the confinement as irksome to the child as possible; but, on the other hand, should do all in her power to alleviate it. "I am very sorry," she might say, "to have to keep you in the house. It would be much pleasanter for you to go out and play in the yard, if it was only safe. I don't blame you very much for running away. It is what foolish little children, as little as you, very often do. I suppose you thought it would be good fun to run out a little way in the street. And it is good fun; but it is not safe. By-and-by, when you grow a little larger, you won't be so foolish, and then I can trust you in the yard at any time without having to watch you at all. And now what can I get for you to amuse you while you stay in the house with me?"

Punishment coming in this way, and administered in this spirit, will irritate the mind and injure the temper comparatively little; and, instead of being less; will be much more effective in accomplishing the *right kind* of cure for the fault, than any stern, severe, and vindictive retribution can possibly be.

The Question of Corporal Punishment.

The question of resorting to corporal punishment in the training of the young has been much, very much, argued and discussed on both sides by writers on education; but it seems to me to be mainly a question of competency and skill. If the parent or teacher has tact or skill enough, and practical knowledge enough of the workings of the youthful mind, he can gain all the necessary ascendency over it without resort to the violent infliction of bodily pain in any form. If he has not these qualities, then he must turn to the next best means at his disposal; for it is better that a child should be trained and governed by the rod than not trained and governed at all. I do not suppose that savages could possibly control their children without blows; while, on the other hand, Maria Edgeworth would have brought under complete submission to her will a family of the most ardent and impulsive juveniles, perhaps without even a harsh word or a frown. If a mother begins with children at the beginning, is just and true in all her dealings with them, gentle in manner, but inflexibly firm in act, and looks constantly for Divine guidance and aid in her conscientious efforts to do her duty, I feel quite confident that it will never be necessary for her to strike them. The necessity may, however, sooner or later come, for aught I know, in the case of those who act on the contrary principle. Under such management, the rod may come to be the only alternative to absolute unmanageableness and anarchy.

There will be occasion, however, to refer to this subject more fully in a future chapter.

CHAPTER VI.

REWARDING OBEDIENCE.

The mode of action described in the last two chapters for training children to habits of obedience consisted in discouraging disobedience by connecting some certain, though mild and gentle disadvantage, inconvenience, or penalty, with every transgression. In this chapter is to be considered another mode, which is in some respects the converse of the first, inasmuch as it consists in the encouragement of obedience, by often—not necessarily always—connecting with it some advantage, or gain, or pleasure; or, as it may be stated summarily, the cautious encouragement of obedience by rewards.

This method of action is more difficult than the other in the sense that it requires more skill, tact, and delicacy of perception and discrimination to carry it successfully into effect. The other demands only firm, but gentle and steady persistence. If the penalty, however slight it may be, *always comes,* the effect will take care of itself. But judiciously to administer a system of rewards, or even of commendations, requires tact, discrimination, and skill. It requires some observation of the peculiar characteristics of the different minds acted upon, and of the effects produced, and often some intelligent modification of the measures is required, to fit them to varying circumstances and times.

Obedience must not be Bought.

If the bestowing of commendation and rewards is made a matter of mere blind routine, as the assigning of gentle penalties may be, the result will become a mere system of *bribing,* or rather paying children to be good; and goodness that is bought, if it deserves the name of virtue at all, is certainly virtue of a very inferior quality.

Whether a reward conferred for obedience shall operate as a bribe, or rather as a price paid—for a *bribe,* strictly speaking, is a price paid, not for doing right, but for doing wrong—depends sometimes on very slight differences in the management of the particular case—differences which an undiscriminating mother will not be very ready to appreciate.

A mother, for example, going into the village on a summer afternoon, leaves her children playing in the yard, under the general charge of Susan, who is at work in the kitchen, whence she can observe them from time to time through the open window. She thinks the children will be safe, provided they remain in the yard. The only thing to be guarded against is the danger that they may go out through the gate into the road.

Two Different Modes of Management.

Under some circumstances, as, for example, where the danger to which they would be exposed in going into the road was very great, or where the mother can not rely upon her power to control her children's conduct by moral means in any way, the only safe method would be to fasten the gate. But if she prefers to depend for their safety on their voluntary obedience to her commands, and wishes, moreover, to promote the spirit of obedience by rewarding rather than punishing, she can make her rewards of the nature of hire or not, according to her mode of management.

If she wishes to *hire* obedience, she has only to say to the children that she is going into the village for a little time, and that they may play in the yard while she is gone, but must not go out of the gate; adding, that she is going to bring home some oranges or candies, which she will give them if she finds that they have obeyed her, but which she will not give them if they have disobeyed.

Such a promise, provided the children have the double confidence in their mother which such a method requires—namely, first, a full belief that she will really bring home the promised rewards, if they obey her; and secondly—and this is a confidence much less frequently felt by children, and much less frequently deserved by their mothers—a conviction that, in case they disobey, no importunities on their part or promises for the next time will induce their mother to give them the good things, but that the rewards will certainly be lost to them unless they are deserved, according to the conditions of the promise—in such a case—that is, when this double confidence exists, the promise will have great influence upon the children. Still, it is, in its nature, *hiring* them to obey. I do not say that this is necessarily a bad plan, though I think there is a better. Children may, perhaps, be trained gradually to habits of obedience by a system of direct rewards, and in a manner, too, far more agreeable to the parent and better for the child than by a system of compulsion through threats and punishment.

The Method of Indirect Rewarding.

But there is another way of connecting pleasurable ideas and associations with submission to parental authority in the minds of children, as a means of alluring them to the habit of obedience—one that is both more efficient in its results and more healthful and salutary in its action than the practice of bestowing direct recompenses and rewards.

Suppose, for example, in the case above described, the mother, on leaving the children, simply gives them the command that they are not to leave the yard, but makes no promises, and then, on returning from the village with the bonbons in her bag, simply asks Susan, when she comes in, whether the children have obeyed her injunction not to leave the yard. If Susan says yes, she nods to them, with a look of satisfaction and pleasure, and adds: "I thought they would obey me. I am very glad. Now I can trust them again."

Then, by-and-by, towards the close of the day, perhaps, and when the children suppose that the affair is forgotten, she takes an opportunity to call them to her, saying that she has something to tell them.

"You remember when I went to the village to-day, I left you in the yard and said that you must not go out of the gate, and you obeyed. Perhaps you would have liked to go out into the road and play there, but you would not go because I had forbidden it. I am very glad that you obeyed. I thought of you when I was in the village, and I thought you would obey me. I felt quite safe about you. If you had been disobedient children, I should have felt uneasy and anxious. But I felt safe. When I had finished my shopping, I thought I would buy you some bonbons, and here they are. You can go and sit down together on the carpet and divide them. Mary can choose one, and then Jane; then Mary, and then Jane again; and so on until they are all chosen."

Difference in the Character of the Effects.

It may, perhaps, be said by the reader that this is substantially the same as giving a direct reward for the obedience. I admit that it is in some sense *substantially* the same thing, but it is not the same in form. And this is one of those cases where the effect is modified very greatly by the form. Where children are directly promised a reward if they do so and so, they naturally regard the transaction as of the nature of a contract or a bargain, such that when they have fulfilled the conditions on their part the reward is their due, as, indeed, it really is; and they come and demand it as such. The tendency, then, is, to divest their minds of all sense of obligation in respect to doing right, and to make them feel that it is in some sense optional with them whether to do right and earn the reward, or not to do right and lose it.

In the case, however, last described, which seems at first view to differ only in form from the preceding one, the commendation and the bonbons would be so connected with the act of obedience as to associate very agreeable ideas with it in the children's minds, and thus to make doing right appear attractive to them on future occasions, while, at the same time, they would not in any degree deprive the act itself of its spontaneous character, as resulting from a sense of duty on their part, or produce the impression on their minds that their remaining within the gate was of the nature of a service rendered to their mother for hire, and afterwards duly paid for.

The lesson which we deduce from this illustration and the considerations connected with it may be stated as follows:

The General Principle.

That the rewards conferred upon children with a view of connecting pleasurable ideas and associations with good conduct should not take the form of compensations stipulated for beforehand, and then conferred according to agreement, as if they were of the nature of payment for a service rendered, but should come as the natural expression of the satisfaction and happiness felt by the mother in the good conduct of her child—expressions as free and spontaneous on her part as the good conduct was on the part of the child.

The mother who understands the full import of this principle, and whose mind becomes fully possessed of it, will find it constantly coming into practical use in a thousand ways. She has undertaken, for example, to teach her little son to read. Of course learning to read is irksome to him. He dislikes extremely to leave his play and come to take his lesson. Sometimes a mother is inconsiderate enough to be pained at this. She is troubled to find that her boy takes so little interest in so useful a work, and even, perhaps, scolds him, and threatens him for not loving study. "If you don't learn to read," she says to him, in a tone of irritation and displeasure, "you will grow up a dunce, and every body will laugh at you, and you will be ashamed to be seen."

Children's Difficulties.

But let her imagine that she herself was to be called away two or three times a day, for half an hour, to study Chinese, with a very exacting teacher, always more or less impatient and dissatisfied with her progress; and yet the irksomeness and difficulty for the mother, in learning to decipher Chinese, would be as nothing compared with that of the child in learning to read. The only thing that could make the work even tolerable to the mother would be a pretty near, distinct, and certain prospect of going to China under circumstances that would make the knowledge of great advantage to her. But the child has no such near, distinct, and certain prospect of the advantages of knowing how to read. He has scarcely any idea of these advantages at all. You can describe them to him, but the description will have no perceptible effect upon his mind. Those faculties by which we bring the future vividly before us so as to influence our present action, are not yet developed. His cerebral organization has not yet advanced to that condition, any more than his bones have advanced to the hardness, rigidness, and strength of manhood. His mind is only capable of being influenced strongly by what is present, or, at least, very near. It is the design of Divine Providence that this should be so. The child is not made to look forward much yet, and the mother who is pained and distressed because he will not look forward, shows a great ignorance of the nature of the infantile mind, and of the manner of its development. If she finds fault with her boy for not feeling distinctly enough the future advantages of learning to lead him to love study now, she is simply finding fault with a boy for not being possessed of the most slowly developed faculties of a man.

The way, then, to induce children to attend to such duties as learning to read, is not to reason with them on the advantages of it, but to put it simply on the ground of authority. "It is very irksome, I know, but you must do it. When you are at play, and having a very pleasant time, I know very well that it is hard for you to be called away to puzzle over your letters and your reading. It was very hard for me when I was a child. It is very hard for all children; but then it must be done."

The way in this, as in all other similar cases, to reduce the irksomeness of disagreeable duties to a minimum is not to attempt to convince or persuade the child, but to put the performance of them simply on the ground of submission to authority. The child must leave his play and come to take his lesson, not because he sees that it is better for him to learn to read than to play all the time, nor because he is to receive a reward in the form of compensation, but because his mother requires him to do it.

Indirect Rewarding.

If, therefore, she concludes, in order to connect agreeable ideas with the hard work of learning to read, that she will often, at the close of the lessons, tell him a little story, or show him a picture, or have a frolic with him, or give him a piece of candy or a lump of sugar, or bestow upon him any other little gratification, it is better not to promise these things beforehand, so as to give to the coming of the child, when called, the character of a service rendered for hire. Let him come simply because he is called; and then let the gratifications be bestowed as the expressions of his mother's satisfaction and happiness, in view of her boy's ready obedience to her commands and faithful performance of his duty.

Obedience, though Implicit, need not be Blind.

It must not be supposed from what has been said that because a mother is not to *rely upon* the reason and forecast of the child in respect to future advantages to accrue from efforts or sacrifices as motives of present action, that she is not to employ the influence of these motives at all. It is true that those faculties of the mind by which we apprehend distant things and govern our conduct by them are not yet developed in the child; but they are *to be* developed, and the aid of the parent will be of the greatest service in promoting the development of them. At proper times, then, the pleasures and advantages of knowing how to read should be described to the child, and presented moreover in the most attractive form. The proper time for doing this would be when no lesson is in question— during a ride or a walk, or in the midst of a story, or while looking at a book of pictures. A most improper time would be when a command had been given and was disregarded, or was reluctantly obeyed; for then such representations would only tend to enfeeble the principle of authority by bringing in the influence of reasonings and persuasions to make up for its acknowledged inefficiency. It is one of those cases where a force is weakened by reinforcement—as a plant, by being long held up by a stake, comes in the end not to be able to stand alone.

So a mother can not in any way more effectually undermine her authority, as *authority*, than by attempting to eke out its force by arguments and coaxings.

Authority not to be made Oppressive.

While the parent must thus take care to establish the *principle of authority* as the ground of obedience on the part of his children, and must not make their doing what he requires any the less acts of *obedience*, through vainly attempting to diminish the hardship of obeying a command by mingling the influence of reasonings and persuasions with it, he may in other ways do all in his power—and that will be a great deal —to make the acts of obedience easy, or, at least, to diminish the difficulty of them and the severity of the trial which they often bring to the child.

One mode by which this may be done is by not springing disagreeable obligations upon a child suddenly, but by giving his mind a little time to form itself to the idea of what is to come. When Johnny and Mary are playing together happily with their blocks upon the floor, and are, perhaps, just completing a tower which they have been building, if their mother comes suddenly into the room, announces to them abruptly that it is time for them to go to bed, throws down the tower and brushes the blocks into the basket, and then hurries the children away to the undressing, she gives a sudden and painful shock to their whole nervous system, and greatly increases the disappointment and pain which they experience in being obliged to give up their play. The delay of a single minute would be sufficient to bring their minds round easily and gently into submission to the necessity of the case. If she comes to them with a smile, looks upon their work a moment with an expression of interest and pleasure upon her countenance, and then says,

"It is bed-time, children, but I would like to see you finish your tower."

One minute of delay like this, to soften the suddenness of the transition, will make the act of submission to the necessity of giving up play and going to bed, in obedience to the mother's command, comparatively easy, instead of being, as it very likely would otherwise have been, extremely vexatious and painful.

Give a Little Time.

In the same way, in bringing to a close an evening party of children at play, if the lady of the house comes a little before the time and says to them that after "one more play," or "two more plays," as the case may be," the party must come to an end," the closing of it would be made easy; while by waiting till the hour had come, and then suddenly interrupting the gayety, perhaps in the middle of a game, by the abrupt announcement to the children that the clock has struck, and they must stop their plays and begin to get ready to go home, she brings upon them a sudden shock of painful surprise, disappointment, and, perhaps, irritation.

So, if children are to be called away from their play for any purpose whatever, it is always best to give them a little notice, if it be only a moment's notice, beforehand. "John, in a minute or two I shall wish you to go and get some wood. You can be getting your things ready to be left." "Mary, it is almost time for your lesson. You had better put Dolly to sleep and lay her in the cradle." "Boys, in ten minutes it will be time for you to go to school. So do not begin any new whistles, but only finish what you have begun."

On the same principle, if boys are at play in the open air—at ball, or skating, or flying kites—and are to be recalled by a bell, obedience to the call will be made much more easy to them by a preliminary signal, as a warning, given five minutes before the time.

Of course, it will not always be convenient to give these signals and these times of preparation. Nor will it be always necessary to give them. To determine how and in what cases it is best to apply the principle here explained will require some tact and good judgment on the part of the parent. It would be folly to lay down a rigid rule of this kind to be considered as always obligatory. All that is desirable is that the mother should understand the principle, and that she should apply it as far as she conveniently and easily can do so. She will find in practice that when she once appreciates the value of it, and observes its kind and beneficent working, she will find it convenient and easy to apply it far more generally than she would suppose.

No weakening of Authority in this.

It is very plain that softening thus the hardship for the child of any act of obedience required of him by giving him a little time implies no abatement of the authority of the parent, nor does it detract at all from the implicitness of the obedience on the part of the child. The submission to authority is as complete in doing a thing in five minutes if the order was to do it in five minutes, as in doing it at once if the order was to do it at once. And the mother must take great care, when thus trying to make obedience more easy by allowing time, that it should be prompt and absolute when the time has expired.

The idea is, that though the parent is bound fully to maintain his authority over his children, in all its force, he is also bound to make the exercise of it as little irksome and painful to them as possible, and to prevent as much as possible the pressure of it from encroaching upon their juvenile joys. He must insist inexorably on being obeyed; but he is bound to do all in his power to make the yoke of obedience light and easily to be borne.

Influence on the healthful Development of the Brain.

Indeed, besides the bearing of these views on the happiness of the children, it is not at all improbable that the question of health may be seriously involved in them. For, however certain we may be of the immateriality of the soul in its essence, it is a perfectly well established fact that all its operations and functions, as an animating spirit in the human body, are fulfilled through the workings of material organs in the brain; that these organs are in childhood in an exceedingly immature, tender, and delicate condition; and that all sudden, sharp, and, especially, painful emotions, greatly excite, and sometimes cruelly irritate them.

When we consider how seriously the action of the digestive organs, in persons in an ordinary state of health, is often interfered with by mental anxiety or distress; how frequently, in persons subject to headaches, the paroxysm is brought on by worryings or perplexities endured incidentally on the preceding day; and especially how often violent and painful emotions, when they are extreme, result in decided and sometimes in permanent and hopeless insanity—that is, in an irreparable damage to some delicate mechanism in the brain—we shall see that there is every reason for supposing that all sudden shocks to the nervous system of children, all violent and painful excitements, all vexations and irritations, and ebullitions of ill-temper and anger, have a tendency to disturb the healthy development of the cerebral organs, and may, in many cases, seriously affect the future health and welfare, as well as the present happiness, of the child.

It is true that mental disturbances and agitations of this kind can not be wholly avoided. But they should be avoided as far as possible; and the most efficient means for avoiding them is a firm, though calm and gentle, establishment and maintenance of parental authority, and not, as many mothers very mistakingly imagine, by unreasonable indulgences, and by endeavors to manage their children by persuasions, bribings, and manoeuvrings, instead of by commands. The most indulged children, and the least governed, are always the most petulant and irritable; while a strong government, if regular, uniform, and just, and if administered by gentle measures, is the most effectual of all possible instrumentalities for surrounding childhood with an atmosphere of calmness and peace.

In a word, while the mother is bound to do all in her power to render submission to her authority easy and agreeable to her children, by softening as much as possible the disappointment and hardship which her commands sometimes occasion, and by connecting pleasurable ideas and sensations with acts of obedience on the part of the child, she must not at all relax the authority itself, but must maintain it under all circumstances in its full force, with a very firm and decided, though still gentle hand.

CHAPTER VII.

THE ART OF TRAINING.

It is very clear that the most simple and the most obvious of the modes by which a parent may establish among his children the habit of submission to his authority, are those which have been already described, namely, punishments and rewards—punishments, gentle in their character, but invariably enforced, as the sure results of acts of insubordination; and rewards for obedience, occasionally and cautiously bestowed, in such a manner that they may be regarded as recognitions simply, on the part of the parent, of the good conduct of his children, and expressions of his gratification, and not in the light of payment or hire. These are obviously the most simple modes, and the ones most ready at hand. They require no exalted or unusual qualities on the part of father or mother, unless, indeed, we consider gentleness, combined with firmness and good sense, as an assemblage of rare and exalted qualities. To assign, and firmly and uniformly to enforce, just but gentle penalties for disobedience, and to recognize, and sometimes reward, special acts of obedience and submission, are measures fully within the reach of every parent, however humble may be the condition of his intelligence or his attainments of knowledge.

Another Class of Influences.

There is, however, another class of influences to be adopted, not as a substitute for these simple measures, but in connection and co-operation with them, which will be far more deep, powerful, and permanent in their results, though they require much higher qualities in the parent for carrying them successfully into effect. This higher method consists in a *systematic effort to develop in the mind of the child a love of the principle of obedience*, by express and appropriate training.

Parents not aware of the Extent of their Responsibility.

Many parents, perhaps indeed nearly all, seem, as we have already shown, to act as if they considered the duty of obedience on the part of their children as a matter of course. They do not expect their children to read or to write without being taught; they do not expect a dog to fetch and carry, or a horse to draw and to understand commands and signals, without being *trained*. In all these cases they perceive the necessity of training and instruction, and understand that the initiative is with *them*. If a horse, endowed by nature with average good qualities, does not work well, the fault is attributed at once to the man who undertook to train him. But what mother, when her child, grown large and strong, becomes the trial and sorrow of her life by his ungovernable disobedience and insubordination, takes the blame to herself in reflecting that he was placed in her hands when all the powers and faculties of his soul were in embryo, tender, pliant, and unresisting, to be formed and fashioned at her will?

The Spirit of filial Obedience not Instinctive.

Children, as has already been remarked, do not require to be taught and trained to eat and drink, to resent injuries, to cling to their possessions, or to run to their mother in danger or pain. They have natural instincts which provide for all these things. But to speak, to read, to write, and to calculate; to tell the truth, and to obey their parents; to forgive injuries, to face bravely fancied dangers and bear patiently unavoidable pain, are attainments for which no natural instincts can adequately provide. There are instincts that will aid in the work, but none that can of themselves be relied upon without instruction and training. In actual fact, children usually receive their instruction and training in respect to some of these things incidentally—as it happens—by the rough knocks and frictions, and various painful experiences which they encounter in the early years of life. In respect to others, the guidance and aid afforded them is more direct and systematic. Unfortunately the establishment in their minds of the principle of obedience comes ordinarily under the former category. No systematic and appropriate efforts are made by the parent to implant it. It is left to the uncertain and fitful influences of accident—to remonstrances, reproaches, and injunctions called forth under sudden excitement in the various emergencies of domestic discipline, and to other means, vague, capricious, and uncertain, and having no wise adaptedness to the attainment of the end in view.

Requires appropriate Training.

How much better and more successfully the object would be accomplished if the mother were to understand distinctly at the outset that the work of training her children to the habit of submission to her authority is a duty, the responsibility of which devolves not upon her children, but upon her; that it is a duty, moreover, of the highest importance, and one that demands careful consideration, much forethought, and the wise adaptation of means to the end.

Methods.

The first thought of some parents may possibly be, that they do not know of any other measures to take in order to teach their children submission to their authority, than to reward them when they obey and punish them when they disobey. To show that there are other methods, we will consider a particular case.

Mary, a young lady of seventeen, came to make a visit to her sister. She soon perceived that her sister's children, Adolphus and Lucia, were entirely ungoverned. Their mother coaxed, remonstrated, advised, gave reasons, said "I wouldn't do this," or "I wouldn't do that,"—did every thing, in fact, except simply to command; and the children, consequently, did pretty much what they pleased. Their mother wondered at their disobedience and insubordination, and in cases where these faults resulted in special inconvenience for herself she bitterly reproached the children for their undutiful behavior. But the reproaches produced no effect.

"The first thing that I have to do," said Mary to herself, in observing this state of things, "is to teach the children to obey—at least to obey *me*. I will give them their first lesson at once."

Mary makes a Beginning.

So she proposed to them to go out with her into the garden and show her the flowers, adding that if they would do so she would make each of them a bouquet. She could make them some very pretty bouquets, she said, provided they would help her, and would follow her directions and obey her implicitly while gathering and arranging the flowers.

This the children promised to do, and Mary went with them into the garden. There, as she passed about from border to border, she gave them a great many different directions in respect to things which they were to do, or which they were not to do. She gathered flowers, and gave some to one child, and some to the other, to be held and carried—with special instructions in respect to many details, such as directing some flowers to be put together, and others to be kept separate, and specifying in what manner they were to be held or carried. Then she led them to a bower where there was a long seat, and explained to them how they were to lay the flowers in order upon the seat, and directed them to be very careful not to touch them after they were once laid down. They were, moreover, to leave a place in the middle of the seat entirely clear. They asked what that was for. Mary said that they would see by-and-by. "You must always do just as I say," she added, "and perhaps I shall explain the reason afterwards, or perhaps you will see what the reason is yourselves."

After going on in this way until a sufficient number and variety of flowers were collected, Mary took her seat in the vacant place which had been left, and assigned the two portions of the seat upon which the flowers had been placed to the children, giving each the charge of the flowers upon one portion, with instructions to select and give to her such as she should call for. From the flowers thus brought she formed two bouquets, one for each of the children. Then she set them both at work to make bouquets for themselves, giving them minute and special directions in regard to every step. If her object had been to cultivate their taste and judgment, then it would have been better to allow them to choose the flowers and determine the arrangement for themselves; but she was teaching them *obedience*, or, rather, beginning to form in them the *habit* of obedience; and so, the more numerous and minute the commands the better, provided that they were not in them selves unreasonable, nor so numerous and minute as to be vexatious, so as to incur any serious danger of their not being readily and good-humoredly obeyed.

THE ART OF TRAINING. 101

When the bouquets were finished Mary gave the children, severally, the two which had been made for them; and the two which they had made for themselves she took into the house and placed them in glasses upon the parlor mantel-piece, and then stood back with the children in the middle of the room to admire them.

"See how pretty they look! And how nicely the work went on while we were making them! That was because you obeyed me so well while we were doing it. You did exactly as I said in every thing."

A Beginning only.

Now this was an excellent *first lesson* in training the children to the habit of obedience. It is true that it was *only* a first lesson. It was a beginning, but it was a very good beginning. If, on the following day, Mary had given the children a command which it would be irksome to them to obey, or one which would have called for any special sacrifice or self-denial on their part, they would have disregarded it. Still they would have been a little less inclined to disregard it than if they had not received their first lesson; and there can be no doubt that if Mary were to continue her training in the same spirit in which she commenced it she would, before many weeks, acquire a complete ascendency over them, and make them entirely submissive to her will.

And yet this is a species of training the efficacy of which depends on influences in which the hope of reward or the fear of punishment does not enter. The bouquets were not promised to the children at the outset, nor were they given to them at last as rewards. It is true that they saw the advantages resulting from due subordination of the inferiors to the superior in concerted action, and at the end they felt a satisfaction in having acted right; but these advantages did not come in the form of rewards. The efficacy of the lesson depended on a different principle altogether.

The Philosophy of it.

The philosophy of it was this: Mary, knowing that the principle of obedience in the children was extremely weak, and that it could not stand any serious test, contrived to bring it into exercise a great many times under the lightest possible pressure. She called upon them to do a great many different things, each of which was very easy to do, and gave them many little prohibitions which it required a very slight effort of self-denial on their part to regard; and she connected agreeable associations in their minds with the idea of submission to authority, through the interest which she knew they would feel in seeing the work of gathering the flowers and making the bouquets go systematically and prosperously on, and through the commendation of their conduct which she expressed at the end.

Such persons as Mary do not analyze distinctly, in their thoughts, nor could they express in words, the principles which underlie their management; but they have an instinctive mental perception of the adaptation of such means to the end in view. Other people, who observe how easily and quietly they seem to obtain an ascendency over all children coming within their influence, and how absolute this ascendency often becomes, are frequently surprised at it. They think there is some mystery about it; they say it is "a knack that some people have;" but there is no mystery about it at all, and nothing unusual or strange, except so far as practical good sense, considerate judgment, and intelligent observation and appreciation of the characteristics of childhood are unusual and strange.

Mary was aware that, although the principle of obedience is seldom or never entirely obliterated from the hearts of children—that is, that the impression upon their minds, which, though it may not be absolutely instinctive, is very early acquired, that it is incumbent on them to obey those set in authority over them, is seldom wholly effaced, the sentiment had become extremely feeble in the minds of Adolphus and Lucia; and that it was like a frail and dying plant, which required very delicate and careful nurture to quicken it to life and give it its normal health and vigor. Her management was precisely of this character. It called the weak and feeble principle into gentle exercise, without putting it to any severe test, and thus commenced the formation of a *habit of action*. Any one will see that a course of training on these principles, patiently and perseveringly continued for the proper time, could not fail of securing the desired end, except in cases of children characterized by unusual and entirely abnormal perversity.

We can not here follow in detail the various modes in which such a manager as Mary would adapt her principle to the changing incidents of each day, and to the different stages of progress made by her pupils in learning to obey, but can only enumerate certain points worthy of the attention of parents who may feel desirous to undertake such a work of training.

Three practical Directions.

1. Relinquish entirely the idea of expecting children to

be *spontaneously* docile and obedient, and the practice of scolding or punishing them vindictively when they are not so. Instead of so doing, understand that docility and obedience on their part is to be the result of wise, careful, and persevering, though gentle training on the part of the parent.

2. If the children have already formed habits of disobedience and insubordination, do not expect that the desirable change can be effected by sudden, spasmodic, and violent efforts, accompanied by denunciations and threats, and declarations that you are going to "turn over a new leaf." The attempt to change perverted tendencies in children by such means is like trying to straighten a bend in the stem of a growing tree by blows with a hammer.

3. Instead of this, begin without saying at all what you are going to do, or finding any fault with the past, and, with a distinct recognition of the fact that whatever is bad in the *native tendencies* of your children's minds is probably inherited from their parents, and, perhaps, specially from yourself, and that whatever is wrong in their *habits of action* is certainly the result of bad training, proceed cautiously and gently, but perseveringly and firmly, in bringing the bent stem gradually up to the right position. In doing this, there is no amount of ingenuity and skill, however great, that may not be usefully employed; nor is there, on the other hand, except in very rare and exceptional cases, any parent who has an allotment so small as not to be sufficient to accomplish the end, if conscientiously and faithfully employed.

CHAPTER VIII.

METHODS EXEMPLIFIED.

In order to give a more clear idea of what I mean by forming habits of obedience in children by methods other than those connected with a system of rewards and punishments, I will specify some such methods, introducing them, however, only as illustrations of what is intended. For, while in respect to rewards and punishments something like special and definite rules and directions may be given, these other methods, as they depend on the tact, ingenuity, and inventive powers of the parents for their success, depend also in great measure upon these same qualities for the discovery of them. The only help that can be received from without must consist of suggestions and illustrations, which can only serve to communicate to the mind some general ideas in respect to them.

Recognizing the Right.

1. A very excellent effect is produced in forming habits of obedience in children, by simply *noticing* their good conduct when they do right, and letting them see that you notice it. When children are at play upon the carpet, and their mother from time to time calls one of them—Mary, we will say—to come to her to render some little service, it is very often the case that she is accustomed, when Mary obeys the call at once, leaving her play immediately and coming directly, to say nothing about the prompt obedience, but to treat it as a matter of course. It is only in the cases of failure that she seems to notice the action. When Mary, greatly interested in what for the moment she is doing, delays her coming, she says, "You ought to come at once, Mary, when I call you, and not make me wait in this way." In the cases when Mary did come at once, she had said nothing.

Mary goes back to her play after the reproof, a little disturbed in mind, at any rate, and perhaps considerably out of humor.

Now Mary may, perhaps, be in time induced to obey more promptly under this management, but she will have no heart in making the improvement, and she will advance reluctantly and slowly, if at all. But if, at the first time that she comes promptly, and then, after doing the errand, is ready to go back to her play, her mother says, "You left your play and came at once when I called you. That was right. It pleases me very much to find that I can depend upon your being so prompt, even when you are at play," Mary will go back to her play pleased and happy; and the tendency of the incident will be to cause her to feel a spontaneous and cordial interest in the principle of prompt obedience in time to come.

Johnny is taking a walk through the fields with his mother. He sees a butterfly and sets off in chase of it. When he has gone away from the path among the rocks and bushes as far as his mother thinks is safe, she calls him to come back. In many cases, if the boy does not come at once in obedience to such a call, he would perhaps receive a scolding. If he does come back at once, nothing is said. In either case no decided effect would be produced upon him.

But if his mother says, "Johnny, you obeyed me at once when I called you. It must be hard, when you are after a butterfly and think you have almost caught him, to stop immediately and come back to your mother when she calls you; but you did it," Johnny will be led by this treatment to feel a desire to come back more promptly still the next time.

A Caution.

Of course there is an endless variety of ways by which you can show your children that you notice and appreciate the efforts they make to do right. Doubtless there is a danger to be guarded against. To adopt the practice of noticing and commending what is right, and paying *no attention whatever* to what is wrong, would be a great perversion of this counsel. There is a danger more insidious than this, but still very serious and real, of fostering a feeling of vanity and self-conceit by constant and inconsiderate praise. These things must be guarded against; and to secure the good aimed at, and at the same time to avoid the evil, requires the exercise of the tact and ingenuity which has before been referred to. But with proper skill and proper care the habit of noticing and commending, or even noticing alone, when children do right, and of even being more quick to notice and to be pleased with the right than to detect and be dissatisfied with the wrong, will be found to be a very powerful means of training children in the right way.

Children will act with a great deal more readiness and alacrity to preserve a good character which people already attribute to them, than to relieve themselves of the opprobrium of a bad one with which they are charged. In other words, it is much easier to allure them to what is right than to drive them from what is wrong.

Giving Advice.

2. There is, perhaps, nothing more irksome to children than to listen to advice given to them in a direct and simple form, and perhaps there is nothing that has less influence upon them in the formation of their characters than advice so given. And there is good reason for this; for either the advice must be general, and of course more or less abstract, when it is necessarily in a great measure lost upon them, since their powers of generalization and abstraction are not yet developed; or else, if it is practical and particular at all, it must be so with reference to their own daily experience in life—in which case it becomes more irksome still, as they necessarily regard it as an indirect mode of fault-finding. Indeed, this kind of advice is almost certain to assume the form of half-concealed fault-finding, for the subject of the counsel given would be, in almost all cases, suggested by the errors, or shortcomings, or failures which had been recently observed in the conduct of the children. The art, then, of giving to children general advice and instruction in respect to their conduct and behavior, consists in making it definite and practical, and at the same time contriving some way of divesting it entirely of all direct application to themselves in respect to their *past* conduct. Of course, the more we make it practically applicable to them in respect to the future the better.

There are various ways of giving advice of this character. It requires some ingenuity to invent them, and some degree of tact and skill to apply them successfully. But the necessary tact and skill would be easily acquired by any mother whose heart is really set upon finding gentle modes of leading her child into the path of duty.

James and his Cousins.

James, going to spend one of his college vacations at his uncle's, was taken by his two cousins, Walter and Ann—eight and six years old—into their room. The room was all in confusion. There was a set of book-shelves upon one side, the books upon them lying tumbled about in all directions. There was a case containing playthings in another place, the playthings broken and in disorder; and two tables, one against the wall, and the other in the middle of the room, both covered with litter. Now if James had commenced his conversation by giving the children a lecture on the disorder of their room, and on the duty, on their part, of taking better care of their things, the chief effect would very probably have been simply to prevent their wishing to have him come to their room again.

But James managed the case differently. After going about the room for a few minutes with the children, and looking with them at their various treasures, and admiring what they seemed to admire, but without finding any fault, he sat down before the fire and took the children upon his lap —one upon each knee—and began to talk to them. Ann had one of her picture-books in her hand, some of the leaves torn, and the rest defaced with dog's-ears.

"Now, Walter," said James, "I'm going to give you some advice. I am going to advise you what to do and how to act when you go to college. By-and-by you will grow to be a young man, and will then, perhaps, go to college."

The idea of growing to be a young man and going to college was very pleasing to Walter's imagination, and brought his mind into what may be called a receptive condition—that is, into a state to receive readily, and entertain with favor, the thoughts which James was prepared to present.

James then went on to draw a very agreeable picture of Walter's leaving home and going to college, with many details calculated to be pleasing to his cousin's fancy, and came at length to his room, and to the circumstances under which he would take possession of it. Then he told him of the condition in which different scholars kept their respective rooms—how some were always in disorder, and every thing in them topsy-turvy, so that they had no pleasant or home-like aspect at all; while in others every thing was well arranged, and kept continually in that condition, so as to give the whole room, to every one who entered it, a very charming appearance.

"The books on their shelves were all properly arranged," he said, "all standing up in order—those of a like size together. Jump down, Ann, and go to your shelves, and arrange the books on the middle shelf in that way, to show him what I mean."

Ann jumped down, and ran with great alacrity to arrange the books according to the directions. When she had arranged one shelf, she was proceeding to do the same with the next, but James said she need not do any more then. She could arrange the others, if she pleased, at another time, he said. "But come back now," he added, "and hear the rest of the advice."

"I advise you to keep your book-shelves in nice order at college," he continued; "and so with your apparatus and your cabinet. For at college, you see, you will perhaps have articles of philosophical apparatus, and a cabinet of specimens, instead of playthings. I advise you, if you should have such things, to keep them all nicely arranged upon their shelves."

Here James turned his chair a little, so that he and the children could look towards the cabinet of playthings. Walter climbed down from his cousin's lap and ran off to that side of the room, and there began hastily to arrange the playthings.

"Yes," said James, "that is the way. But never mind that now. I think you will know how to arrange your philosophical instruments and your cabinet very nicely when you are in college; and you can keep your playthings in order in your room here, while you are a boy, if you please. But come back now and hear the rest of the advice."

So Walter came back and took his place again upon James's knee.

"And I advise you," continued James, "to take good care of your books when you are in college. It is pleasanter, at the time, to use books that are clean and nice, and then, besides, you will like to take your college books with you, after you leave college, and keep them as long as you live, as memorials of your early days, and you will value them a great deal more if they are in good order."

Here Ann opened the book which was in her hand, and began to fold back the dog's-ears and to smooth down the leaves.

The Principle Involved.

In a word, by the simple expedient of shifting the time, in the imagination of the children, when the advice which he was giving them would come to its practical application, he divested it of all appearance of fault-finding in respect to their present conduct, and so secured not merely its ready admission, but a cordial welcome for it, in their minds.

Any mother who sees and clearly apprehends the principle here illustrated, and has ingenuity enough to avail herself of it, will find an endless variety of modes by which she can make use of it, to gain easy access to the hearts of her children, for instructions and counsels which, when they come in the form of fault-finding advice, make no impression whatever.

Expectations of Results must be Reasonable.

Some persons, however, who read without much reflection, and who do not clearly see the principle involved in the case above described, and do not understand it as it is intended—that is, as a single specimen or example of a mode of action capable of an endless variety of applications, will perhaps say, "Oh, that was all very well. James's talk was very good for the purpose of amusing the children for a few minutes while he was visiting them, but it is idle to suppose that such a conversation could produce any permanent or even lasting impression upon them; still less, that it could work any effectual change in respect to their habits of order."

That is very true. In the work of forming the hearts and minds of children it is "line upon line, and precept upon precept" that is required; and it can not be claimed that one such conversation as that of James is any thing more than *one line*. But it certainly is that. It would be as unreasonable to expect that one single lesson like that could effectually and completely accomplish the end in view, as that one single watering of a plant will suffice to enable it to attain completely its growth, and enable it to produce in perfection its fruits or its flowers.

But if a mother often clothes thus the advice or instruction which she has to give to her children in some imaginative guise like this, advising them what to do when they are on a journey, for example, or when they are making a visit at the house of a friend in the country; or, in the case of a boy, what she would counsel him to do in case he were a young man employed by a farmer to help him on his farm, or a clerk in a store, or a sea-captain in charge of a ship, or a general commanding a force in the field; or, if a girl, what dangers or what undesirable habits or actions she should avoid when travelling in Europe, or when, as a young lady, she joins in picnics or goes on excursions, or attends concerts or evening parties, or in any of the countless other situations which it is pleasant for young persons to picture to their minds, introducing into all, so far as her ingenuity and skill enable her to do it, interesting incidents and details, she will find that she is opening to herself an avenue to her children's hearts for the sound moral principles that she wishes to inculcate upon them, which she can often employ easily, pleasantly, and very advantageously, both to herself and to them.

When a child is sick, it may be of little consequence whether the medicine which is required is agreeable or disagreeable to the taste. But with moral remedies the case is different. Sometimes the whole efficiency of the treatment administered as a corrective for a moral disorder depends upon the readiness and willingness with which it is taken. To make it disagreeable, consequently, in such cases, is to neutralize the intended action of it—a result which the methods described in this chapter greatly tend to avoid.

CHAPTER IX.

DELLA AND THE DOLLS.

This book may, perhaps, sometimes fall into the hands of persons who have, temporarily or otherwise, the charge of young children without any absolute authority over them, or any means, or even any right, to enforce their commands, as was the case, in fact, with the older brothers or sister referred to in the preceding illustrations. To such persons, these indirect modes of training children in habits of subordination to their will, or rather of yielding to their influence, are specially useful. Such persons may be interested in the manner in which Delia made use of the children's dolls as a means of guiding and governing their little mothers.

Della.

Della had a young sister named Maria, and a cousin whose name was Jane. Jane used often to come to make Maria a visit, and when together the children were accustomed to spend a great deal of time in playing with their dolls. Besides dressing and undressing them, and playing take them out to excursions and visits, they used to talk with them a great deal, and give them much useful and valuable information and instruction.

Now Delia contrived to obtain a great influence and ascendency over the minds of the children by means of these dolls. She fell at once into the idea of the children in regard to them, and treated them always as if they were real persons; often speaking of them and to them, in the presence of the other children, in the most serious manner. This not only pleased the children very much, but enabled Della, under pretense of talking to the dolls, to communicate a great deal of useful instruction to the children, and sometimes to make very salutary and lasting impressions upon their minds.

Lectures to the Dolls.

For instance, sometimes when Jane was making Maria a visit, and the two children came into her room with their dolls in their arms, she would speak to them as if they were real persons, and then taking them in her hands would set them before her on her knee, and give them a very grave lecture in respect to the proper behavior which they were to observe during the afternoon. If Delia had attempted to give precisely the same lecture to the children themselves, they would very soon have become restless and uneasy, and it would have made very little impression upon them. But being addressed to the dolls, they would be greatly interested in it, and would listen with the utmost attention; and there is no doubt that the counsels and instructions which she gave made a much stronger impression upon their minds than if they had been addressed directly to the children themselves. To give an idea of these conversations I will report one of them in full.

"How do you do, my children?" she said, on one such occasion. "I am very glad to see you. How nice you look! You have come, Andella (Andella was the name of Jane's doll), to make Rosalie a visit. I am very glad. You will have a very pleasant time, I am sure; because you never quarrel. I observe that, when you both wish for the same thing, you don't quarrel for it and try to pull it away from one another; but one waits like a lady until the other has done with it. I expect you have been a very good girl, Andella, since you were here last."

Then, turning to Jane, she asked, in a somewhat altered tone, "Has she been a good girl, Jane?"

"She has been a *pretty* good girl," said Jane, "but she has been sick."

"Ah!" said Della in a tone of great concern, and looking again at Andella, "I heard that you had been sick. I heard that you had an attack of Aurora Borealis, or something like that. And you don't look very well now. You must take good care of yourself, and if you don't feel well, you must ask your mother to bring you in to me and I will give you a dose of my medicine—my *aqua saccharina*. I know you always take your medicine like a little heroine when you are sick, without making any difficulty or trouble at all."

Aqua saccharina was the Latin name which Delia gave to a preparation of which she kept a supply in a small phial on her table, ready to make-believe give to the dolls when they were sick. Maria and Jane were very fond of playing that their dolls were sick and bringing them to Della for medicine, especially as Della always recommended to them to taste the medicine themselves from a spoon first, in order to set their children a good example of taking it well.

Sometimes Della would let the children take the phial away, so as to have it always at hand in case the dolls should be taken suddenly worse. But in such cases as this the attacks were usually so frequent, and the mothers were obliged to do so much tasting to encourage the patients, that the phial was soon brought back nearly or quite empty, when Delia used to replenish it by filling it nearly full of water, and then pouring a sufficient quantity of the saccharine powder into the mouth of it from the sugar-bowl with a spoon. Nothing more was necessary except to shake up the mixture in order to facilitate the process of solution, and the medicine was ready.

A Medium of Reproof.

Delia was accustomed to use the dolls not only for the purpose of instruction, but sometimes for reproof, in many ingenious ways. For instance, one day the children had been playing upon the piazza with blocks and other playthings, and finally had gone into the house, leaving all the things on the floor of the piazza, instead of putting them away in their places, as they ought to have done. They were now playing with their dolls in the parlor.

Delia came to the parlor, and with an air of great mystery beckoned the children aside, and said to them, in a whisper, "Leave Andella and Rosalie here, and don't say a word to them. I want you to come with me. There is a secret—something I would not have them know on any account."

So saying, she led the way on tiptoe, followed by the children out of the room, and round by a circuitous route to the piazza.

"There!" said she, pointing to the playthings; "see! all your playthings left out! Put them away quick before Andella and Rosalie see them. I would not have them know that their mothers leave their playthings about in that way for any consideration. They would think that they might do so too, and that would make you a great deal of trouble. You teach them, I have no doubt, that they must always put their playthings away, and they must see that you set them a good example. Put these playthings all away quick, and carefully, and we will not let them know any thing about your leaving them out."

So the children went to work with great alacrity, and put the playthings all away. And this method of treating the case was much more effectual in making them disposed to avoid committing a similar fault another time than any direct rebukes or expressions of displeasure addressed personally to them would have been.

Besides, a scolding would have made them unhappy, and this did not make them unhappy at all; it amused and entertained them. If you can lead children to cure themselves of their faults in such a way that they shall have a good time in doing it, there is a double gain.

In due time, by this kind of management, and by other modes conceived and executed in the same spirit, Bella gained so great an ascendency over the children that they were far more ready to conform to her will, and to obey all her directions, than they would have been to submit to the most legitimate authority that was maintained, as such authority too often is, by fault-finding and threats, and without any sympathy with the fancies and feelings which reign over the hearts of the children in the little world in which they live.

CHAPTER X.

SYMPATHY:—1. THE CHILD WITH THE PARENT.

The subject of sympathy between children and parents is to be considered in two aspects: first, that of the child with the parent; and secondly, that of the parent with the child. That is to say, an emotion may be awakened in the child by its existence and manifestation in the parent, and secondly, it may be awakened in the parent by its existence in the child.

We are all ready to acknowledge in words the great power and influence of sympathy, but very few are aware how very vast this power is, and how inconceivably great is the function which this principle fulfills in the formation of the human character, and in regulating the conduct of men.

Mysterious Action of the Principle of Sympathy.

There is a great mystery in the nature of it, and in the manner of its action. This we see very clearly in the simplest and most striking material form of it—the act of gaping. Why and how does the witnessing of the act of gaping in one person, or even the thought of it, produce a tendency to the same action in the nerves and muscles of another person? When we attempt to trace the chain of connection through the eye, the brain, and the thoughts—through which line of agencies the chain of cause and effect must necessarily run—we are lost and bewildered.

Other states and conditions in which the mental element is more apparent are communicated from one to another in the same or, at least, in some analogous way. Being simply in the presence of one who is amused, or happy, or sad, causes us to feel amused, or happy, or sad ourselves—or, at least, has that tendency—even if we do not know from what cause the emotion which is communicated to us proceeds. A person of a joyous and happy disposition often brightens up at once any little circle into which he enters, while a morose and melancholy man carries gloom with him wherever he goes. Eloquence, which, if we were to hear it addressed to us personally and individually, in private conversation, would move us very little, will excite us to a pitch of the highest enthusiasm if we hear it in the midst of a vast audience; even though the words, and the gestures, and the inflections of the voice, and the force with which it reaches our ears, were to be precisely the same in the two cases. And so a joke, which would produce only a quiet smile if we read it by ourselves at the fireside alone, will evoke convulsions of laughter when heard in a crowded theatre, where the hilarity is shared by thousands.

A new element, indeed, seems to come into action in these last two cases; for the mental condition of one mind is not only communicated to another, but it appears to be increased and intensified by the communication. Each does not feel *merely* the enthusiasm or the mirth which would naturally be felt by the other, but the general emotion is vastly heightened by its being so largely shared. It is like the case of the live coal, which does not merely set the dead coal on fire by being placed in contact with it, but the two together, when together, burn far more brightly than when apart.

Wonderful Power of Sympathy.

So much for the reality of this principle; and it is almost impossible to exaggerate the extent and the magnitude of the influence it exerts in forming the character and shaping the ideas and opinions of men, and in regulating all their ordinary habits of thought and feeling. People's opinions are not generally formed or controlled by arguments or reasonings, as they fondly suppose. They are imbibed by sympathy from those whom they like or love, and who are, or have been, their associates. Thus people, when they arrive at maturity, adhere in the main to the associations, both in religion and in politics, in which they have been brought up, from the influence of sympathy with those whom they love. They believe in this or that doctrine or system, not because they have been convinced by proof, but chiefly because those whom they love believe in them. On religious questions the arguments are presented to them, it is true, while they are young, in catechisms and in other forms of religious instruction, and in politics by the conversations which they overhear; but it is a mistake to suppose that arguments thus offered have any material effect as processes of ratiocination in producing any logical conviction upon their minds. An English boy is Whig or Tory because his father, and his brothers, and his uncles are Whigs or Tories. He may, indeed, have many arguments at his command with which to maintain his opinions, but it is not the force of the arguments that has convinced him, nor do they have any force as a means of convincing the other boys to whom he offers them. *They* are controlled by their sympathies, as he is by his. But if he is a popular boy, and makes himself a favorite among his companions, the very fact that he is of this or that party will have more effect upon the other boys than the most logical and conclusive trains of reasoning that can be conceived.

So it is with the religious and political differences in this and in every other country. Every one's opinions—or rather the opinion of people in general, for of course there are many individual exceptions—are formed from sympathy with those with whom in mind and heart they have been in friendly communication during their years of childhood and youth. And even in those cases where persons change their religious opinions in adult age, the explanation of the mystery is generally to be found, not in seeking for the *argument that convinced them*, but for the *person that led them*, in the accomplishment of the change. For such changes can very often, and perhaps generally, be traced to some person or persons whose influence over them, if carefully scrutinized, would be found to consist really not in the force of the arguments they offered, but in the magic power of a silent and perhaps unconscious sympathy. The way, therefore, to convert people to our ideas and opinions is to make them like us or love us, and then to avoid arguing with them, but simply let them perceive what our ideas and opinions are.

The well-known proverb, "Example is better than precept," is only another form of expressing the predominating power of sympathy; for example can have little influence except so far as a sympathetic feeling in the observer leads him to imitate it. So that, example is better than precept means only that sympathy has more influence in the human heart than reasoning.

The Power of Sympathy in Childhood.

This principle, so powerful at every period of life, is at its maximum in childhood. It is the origin, in a very great degree, of the spirit of imitation which forms so remarkable a characteristic of the first years of life. The child's thoughts and feelings being spontaneously drawn into harmony with the thoughts and feelings of those around him whom he loves, leads, of course, to a reproduction of their actions, and the prevalence and universality of the effect shows how constant and how powerful is the cause. So the great secret of success for a mother, in the formation of the character of her children, is to make her children respect and love her, and then simply to *be* herself what she wishes them to be.

And to make them respect and love her, is to control them by a firm government where control is required, and to indulge them almost without limit where indulgence will do no harm.

Special Application of the Principle.

But besides this general effect of the principle of sympathy in aiding parents in forming the minds and hearts of their children, there are a great many cases in which a father or mother who understands the secret of its wonderful and almost magic power can avail themselves of it to produce special effects. One or two examples will show more clearly what I mean.

William's aunt Maria came to pay his mother a visit in the village where

William's mother lived. On the same day she went to take a walk with William—who is about nine years old—to see the village. As they went along together upon the sidewalk, they came to two small boys who were trying to fly a kite. One of the boys was standing upon the sidewalk, embarrassed a little by some entanglement of the string.

"Here, you fellow!" said William, as he and his aunt approached the spot, "get out of the way with your kite, and let us go by."

The boy hurried out of the way, and, in so doing, got his kite-string more entangled still in the branches of a tree which grew at the margin of the sidewalk.

Now William's aunt might have taken the occasion, as she and her nephew walked along, to give him some kind and friendly instruction or counsel about the duty of being kind to every body in any difficulty, trouble, or perplexity, whether they are young or old; showing him how we increase the general sum of happiness in so doing, and how we feel happier ourselves when we have done good to any one, than when we have increased in any way, or even slighted or disregarded, their troubles. How William would receive such a lecture would depend a great deal upon his disposition and state of mind. But in most cases such counsels, given at such a time, involving, as they would, some covert though very gentle censure, would cause the heart of the boy to close itself in a greater or less degree against them, like the leaves of a sensitive-plant shrinking from the touch. The reply would very probably be, "Well, he had no business to be on the sidewalk, right in our way."

William and his aunt walked on a few steps. His aunt then stopped, hesitatingly, and said,

"How would it do to go back and help that boy disentangle his kite-string? He's a little fellow, and does not know so much about kites and kite-strings as you do."

Here the suggestion of giving help to perplexity and distress came associated with a compliment instead of what implied censure, and the leaves of the sensitive-plant expanded at once, and widely, to the genial influence.

"Yes," said William; "let's go."

So his aunt turned and went back a step or two, and then said, "You can go and do it without me. I'll wait here till you come back. I don't suppose you want any help from me. If you do, I'll come."

"No," aid William, "I can do it alone."

So William ran on with great alacrity to help the boys clear the string, and then came back with a beaming face to his aunt, and they walked on.

William's aunt made no further allusion to the affair until the end of the walk, and then, on entering the gate, she said, "We have had a very pleasant walk, and you have taken very good care of me. And I am glad we helped those boys out of their trouble with the kite."

"So am I," said William.

Analysis of the Incident.

Now it is possible that some one may say that William was wrong in his harsh treatment of the boys, or at least in his want of consideration for their perplexity; and that his aunt, by her mode of treating the case, covered up the wrong, when it ought to have been brought distinctly to view and openly amended. But when we come to analyze the case, we shall find that it is not at all certain that there was any thing wrong on William's part in the transaction, so far as the state of his heart, in a moral point of view, is concerned. All such incidents are very complicated in their nature, and in their bearings and relations. They present many aspects which vary according to the point of view from which they are regarded. Even grown people do not always see all the different aspects of an affair in respect to which they are called upon to act or to form an opinion, and children, perhaps, never; and in judging their conduct, we must always consider the aspect in which the action is presented to their minds. In this case, William was thinking only of his aunt. He wished to make her walk convenient and agreeable to her. The boy disentangling his string on the sidewalk was to him, at that time, simply an obstacle in his aunt's way, and he dealt with it as such, sending the boy off as an act of kindness and attention to his aunt solely. The idea of a sentient being suffering distress which he might either increase by harshness or relieve by help was not present in his mind at all. We may say that he ought to have thought of this. But a youthful mind, still imperfect in its development, can not be expected to take cognizance at once of all the aspects of a transaction which tends in different directions to different results. It is true, that he ought to have thought of the distress of the boys, if we mean that he ought to be taught or trained to think of such distress when he witnessed it; and that was exactly what his aunt was endeavoring to do. We ourselves have learned, by long experience of life, to perceive at once the many different aspects which an affair may present, and the many different results which may flow in various directions from the same action; and we often inconsiderately blame children, simply because their minds are yet so imperfectly developed that they can not take simultaneous cognizance of more than one or two of them. This is the true philosophy of most of what is called heedlessness in children, and for which, poor things, they receive so many harsh reprimands and so much punishment.

A little girl, for example, undertakes to water her sister's plants. In her praiseworthy desire to do her work well and thoroughly, she fills the mug too full, and spills the water upon some books that are lying upon the table. The explanation of the misfortune is simply that her mind was filled, completely filled, with the thoughts of helping her sister. The thought of the possibility of spilling the water did not come into it at all. There was no room for it while the other thought, so engrossing, was there; and to say that she *ought* to have thought of both the results which might follow her action, is only to say that she ought to be older.

Sympathy as the Origin of childish Fears.

The power of sympathy in the mind of a child—that is, its tendency to imbibe the opinions or sentiments manifested by others in their presence —may be made very effectual, not only in inculcating principles of right and wrong, but in relation to every other idea or emotion. Children are afraid of thunder and lightning, or of robbers at night, or of ghosts, because they perceive that their parents, or older brothers or sisters, are afraid of them. Where the parents do not believe in ghosts, the children are not afraid of them; unless, indeed, there are domestics in the house, or playmates at school, or other companions from whom they take the contagion. So, what they see that their parents value they prize themselves. They imbibe from their playmates at school a very large proportion of their tastes, their opinions, and their ideas, not through arguments or reasoning, but from sympathy; and most of the wrong or foolish notions of any kind that they have acquired have not been established in their minds by false reasoning, but have been taken by sympathy, as a disease is communicated by infection; and the remedy is in most cases, not reasoning, but a countervailing sympathy.

Afraid of a Kitten.

Little Jane was very much afraid of a kitten which her brother brought home—the first that she had known. She had, however, seen a picture of a tiger or some other feline animal devouring a man in a forest, and had been frightened by it; and she had heard too, perhaps, of children being scratched by cats or kittens. So, when the kitten was brought in and put down on the floor, she ran to her sister in great terror, and began to cry.

Now her sister might have attempted to reason with her by explaining the difference between the kitten and the wild animals of the same class in the woods, and by assuring her that thousands of children have kittens to play with and are never scratched by them so long as they treat them kindly—and all without producing any sensible effect. But, instead of this, she adopted a different plan. She took the child up into her lap, and after quieting her fears, began to talk to the kitten.

"Poor little pussy," said she, "I am glad you have come. You never scratch any body, I am sure, if they are kind to you. Jennie will give you some milk some day, and she and I will like to see you lap it up with your pretty little tongue. And we will give you a ball to play with some day upon the carpet. See, Jennie, see! She is going to lie down upon the rug. She is glad that she has come to such a nice home. Now she is putting her head down, but she has not any pillow to lay it upon. Wouldn't you like a pillow, kitty? Jennie will make you a pillow some day, I am sure, if you would like one. Jennie is beginning to learn to sew, and she could make you a nice pillow, and stuff it with cotton wool. Then we can see you lying down upon the rug, with the pillow under your head that Jennie will have made for you—all comfortable."

Such a talk as this, though it could not be expected entirely and at once to dispel Jennie's unfounded fears, would be far more effectual towards beginning the desired change than any arguments or reasoning could possibly be.

Any mother who will reflect upon the principle here explained will at once recall to mind many examples and illustrations of its power over the hearts and minds of children which her own experience has afforded. And if she begins practically and systematically to appeal to it, she will find herself in possession of a new element of power—new, at least, to her realization—the exercise of which will be as easy and agreeable to herself as it will be effective in its influence over her children.

CHAPTER XI.

SYMPATHY:—II. THE PARENT WITH THE CHILD.

I think there can be no doubt that the most effectual way of securing the confidence and love of children, and of acquiring an ascendency over them, is by sympathizing with them in their child-like hopes and fears, and joys and sorrows—in their ideas, their fancies, and even in their caprices, in all cases where duty is not concerned. Indeed, the more child-like, that is, the more peculiar to the children themselves, the feelings are that we enter into with them, the closer is the bond of kindness and affection that is formed.

An Example.

If a gentleman coming to reside in a new town concludes that it is desirable that he should be on good terms with the boys in the streets, there are various ways by which he can seek to accomplish the end.

Fortunately for him, the simplest and easiest mode is the most effectual. On going into the village one day, we will suppose he sees two small boys playing horse. One boy is horse, and the other driver. As they draw near, they check the play a little, to be more decorous in passing by the stranger. He stops to look at them with a pleased expression of countenance, and then says, addressing the driver, with a face of much seriousness, "That's a first-rate horse of yours. Would you like to sell him? He seems to be very spirited." The horse immediately begins to prance and caper. "You must have paid a high price for him. You must take good care of him. Give him plenty of oats, and don't drive him hard when it is hot weather. And if ever you conclude to sell him, I wish you would let me know."

So saying, the gentleman walks on, and the horse, followed by his driver, goes galloping forward in high glee.

Now, by simply manifesting thus a fellow-feeling with the boys in their childish play, the stranger not only gives a fresh impulse to their enjoyment at the time, but establishes a friendly relationship between them and him which, without his doing any thing to strengthen or perpetuate it, will of itself endure for a long time. If he does not speak to the boys again for months, every time they meet him they will be ready to greet him with a smile.

The incident will go much farther towards establishing friendly relations between him and them than any presents that he could make them—except so far as his presents were of such a kind, and were given in such a way, as to be expressions of kindly feeling towards them—that is to say, such as to constitute of themselves a manifestation of sympathy.

The uncle who gives his nephews and nieces presents, let them be ever so costly or beautiful, and takes no interest in their affairs, never inspires them with any feeling of personal affection. They like him as they like the apple-tree which bears them sweet and juicy apples, or the cow that gives them milk—which is on their part a very different sentiment from that which they feel for the kitten that plays with them and shares their joys—or even for their dolls, which are only pictured in their imagination as sharing them.

Sophronia and Aurelia.

Miss Sophronia calls at a house to make a visit. A child of seven or eight years of age is playing upon the floor. After a little time, at a pause in the conversation, she calls the child—addressing her as "My little girl"—to come to her. The child—a shade being cast over her mind by being thus unnecessarily reminded of her littleness—hesitates to come. The mother says, "Come and shake hands with the lady, my dear!" The child comes reluctantly. Miss Sophronia asks what her name is, how old she is, whether she goes to school, what she studies there, and whether she likes to go to school, and at length releases her. The child, only too glad to be free from such a tiresome visitor, goes back to her play, and afterwards the only ideas she has associated with the person of her visitor are those relating to her school and her lessons, which may or may not be of an agreeable character.

Presently, after Miss Sophronia has gone, Miss Aurelia comes in. After some conversation with the mother, she goes to see what the child is building with her blocks. After looking on for a moment with an expression of interest in her countenance, she asks her if she has a doll. The child says she has four. Miss Aurelia then asks which she likes best, and expresses a desire to see that one. The child, much pleased, runs away to bring it, and presently comes back with all four. Miss Aurelia takes them in her hands, examines them, talks about them, and talks to them; and when at last the child goes back to her play, she goes with the feeling in her heart that she has found a new friend.

Thus, to bring ourselves near to the hearts of children, we must go to them by entering into *their world*. They can not come to us by entering ours. They have no experience of it, and can not understand it. But we have had experience of theirs, and can enter it if we choose; and in that way we bring ourselves very near to them.

Sympathy must be Sincere.

But the sympathy which we thus express with children, in order to be effectual, must be sincere and genuine, and not pretended. We must renew our own childish ideas and imaginations, and become for the moment, in feeling, one with them, so that the interest which we express in what they are saying or doing may be real, and not merely assumed. They seem to have a natural instinct to distinguish between an honest and actual sharing of their thoughts and emotions, and all mere condescension and pretense, however adroitly it may be disguised.

Want of Time.

Some mothers may perhaps say that they have not time thus to enter into the ideas and occupations of their children. They are engrossed with the serious cares of life, or busy with its various occupations. But it does not require time. It is not a question of time, but of manner. The farmer's wife, for example, is busy ironing, or sewing, or preparing breakfast for her husband and sons, who are expected every moment to come in hungry from their work. Her little daughter, ten years old, comes to show her a shawl she has been making from a piece of calico for her doll. The busy mother thinks she must say, "Yes; but run away now, Mary; I am very busy!"—because that is the easiest and quickest thing to say; but it is just as easy and just as quick to say, "What a pretty shawl! Play now that you are going to take Minette out for a walk in it!" The one mode sends the child away repulsed and a little disappointed; the other pleases her and makes her happy, and tends, moreover, to form a new bond of union and sympathy between her mother's heart and her own. A merchant, engrossed all day in his business, comes home to his house at dinner-time, and meets his boy of fifteen on the steps returning from his school. "Well, James," he says, as they walk together up stairs, "I hope you have been a good boy at school to-day." James, not knowing what to say, makes some inaudible or unmeaning reply. His father then goes on to say that he hopes his boy will be diligent and attentive to his studies, and improve his time well, as his future success in life will depend upon the use which he makes of his advantages while he is young; and then leaves him at the head of the stairs, each to go to his room.

All this is very well. Advice given under such circumstances and in such a way produces, undoubtedly, a certain good effect, but it does not tend at all to bring the father and son together. But if, instead of giving this common-place advice, the father asks—supposing it to be winter at the time—"Which kind of skates are the most popular among the boys nowadays, James?" Then, after hearing his reply, he asks him what *his* opinion is, and whether any great improvement has been made within a short time, and whether the patent inventions are any of them of much consequence. The tendency of such a conversation as this, equally brief with the other, will be to draw the father and son more together. Even in a moral point of view, the influence would be, indirectly, very salutary; for although no moral counsel or instruction was given at the time, the effect of such a participation in the thoughts with which the boy's mind is occupied is to strengthen the bond of union between the heart of the boy and that of his father, and thus to make the boy far more ready to receive and be guided by the advice or admonitions of his father on other occasions.

Let no one suppose, from these illustrations, that they are intended to inculcate the idea that a father is to lay aside the parental counsels and instructions that he has been accustomed to give to his children, and replace them by talks about skates! They are only intended to show one aspect of the difference of effect produced by the two kinds of conversation, and that the father, if he wishes to gain and retain an influence over the hearts of his boys, must descend sometimes into the world in which they live, and with which their thoughts are occupied, and must enter it, not merely as a spectator, or a fault-finder, or a counsellor, but as a sharer, to some extent, in the ideas and feelings which are appropriate to it.

Ascendency over the Minds of Children.

Sympathizing with children in their own pleasures and enjoyments, however childish they may seem to us when we do not regard them, as it were, with children's eyes, is, perhaps, the most powerful of all the means at our command for gaining a powerful ascendency over them. This will lead us not to interfere with their own plans and ideas, but to be willing that they should be happy in their own way. In respect to their duties, those connected, for example, with their studies, their serious employments, and their compliance with directions of any kind emanating from superior authority, of course their will must be under absolute subjection to that of those who are older and wiser than they. In all such things they must bring their thoughts and actions into accord with ours. In these things they must come to us, not we to them. But in every thing that relates to their child-like pleasures and joys, their modes of recreation and amusement, their playful explorations of the mysteries of things, and the various novelties around them in the strange world into which they find themselves ushered—in all these things we must not attempt to bring them to us, but must go to them. In this, their own sphere, the more perfectly they are at liberty, the better; and if we join them in it at all, we must do so by bringing our ideas and wishes into accord with theirs.

Foolish Fears.

The effect of our sympathy with children in winning their confidence and love, is all the more powerful when it is exercised in cases where they are naturally inclined not to expect sympathy—that is, in relation to feelings which they would suppose that older persons would be inclined to condemn. Perhaps the most striking example of this is in what is commonly called foolish fears. Now a fear is foolish or otherwise, not according to the absolute facts involving the supposed danger, but according to the means which the person in question has of knowing the facts. A lady, for example, in passing along the sidewalk of a great city comes to a place where workmen are raising an immense and ponderous iron safe, which, slowly rising, hangs suspended twenty feet above the walk. She is afraid to pass under it. The foreman, however, who is engaged in directing the operation, passing freely to and fro under the impending weight, as he has occasion, and without the least concern, smiles, perhaps, at the lady's "foolish fears." But the fears which might, perhaps, be foolish in him, are not so in her, since he *knows* the nature and the strength of the machinery and securities above, and she does not. She only knows that accidents do sometimes happen from want of due precaution in raising heavy weights, and she does not know, and has no means of knowing, whether or not the due precautions have been taken in this case. So she manifests good sense, and not folly, in going out of her way to avoid all possibility of danger.

This is really the proper explanation of a large class of what are usually termed foolish fears. Viewed in the light of the individual's knowledge of the facts in the case, they are sensible fears, and not foolish ones at all.

A girl of twelve, from the city, spending the summer in the country, wishes to go down to the river to join her brothers there, but is stopped by observing a cow in a field which she has to cross. She comes back to the house, and is there laughed at for her foolishness in being; "afraid of a cow!"

But why should she not be afraid of a cow? She has heard stories of people being gored by bulls, and sometimes by cows, and she has no means whatever of estimating the reality or the extent of the danger in any particular case. The farmer's daughters, however, who laugh at her, know the cow in question perfectly well. They have milked her, and fed her, and tied her up to her manger a hundred times; so, while it would be a very foolish thing for them to be afraid to cross a field where the cow was feeding, it is a very sensible thing for the stranger-girl from the city to be so.

Nor would it certainly change the case much for the child, if the farmer's girls were to assure her that the cow was perfectly peaceable, and that there was no danger; for she does not know the girls any better than she does the cow, and can not judge how far their statements or opinions are to be relied upon. It may possibly not be the cow they think it is. They are very positive, it is true; but very positive people are often mistaken. Besides, the cow may be peaceable with them, and yet be disposed to attack a stranger. What a child requires in such a case is sympathy and help, not ridicule.

This, in the case supposed, she meets in the form of the farmer's son, a young man browned in face and plain in attire, who comes along while she stands loitering at the fence looking at the cow, and not daring after all, notwithstanding the assurances she has received at the house, to cross the field. His name is Joseph, and he is a natural gentleman—a class of persons of whom a much larger number is found in this humble guise, and a much smaller number in proportion among the fashionables in elegant life, than is often supposed. "Yes," says Joseph, after hearing the child's statement of the case, "you are right. Cows are sometimes vicious, I know; and you are perfectly right to be on your guard against such as you do not know when you meet them in the country. This one, as it happens, is very kind; but still, I will go through the field with you."

So he goes with her through the field, stopping on the way to talk a little to the cow, and to feed her with an apple which he has in his pocket.

It is in this spirit that the fears, and antipathies, and false imaginations of children are generally to be dealt with; though, of course, there may be many exceptions to the general rule.

When Children are in the Wrong.

There is a certain sense in which we should feel a sympathy with children in the wrong that they do. It would seem paradoxical to say that in any sense there should be sympathy with sin, and yet there is a sense in which this is true, though perhaps, strictly speaking, it is sympathy with the trial and temptation which led to the sin, rather than with the act of transgression itself. In whatever light a nice metaphysical analysis would lead us to regard it, it is certain that the most successful efforts that have been made by philanthropists for reaching the hearts and reforming the conduct of criminals and malefactors have been prompted by a feeling of compassion for them, not merely for the sorrows and sufferings which they have brought upon themselves by their wrongdoing, but for the mental conflicts which they endured, the fierce impulses of appetite and passion, more or less connected with and dependent upon the material condition of the bodily organs, under the onset of which their feeble moral sense, never really brought into a condition of health and vigor, was over-borne. These merciful views of the diseased condition and action of the soul in the commission of crime are not only in themselves right views for man to take of the crimes and sins of his fellow-man, but they lie at the foundation of all effort that can afford any serious hope of promoting reformation.

This principle is eminently true in its application to children. They need the influence of a kind and considerate sympathy when they have done wrong, more, perhaps, than at any other time; and the effects of the proper manifestation of this sympathy on the part of the mother will, perhaps, be greater and more salutary in this case than in any other. Of course the sympathy must be of the right kind, and must be expressed in the right way, so as not to allow the tenderness or compassion for the wrong-doer to be mistaken for approval or justification of the wrong.

Case supposed.

A boy, for instance, comes home from school in a state of great distress, and perhaps of indignation and resentment, on account of having been punished. Mothers sometimes say at once, in such a case, "I don't pity you at all. I have no doubt you deserved it." This only increases the tumult of commotion in the boy's mind, without at all tending to help him to feel a sense of his guilt. His mind, still imperfectly developed, can not take cognizance simultaneously of all the parts and all the aspects of a complicated transaction. The sense of his wrong-doing, which forms in his teacher's and in his mother's mind so essential a part of the transaction, is not present in his conceptions at all. There is no room for it, so totally engrossed are all his faculties with the stinging recollections of suffering, the tumultuous emotions of anger and resentment, and now with the additional thought that even his mother has taken part against him. The mother's conception of the transaction is equally limited and imperfect, though in a different way. She thinks only that if she were to treat the child with kindness and sympathy, she would be taking the part of a bad boy against his teacher; whereas, in reality, she might do it in such a way as only to be taking the part of a suffering boy against his pain.

It would seem that the true and proper course for a mother to take with a child in such a case would be to soothe and calm his agitation, and to listen, if need be, to his account of the affair, without questioning or controverting it at all, however plainly she may see that, under the blinding and distorting influence of his excitement, he is misrepresenting the facts. Let him tell his story. Listen to it patiently to the end. It is not necessary to express or even to form an opinion on the merits of it. The ready and willing hearing of one side of a case does not commit the tribunal to a decision in favor of that side. On the other hand, it is the only way to give weight and a sense of impartiality to a decision against it.

Thus the mother may sympathize with her boy in his troubles, appreciate fully the force of the circumstances which led him into the wrong, and help to soothe and calm his agitation, and thus take his part, and place herself closely to him in respect to his suffering, without committing herself at all in regard to the original cause of it; and then, at a subsequent time, when the tumult of his soul has subsided, she can, if she thinks best, far more easily and effectually lead him to see wherein he was wrong.

CHAPTER XII.

COMMENDATION AND ENCOURAGEMENT.

We are very apt to imagine that the disposition to do right is, or ought to be, the natural and normal condition of childhood, and that doing wrong is something unnatural and exceptional with children. As a consequence, when they do right we think there is nothing to be said. That is, or ought to be, a matter of course. It is only when they do wrong that we notice their conduct, and then, of course, with censure and reproaches. Thus our discipline consists mainly, not in gently leading and encouraging them in the right way, but in deterring them, by fault-finding and punishment, from going wrong.

Now we ought not to forget that in respect to moral conduct as well as to mental attainments children know nothing when they come into the world, but have every thing to learn, either from the instructions or from the example of those around them. We do not propose to enter at all into the consideration of the various theological and metaphysical theories held by different classes of philosophers in respect to the native constitution and original tendencies of the human soul, but to look at the phenomena of mental and moral action in a plain and practical way, as they present themselves to the observation of mothers in the every-day walks of life. And in order the better to avoid any complication with these theories, we will take first an extremely simple case, namely, the fault of making too much noise in opening and shutting the door in going in and out of a room. Georgie and Charlie are two boys, both about five years old, and both prone to the same fault. We will suppose that their mothers take opposite methods to correct them; Georgie's mother depending upon the influence of commendation and encouragement when he does right, and Charlie's, upon the efficacy of reproaches and punishments when he does wrong.

One Method.

Georgie, eager to ask his mother some question, or to obtain some permission in respect to his play, bursts into her room some morning with great noise, opening and shutting the door violently, and making much disturbance. In a certain sense he is not to blame for this, for he is wholly unconscious of the disturbance he makes. The entire cognizant capacity of his mind is occupied with the object of his request. He not only had no intention of doing any harm, but has no idea of his having done any.

His mother takes no notice of the noise he made, but answers his question, and he goes away making almost as much noise in going out as he did in coming in.

The next time he comes in it happens—entirely by accident, we will suppose—that he makes a little less noise than before. This furnishes his mother with her opportunity.

"Georgie," she says, "I see you are improving."

"Improving?" repeats Georgie, not knowing to what his mother refers.

"Yes," said his mother; "you are improving, in coming into the room without making a noise by opening and shutting the door. You did not make nearly as much noise this time as you did before when you came in. Some boys, whenever they come into a room, make so much noise in opening and shutting the door that it is very disagreeable. If you go on improving as you have begun, you will soon come in as still as any gentleman."

The next time that Georgie comes in, he takes the utmost pains to open and shut the door as silently as possible.

He makes his request. His mother shows herself unusually ready to grant it.

"You opened and shut the door like a gentleman," she says. "I ought to do every thing for you that I can, when you take so much pains not to disturb or trouble me."

Another Method.

Charlie's mother, on the other hand, acts on a different principle. Charlie comes in sometimes, we will suppose, in a quiet and proper manner. His mother takes no notice of this. She considers it a matter of course. By-and-by, however, under the influence of some special eagerness, he makes a great noise. Then his mother interposes. She breaks out upon him with,

"Charlie, what a noise you make! Don't you know better than to slam the doer in that way when you come in? If you can't learn to make less noise in going in and out, I shall not let you go in and out at all."

Charlie knows very well that this is an empty threat. Still, the utterance of it, and the scolding that accompanies it, irritate him a little, and the only possible good effect that can be expected to result from it is to make him try, the next time he comes in, to see how small an abatement of the noise he usually makes will do, as a kind of make-believe obedience to his mother's command. He might, indeed, honestly answer his mother's angry question by saying that he does *not* know better than to make such a noise. He does not know why the noise of the door should be disagreeable to his mother. It is not disagreeable to *him*. On the contrary, it is agreeable. Children always like noise, especially if they make it themselves. And although Charlie has often been told that he must not make any noise, the reason for this—namely, that though noise is a source of pleasure, generally, to children, especially when they make it themselves, it is almost always a source of annoyance and pain to grown persons—has never really entered his mind so as to be actually comprehended us a practical reality. His ideas in respect to the philosophy of the transaction are, of course, exceedingly vague; but so far as he forms any idea, it is that his mother's words are the expression of some mysterious but unreasonable sensitiveness on her part, which awakens in her a spirit of fault-finding and ill-humor that vents itself upon him in blaming him for nothing at all; or, as he would express it more tersely, if not so elegantly, that she is "very cross." In other words, the impression made by the transaction upon his moral sense is that of wrong-doing on his *mother's part*, and not at all on his own.

It is evident, when we thus look into the secret workings of this method of curing children of their faults, that even when it is successful in restraining certain kinds of outward misconduct, and is thus the means of effecting some small amount of good, the injury which it does by its reaction on the spirit of the child may be vastly greater, through the irritation and ill-humor which it occasions, and the impairing of his confidence in the justice and goodness of his mother. Before leaving this illustration, it must be carefully observed that in the first-mentioned case —namely, that of Georgie—the work of curing the fault in question is not to be at all considered as *effected* by the step taken by his mother which has been already described. That was only a beginning— a *right* beginning, it is true, but still only a beginning. It produced in him a cordial willingness to do right, in one instance. That is a great thing, but it is, after all, only one single step. The work is not complete until a *habit* of doing right is formed, which is another thing altogether, and requires special and continual measures directed to this particular end. Children have to be *trained* in the way they should go—not merely shown the way, and induced to make a beginning of entering it. We will now try to show how the influence of commendation and encouragement may be brought into action in this more essential part of the process.

Habit to be Formed.

Having taken the first step already described, Georgie's mother finds some proper opportunity, when she can have the undisturbed and undivided attention of her boy—perhaps at night, after he has gone to his crib or his trundle-bed, and just before she leaves him; or, perhaps, at some time while she is at work, and he is sitting by her side, with his mind calm, quiet, and unoccupied.

"Georgie," she says, "I have a plan to propose to you."

Georgie is eager to know what it is.

"You know how pleased I was when you came in so still to-day."

Georgie remembers it very well.

"It is very curious," continued his mother, "that there is a great difference between grown people and children about noise. Children *like* almost all kinds of noises very much, especially, if they make the noises themselves; but grown people dislike them even more, I think, than children like them. If there were a number of boys in the house, and I should tell them that they might run back and forth through the rooms, and rattle and slam all the doors as they went as loud as they could, they would like it very much. They would think it excellent fun."

"Yes," says Georgie, "indeed, they would. I wish you would let us do it some day."

"But grown people," continues his mother, "would not like such an amusement at all. On the contrary, such a racket would be excessively disagreeable to them, whether they made it themselves or whether somebody else made it. So, when children come into a room where grown people are sitting, and make a noise in opening and shutting the door, it is very disagreeable. Of course, grown people always like those children the best that come into a room quietly, and in a gentlemanly and lady-like manner."

As this explanation comes in connection with Georgia's having done right, and with the commendation which he has received for it, his mind and heart are open to receive it, instead of being disposed to resist and exclude it, as he would have been if the same things exactly had been said to him in connection with censure and reproaches for having acted in violation of the principle.

"Yes, mother," says he, "and I mean always to open and shut the door as still as I can."

"Yes, I know you *mean* to do so," rejoined his mother, "but you will forget, unless you have some plan to make you remember it until the *habit is formed*. Now I have a plan to propose to help you form the habit. When you get the habit once formed there will be no more difficulty.

"The plan is this: whenever you come into a room making a noise, I will simply say, *Noise*. Then you will step back again softly and shut the door, and then come in again in a quiet and proper way. You will not go back for punishment, for you would not have made the noise on purpose, and so would not deserve any punishment. It is only to help you remember, and so to form the habit of coming into a room in a quiet and gentlemanly manner."

Now Georgie, especially if all his mother's management of him is conducted in this spirit, will enter into this plan with great cordiality.

"I should not propose this plan," continued his mother, "if I thought that when I say *Noise*, and you have to go out and come in again, it would put you out of humor, and make you cross or sullen. I am sure you will be good-natured about it, and even if you consider it a kind of punishment, that you will go out willingly, and take the punishment like a man; and when you come in again you will come in still, and look pleased and happy to find that you are carrying out the plan honorably."

Then if, on the first occasion when he is sent back, he *does* take it good-naturedly, this must be noticed and commended.

Now, unless we are entirely wrong in all our ideas of the nature and tendencies of the infantile mind, it is as certain that a course of procedure like this will be successful in curing the fault which is the subject of treatment, as that water will extinguish fire. It cures it, too, without occasioning any irritation, annoyance, or ill-humor in the mind either of mother or child. On the contrary, it is a source of real satisfaction and pleasure to them both, and increases and strengthens the bond of sympathy by which their hearts are united to each other.

The Principle involved.

It must be understood distinctly that this case is given only as an illustration of a principle which is applicable to all cases. The act of opening and shutting a door in a noisy manner is altogether too insignificant a fault to deserve this long discussion of the method of curing it, were it not that methods founded on the same principles, and conducted in the same spirit, are applicable universally in all that pertains to the domestic management of children. And it is a method, too, directly the opposite of that which is often—I will not say generally, but certainly very often—pursued. The child tells the truth many times, and in some cases, perhaps, when the inducement was very strong to tell an untruth. We take no notice of these cases, considering it a matter of course that he should tell the truth. We reserve our action altogether for the first case when, overcome by a sudden temptation, he tells a lie, and then interpose with reproaches and punishment. Nineteen times he gives up what belongs to his little brother or sister of his own accord, perhaps after a severe internal struggle. The twentieth time the result of the struggle goes the wrong way, and he attempts to retain by violence what does not belong to him. We take no notice of the nineteen cases when the little fellow did right, but come and box his ears in the one case when he does wrong.

Origin of the Error.

The idea on which this mode of treatment is founded—namely, that it is a *matter of course* that children should do right, so that when they do right there is nothing to be said, and that doing wrong is the abnormal condition and exceptional action which alone requires the parent to interfere—is, to a great extent, a mistake. Indeed, the *matter of course* is all the other way. A babe will seize the plaything of another babe without the least compunction long after it is keenly alive to the injustice and wrongfulness of having its own playthings taken by any other child. So in regard to truth. The first impulse of all children, when they have just acquired the use of language, is to use it in such a way as to effect their object for the time being, without any sense of the sacred obligation of making the words always correspond truly with the facts. The principles of doing justice to the rights of others to one's own damage, and of speaking the truth when falsehood would serve the present purpose better, are principles that are developed or acquired by slow degrees, and at a later period. I say developed *or* acquired—for different classes of metaphysicians and theologians entertain different theories in respect to the way by which the ideas of right and of duty enter into the human mind. But all will agree in this, that whatever may be the origin of the moral sense in man, it does not appear as a *practical element of control for the conduct* till some time after the animal appetites and passions have begun to exercise their power. Whether we regard this sense as arising from a development within of a latent principle of the soul, or as an essential element of the inherited and native constitution of man, though remaining for a time embryonic and inert, or as a habit acquired under the influence of instruction and example, all will admit that the period of its appearance as a perceptible motive of action is so delayed, and the time required for its attaining sufficient strength to exercise any real and effectual control over the conduct extends over so many of the earlier years of life, that no very material help in governing the appetites and passions and impulses can be reasonably expected from it at a very early period. Indeed, conscience, so far as its existence is manifested at all in childhood, seems to show itself chiefly in the form of the simple *fear of detection* in what there is reason to suppose will lead, if discovered, to reproaches or punishment.

At any rate, the moral sense in childhood, whatever may be our philosophy in respect to the origin and the nature of it, can not be regarded as a strong and settled principle on which we can throw the responsibility of regulating the conduct, and holding it sternly to its obligations. It is, on the contrary, a very tender plant, slowly coming forward to the development of its beauty and its power, and requiring the most gentle fostering and care on the part of those intrusted with the training of the infant mind; and the influence of commendation and encouragement when the embryo monitor succeeds in its incipient and feeble efforts, will be far more effectual in promoting its development, than that of censure and punishment when it fails.

Important Caution.

For every good thing there seems to be something in its form and semblance that is spurious and bad. The principle brought to view in this chapter has its counterfeit in the indiscriminate praise and flattery of children by their parents, which only makes them self-conceited and vain, without at all promoting any good end. The distinction between the two might be easily pointed out, if time and space permitted; but the intelligent parent, who has rightly comprehended the method of management here described, and the spirit in which the process of applying it is to be made, will be in no danger of confounding one with the other.

This principle of noticing and commending, within proper limits and restrictions, what is right, rather than finding fault with what is wrong, will be found to be as important in the work of instruction as in the regulation of conduct. We have, in fact, a very good opportunity of comparing the two systems, as it is a curious fact that in certain things it is almost the universal custom to adopt one method, and in certain others, the other.

The two Methods exemplified.

There are, for example, two arts which children have to learn, in the process of their mental and physical development, in which their faults, errors, and deficiencies are never pointed out, but in the dealings of their parents with them all is commendation and encouragement. They are the arts of walking and talking.

The first time that a child attempts to walk alone, what a feeble, staggering, and awkward exhibition it makes. And yet its mother shows, by the excitement of her countenance, and the delight expressed by her exclamations, how pleased she is with the performance; and she, perhaps, even calls in persons from the next room to see how well the baby can walk! Not a word about imperfections and failings, not a word about the tottering, the awkward reaching out of arms to preserve the balance, the crookedness of the way, the anxious expression of the countenance, or any other faults. These are left to correct themselves by the continued practice which encouragement is sure to lead to.

It is true that words would not be available in such a case for fault-finding; for a child when learning to walk would be too young to understand them. But the parent's sense of the imperfections of the performance might be expressed in looks and gestures which the child would understand; but he sees, on the contrary, nothing but indications of satisfaction and pleasure, and it is very manifest how much he is encouraged by them. Seeing the pleasure which his efforts give to the spectators, he is made proud and happy by his success, and goes on making efforts to improve with alacrity and delight.

It is the same with learning to talk. The mistakes, deficiencies, and errors of the first rude attempts are seldom noticed, and still more seldom pointed out by the parent. On the contrary, the child takes the impression, from the readiness with which its words are understood and the delight it evidently gives its mother to hear them, that it is going on triumphantly in its work of learning to talk, instead of feeling that its attempts are only tolerated because they are made by such a little child, and that they require a vast amount of correction, alteration, and improvement, before they will be at all satisfactory. Indeed, so far from criticising and pointing out the errors and faults, the mother very frequently meets the child half way in its progress, by actually adopting the faults and errors herself in her replies. So that when the little beginner in the use of language, as he wakes up in his crib, and stretching out his hands to his mother says, "I want *to get up*" she comes to take him, and replies, her face beaming with delight, "My little darling! you shall *get up*;" thus filling his mind with happiness at the idea that his mother is not only pleased that he attempts to speak, but is fully satisfied, and more than satisfied, with his success.

The result is, that in learning to walk and to talk, children always go forward with alacrity and ardor. They practise continually and spontaneously, requiring no promises of reward to allure them to effort, and no threats of punishment to overcome repugnance or aversion. It might be too much to say that the rapidity of their progress and the pleasure which they experience in making it, are owing wholly to the commendation and encouragement they receive—for other causes may co-operate with these. But it is certain that these influences contribute very essentially to the result. There can be no doubt at all that if it were possible for a mother to stop her child in its efforts to learn to walk and to talk, and explain to it, no matter how kindly, all its shortcomings, failures, and mistakes, and were to make this her daily and habitual practice, the consequence would be, not only a great diminution of the ardor and animation of the little pupil, in pressing forward in its work, but also a great retardation in its progress.

Example of the other Method.

Let us now, for the more full understanding of the subject, go to the other extreme, and consider a case in which the management is as far as possible removed from that above referred to. We can not have a better example than the method often adopted in schools and seminaries for teaching composition; in other words, the art of expressing one's thoughts in written language—an art which one would suppose to be so analogous to that of learning to talk—that is, to express one's thoughts in *oral* language—that the method which was found so eminently successful in the one would be naturally resorted to in the other. Instead of that, the method often pursued is exactly the reverse. The pupil having with infinite difficulty, and with many forebodings and anxious fears, made his first attempt, brings it to his teacher. The teacher, if he is a kind-hearted and considerate man, perhaps briefly commends the effort with some such dubious and equivocal praise as it is "Very well for a beginner," or "As good a composition as could be expected at the first attempt," and then proceeds to go over the exercise in a cool and deliberate manner, with a view of discovering and bringing out clearly and conspicuously to the view, not only of the little author himself, but often of all his classmates and friends, every imperfection, failure, mistake, omission, or other fault which a rigid scrutiny can detect in the performance. However kindly he may do this, and however gentle the tones of his voice, still the work is criticism and fault-finding from beginning to end. The boy sits on thorns and nettles while submitting to the operation, and when he takes his marked and corrected manuscript to his seat, he feels mortified and ashamed, and is often hopelessly discouraged.

How Faults are to be Corrected.

Some one may, perhaps, say that pointing out the errors and faults of pupils is absolutely essential to their progress, inasmuch as, unless they are made to see what their faults are, they can not be expected to correct them. I admit that this is true to a certain extent, but by no means to so great an extent as is often supposed. There are a great many ways of teaching pupils to do better what they are going to do, besides showing them the faults in what they have already done.

Thus, without pointing out the errors and faults which he observes, the teacher may only refer to and commend what is right, while he at the same time observes and remembers the prevailing faults, with a view of adapting his future instructions to the removal of them. These instructions, when given, will take the form, of course, of general information on the art of expressing one's thoughts in writing, and on the faults and errors to be avoided, perhaps without any, or, at least, very little allusion to those which the pupils themselves had committed. Instruction thus given, while it will have at least an equal tendency with the other mode to form the pupils to habits of correctness and accuracy, will not have the effect upon their mind of disparagement of what they have already done, but rather of aid and encouragement for them in regard to what they are next to do. In following the instructions thus given them, the pupils will, as it were, leave the faults previously committed behind them, being even, in many instances, unconscious, perhaps, of their having themselves ever committed them.

The ingenious mother will find various modes analogous to this, of leading her children forward into what is right, without at all disturbing their minds by censure of what is wrong—a course which it is perfectly safe to pursue in the case of all errors and faults which result from inadvertence or immaturity. There is, doubtless, another class of faults—those of willful carelessness or neglect—which must be specially pointed out to the attention of the delinquents, and a degree of discredit attached to the commission of them, and perhaps, in special cases, some kind of punishment imposed, as the most proper corrective of the evil. And yet, even in cases of carelessness and neglect of duty, it will generally be found much more easy to awaken ambition, and a desire to improve, in a child, by discovering, if possible, something good in his work, and commending that, as an encouragement to him to make greater exertion the next time, than to attempt to cure him of his negligence by calling his attention to the faults which he has committed, as subjects of censure, however obvious the faults may be, and however deserving of blame.

The advice, however, made in this chapter, to employ commendation and encouragement to a great extent, rather than criticism and fault-finding, in the management and instruction of children, must, like all other general counsels of the kind, be held subject to all proper limitations and restrictions. Some mother may, perhaps, object to what is here advanced, saying, "If I am always indiscriminately praising my child's doings, he will become self-conceited and vain, and he will cease to make progress, being satisfied with what he has already attained." Of course he will, and therefore you must take care not to be always and indiscriminately praising him. You must exercise tact and good judgment, or at any rate, common sense, in properly proportioning your criticism and your praise. There are no principles of management, however sound, which may not be so exaggerated, or followed with so blind a disregard of attendant circumstances, as to produce more harm than good.

It must be especially borne in mind that the counsels here given in relation to curing the faults of children by dealing more with what is good in them than what is bad, are intended to apply to faults of ignorance, inadvertence, or habit only, and not to acts of known and willful wrong. When we come to cases of deliberate and intentional disobedience to a parent's commands, or open resistance to his authority, something different, or at least something more, is required.

The Principle of Universal Application.

In conclusion, it is proper to add that the principle of influencing human character and action by noticing and commending what is right, rather than finding fault with what is wrong, is of universal application, with the mature as well as with the young. The susceptibility to this influence is in full operation in the minds of all men everywhere, and acting upon it will lead to the same results in all the relations of society. The way to awaken a penurious man to the performance of generous deeds is not by remonstrating with him, however kindly, on his penuriousness, but by watching his conduct till we find some act that bears some semblance of liberality, and commending him for that. If you have a neighbor who is surly and troublesome—tell him that he is so, and you make him worse than ever. But watch for some occasion in which he shows you some little kindness, and thank him cordially for such a good neighborly act, and he will feel a strong desire to repeat it. If mankind universally understood this principle, and would generally act upon it in their dealings with others—of course, with such limitations and restrictions as good sense and sound judgment would impose—the world would not only go on much more smoothly and harmoniously than it does now, but the progress of improvement would, I think, in all respects be infinitely more rapid.

CHAPTER XIII.

FAULTS OF IMMATURITY.

A great portion of the errors and mistakes, and of what we call the follies, of children arise from simple ignorance. Principles of philosophy, whether pertaining to external nature or to mental action, are involved which have never come home to their minds. They may have been presented, but they have not been understood and appreciated. It requires some tact, and sometimes delicate observation, on the part of the mother to determine whether a mode of action which she sees ought to be corrected results from childish ignorance and inexperience, or from willful wrong-doing. Whatever may be the proper treatment in the latter case, it is evident that in the former what is required is not censure, but instruction.

Boasting.

A mother came into the room one day and found Johnny disputing earnestly with his Cousin Jane on the question which was the tallest—Johnny very strenuously maintaining that he was the tallest, *because he was a boy*. His older brother, James, who was present at the time, measured them, and found that Johnny in reality was the tallest.

Now there was nothing wrong in his feeling a pride and pleasure in the thought that he was physically superior to his cousin, and though it was foolish for him to insist himself on this superiority in a boasting way, it was the foolishness of ignorance only. He had not learned the principle—which half mankind do not seem ever to learn during the whole course of their lives—that it is far wiser and better to let our good qualities appear naturally of themselves, than to claim credit for them beforehand by boasting. It would have been much wiser for Johnny to have admitted at the outset that Jane might possibly be taller than he, and then to have awaited quietly the result of the measuring.

But we can not blame him much for not having learned this particular wisdom at five years of age, when so many full-grown men and women never learn it at all.

Nor was there any thing blameworthy in him in respect to the false logic involved in his argument, that his being a boy made him necessarily taller than his cousin, a girl of the same age. There was a *semblance* of proof in that fact—what the logicians term a presumption. But the reasoning powers are very slowly developed in childhood. They are very seldom aided by any instruction really adapted to the improvement of them; and we ought not to expect that such children can at all clearly distinguish a semblance from a reality in ideas so extremely abstruse as those relating to the logical connection between the premises and the conclusion in a process of ratiocination.

In this case as in the other we expect them to understand at once, without instruction, what we find it extremely difficult to learn ourselves; for a large portion of mankind prove themselves utterly unable ever to discriminate between sound arguments and those which are utterly inconsequent and absurd.

In a word, what Johnny requires in such a case as this is, not ridicule to shame him out of his false reasoning, nor censure or punishment to cure him of his boasting, but simply instruction.

And this instruction it is much better to give *not* in direct connection with the occurrence which indicated the want of it. If you attempt to explain to your boy the folly of boasting in immediate connection with some act of boasting of his own, he feels that you are really finding fault with him; his mind instinctively puts itself into a position of defense, and the truth which you wish to impart to it finds a much less easy admission.

If, for example, in this case Johnny's mother attempts on the spot to explain to him the folly of boasting, and to show how much wiser it is for us to let our good qualities, if we have any, speak for themselves, without any direct agency of ours in claiming the merit of them, he listens reluctantly and nervously as to a scolding in disguise. If he is a boy well managed, he waits, perhaps, to hear what his mother has to say, but it makes no impression. If he is badly trained, he will probably interrupt his mother in the midst of what she is saying, or break away from her to go on with his play.

A right Mode of Treatment.

If now, instead of this, the mother waits until the dispute and the transaction of measuring have passed by and been forgotten, and then takes some favorable opportunity to give the required *instruction*, the result will be far more favorable. At some time, when tired of his play, he comes to stand by her to observe her at her work, or perhaps to ask her for a story; or, after she has put him to bed and is about to leave him for the night, she says to him as follows:

"I'll tell you a story about two boys, Jack and Henry, and you shall tell me which of them came off best. They both went to the same school and were in the same class, and there was nobody else in the class but those two. Henry, who was the most diligent scholar, was at the head of the class, and Jack was below him, and, of course, as there were only two, he was at the foot.

"One day there was company at the house, and one of the ladies asked the boys how they got along at school. Jack immediately said, 'Very well. I'm next to the head of my class.' The lady then praised him, and said that he must be a very good scholar to be so high in his class. Then she asked Henry how high he was in his class. He said he was next to the foot.

"The lady was somewhat surprised, for she, as well as the others present, supposed that Henry was the best scholar; they were all a little puzzled too, for Henry looked a little roguish and sly when he said it. But just then the teacher came in, and she explained the case; for she said that the boys were in the same class, and they were all that were in it; so that Henry, who was really at the head, was next but one to the foot, while Jack, who was at the foot, was next but one to the head. On having this explanation made to the company, Jack felt very much confused and ashamed, while Henry, though he said nothing, could not help feeling pleased.

"And now," asks the mother, in conclusion, "which of these boys do you think came off the best?"

Johnny answers that Henry came out best.

"Yes," adds his mother, "and it is always better that people's merits, if they have any, should come out in other ways than by their own boasting of them."

It is true that this case of Henry and Jack does not correspond exactly—not even nearly, in fact—with that of Johnny and his cousin. Nor is it necessary that the instruction given in these ways should logically conform to the incident which calls them forth. It is sufficient that there should be such a degree of analogy between them, that the interest and turn of thought produced by the incident may prepare the mind for appreciating and receiving the lesson. But the mother may bring the lesson nearer if she pleases.

"I will tell you another story," she says. "There were two men at a fair. Their names were Thomas and Philip.

"Thomas was boasting of his strength. He said he was a great deal stronger than Philip. 'Perhaps you are,' said Philip. Then Thomas pointed to a big stone which was lying upon the ground, and dared Philip to try which could throw it the farthest. 'Very well,' said Philip, 'I will try, but I think it very likely you will beat me, for I know you are very strong.' So they tried, and it proved that Philip could throw it a great deal farther than Thomas could. Then Thomas went away looking very much incensed and very much ashamed, while Philip's triumph was altogether greater for his not having boasted."

"Yes," says Johnny, "I think so."

The mother may, if she pleases, come still nearer than this, if she wishes to suit Johnny's individual case, without exciting any resistance in his heart to the reception of her lesson. She may bring his exact case into consideration, provided she changes the names of the actors, so that Johnny's mind may be relieved from the uneasy sensitiveness which it is so natural for a child to feel when his own conduct is directly the object of unfavorable comment. It is surprising how slight a change in the mere outward incidents of an affair will suffice to divert the thoughts of the child from himself in such a case, and enable him to look at the lesson to be imparted without personal feeling, and so to receive it more readily.

Johnny's mother may say, "There might be a story in a book about two boys that were disputing a little about which was the tallest. What do you think would be good names for the boys, if you were making up such a story?"

When Johnny has proposed the names, his mother could go on and give an almost exact narrative of what took place between Johnny and his cousin, offering just such instructions and such advice as she would like to offer; and she will find, if she manages the conversation with ordinary tact and discretion, that the lessons which she desires to impart will find a ready admission to the mind of her child, simply from the fact that, by divesting them of all direct personal application, she has eliminated from them the element of covert censure which they would otherwise have contained. Very slight disguises will, in all such cases, be found to be sufficient to veil the personal applicability of the instruction, so far as to divest it of all that is painful or disagreeable to the child. He may have a vague feeling that you mean him, but the feeling will not produce any effect of irritation or repellency.

Now, the object of these illustrations is to show that those errors and faults which, when we look at their real and intrinsic character, we see to be results of ignorance and inexperience, and not instances of willful and intentional wrong-doing, are not to be dealt with harshly, and made occasions of censure and punishment. The child does not deserve censure or punishment in such cases; what he requires is instruction. It is the bringing in of light to illuminate the path that is before him which he has yet to tread, and not the infliction of pain, to impress upon him the evil of the missteps he made, in consequence of the obscurity, in the path behind him.

Indeed, in such cases as this, it is the influence of pleasure rather than pain that the parent will find the most efficient means of aiding him; that is, in these cases, the more pleasant and agreeable the modes by which he can impart the needed knowledge to the child—in other words, the more attractive he can make the paths by which he can lead his little charge onward in its progress towards maturity—the more successful he will be.

Ignorance of Material Properties and Laws.

In the example already given, the mental immaturity consisted in imperfect acquaintance with the qualities and the action of the mind, and the principles of sound reasoning; but a far larger portion of the mistakes and failures into which children fall, and for which they incur undeserved censure, are due to their ignorance of the laws of external nature, and of the properties and qualities of material objects.

A boy, for example, seven or eight years old, receives from his father a present of a knife, with a special injunction to be careful of it. He is, accordingly, very careful of it in respect to such dangers as he understands, but in attempting to bore a hole with it in a piece of wood, out of which he is trying to make a windmill, he breaks the small blade. The accident, in such a case, is not to be attributed to any censurable carelessness, but to want of instruction in respect to the strength of such a material as steel, and the nature and effects of the degree of tempering given to knife-blades. The boy had seen his father bore holes with a gimlet, and the knife-blade was larger—in one direction at least, that is, in breadth—than the gimlet, and it was very natural for him to suppose that it was stronger. What a boy needs in such a case, therefore, is not a scolding, or punishment, but simply information.

A girl of about the same age—a farmer's daughter, we will suppose—under the influence of a dutiful desire to aid her mother in preparing the table for breakfast, attempts to carry across the room a pitcher of milk which is too full, and she spills a portion of it upon the floor.

The Intention good.

The mother, forgetting the good intention which prompted the act, and thinking only of the inconvenience which it occasions her, administers at once a sharp rebuke. The cause of the trouble was, simply, that the child was not old enough to understand the laws of momentum and of oscillation that affect the condition of a fluid when subjected to movements more or less irregular. She has had no theoretical instruction on the subject, and is too young to have acquired the necessary knowledge practically, by experience or observation.

It is so with a very large portion of the accidents which befall children. They arise not from any evil design, nor even any thing that can properly be called carelessness, on their part, but simply from the immaturity of their knowledge in respect to the properties and qualities of the material objects with which they have to deal.

It is true that children may be, and often, doubtless, are, in fault for these accidents. The boy may have been warned by his father not to attempt to bore with his knife-blade, or the girl forbidden to attempt to carry the milk-pitcher. The fault, however, would be, even in these cases, in the disobedience, and not in the damage that accidentally resulted from it. And it would be far more reasonable and proper to reprove and punish the fault when no evil followed than when a damage was the result; for in the latter case the damage itself acts, ordinarily, as a more than sufficient punishment.

Misfortunes befalling Men.

These cases are exactly analogous to a large class of accidents and calamities that happen among men. A ship-master sails from port at a time when there are causes existing in the condition of the atmosphere, and in the agencies in readiness to act upon it, that must certainly, in a few hours, result in a violent storm. He is consequently caught in the gale, and his topmasts and upper rigging are carried away. The owners do not censure him for the loss which they incur, if they are only assured that the meteorological knowledge at the captain's command at the time of leaving port was not such as to give him warning of the danger; and provided, also, that his knowledge was as advanced as could reasonably be expected from the opportunities which he had enjoyed. But we are very much inclined to hold children responsible for as much knowledge of the sources of danger around them as we ourselves, with all our experience, have been able to acquire, and are accustomed to condemn and sometimes even to punish them, for want of this knowledge.

Indeed, in many cases, both with children and with men, the means of knowledge in respect to the danger may be fully within reach, and yet the situation may be so novel, and the combination of circumstances so peculiar, that the connection between the causes and the possible evil effects does not occur to the minds of the persons engaged. An accident which has just occurred at the time of this present writing will illustrate this. A company of workmen constructing a tunnel for a railway, when they had reached the distance of some miles from the entrance, prepared a number of charges for blasting the rock, and accidentally laid the wires connected with the powder in too close proximity to the temporary railway-track already laid in the tunnel. The charges were intended to be fired from an electric battery provided for the purpose; but a thunder-cloud came up, and the electric force from it was conveyed by the rails into the tunnel and exploded the charges, and several men were killed. No one was inclined to censure the unfortunate men for carelessness in not guarding against a contingency so utterly unforeseen by them, though it is plain that, as is often said to children in precisely analogous cases, they *might have known*.

Children's Studies.—Spelling.

There is, perhaps, no department of the management of children in which they incur more undeserved censure, and even punishment, and are treated with so little consideration for faults arising solely from the immaturity of their minds, than in the direction of what may be called school studies. Few people have any proper appreciation of the enormous difficulties which a child has to encounter in learning to read and spell. How many parents become discouraged, and manifest their discouragement and dissatisfaction to the child in reproving and complaints, at what they consider his slow progress in learning to spell— forgetting that in the English language there are in common, every-day use eight or ten thousand words, almost all of which are to be learned separately, by a bare and cheerless toil of committing to memory, with comparatively little definite help from the sound. We have ourselves become so accustomed to seeing the word *bear*, for example, when denoting the animal, spelt *b e a r*, that we are very prone to imagine that there is something naturally appropriate in those letters and in that collocation of them, to represent that sound when used to denote that idea. But what is there in the nature and power of the letters to aid the child in perceiving—or, when told, in remembering—whether, when referring to the animal, he is to write *bear*, or *bare*, or *bair*, or *bayr*, or *bere*, as in *where*. So with the word *you*. It seems to us the most natural thing in the world to spell it *y o u*. And when the little pupil, judging by the sound, writes it *y u*, we mortify him by our ridicule, as if he had done something in itself absurd. But how is he to know, except by the hardest, most meaningless, and distasteful toil of the memory, whether he is to write *you*, or *yu*, or *yoo,* or *ewe*, or *yew*, or *yue*, as in *flue*, or even *yo* as in *do*, and to determine when and in what cases respectively he is to use those different forms?

The truth is, that each elementary sound that enters into the composition of words is represented in our language by so many different combinations of letters, in different cases, that the child has very little clue from the sound of a syllable to guide him in the spelling of it. We ourselves, from long habit, have become so accustomed to what we call the right spelling—which, of course, means nothing more than the customary one—that we are apt to imagine, as has already been said, that there is some natural fitness in it; and a mode of representing the same sound, which in one case seems natural and proper, in another appears ludicrous and absurd. We smile to see *laugh* spelled *larf,* just as we should to see *scarf* spelled *scaugh,* or *scalf,* as in *half;* and we forget that this perception of apparent incongruity is entirely the result of long habit in us, and has no natural foundation, and that children can not be sensible of it, or have any idea of it whatever. They learn, in learning to talk, what sound serves as the name by which the drops of water that they find upon the grass in the morning is denoted, but they can have no clue whatever to guide them in determining which of the various modes by which precisely that sound is represented in different words, as *dew, do, due, du, doo,* and *dou,* is to be employed in this case, and they become involved in hopeless perplexity if they attempt to imagine "*how it ought to be spelled;*" and we think them stupid because they can not extricate themselves from the difficulty on our calling upon them to "think!" No doubt there is a reason for the particular mode of spelling each particular word in the language—but that reason is hidden in the past history of the word and in facts connected with its origin and derivation from some barbarous or dead language, and is as utterly beyond the reach of each generation of spellers as if there were no such reasons in existence. There can not be the slightest help in any way from the exercise of the thinking or the reasoning powers.

It is true that the variety of the modes by which a given sound may be represented is not so great in all words as it is in these examples, though with respect to a vast number of the words in common use the above are fair specimens. They were not specially selected, but were taken almost at random. And there are very few words in the language the sound of which might not be represented by several different modes.

Take, for example, the three last words of the last sentence, which, as the words were written without any thought of using them for this purpose, may be considered, perhaps, as a fair specimen of words taken actually at random. The sound of the word *several* might be expressed in perfect accordance with the usage of English spelling, as *ceveral, severul, sevaral, cevural*, and in many other different modes. The combinations *dipherant, diferunt, dyfferent, diffurunt*, and many others, would as well represent the sound of the second word as the usual mode. And so with *modes*, which, according to the analogy of the language, might as well be expressed by *moads, mowdes, moades, mohdes*, or even *mhodes*, as in *Rhodes*.

An exceptionally precise speaker might doubtless make some slight difference in the sounds indicated by the different modes of representing the same syllable as given above; but to the ordinary appreciation of childhood the distinction in sound between such combinations, for example, as *a n t* in *constant* and *e n t* in *different* would not be perceptible.

Now, when we consider the obvious fact that the child has to learn mechanically, without any principles whatever to guide him in discovering which, out of the many different forms, equally probable, judging simply from analogy, by which the sound of the word is to be expressed, is the right one; and considering how small a portion of his time each day is or can be devoted to this work, and that the number of words in common use, all of which he is expected to know how to spell correctly by the time that he is twelve or fifteen years of age, is probably ten or twelve thousand (there are in Webster's dictionary considerably over a hundred thousand); when we take these considerations into account, it would seem that a parent, on finding that a letter written by his daughter, twelve or fourteen years of age, has all but three or four words spelled right, ought to be pleased and satisfied, and to express his satisfaction for the encouragement of the learner, instead of appearing to think only of the few words that are wrong, and disheartening and discouraging the child by attempts to make her ashamed of her spelling.

The case is substantially the same with the enormous difficulties to be encountered in learning to read and to write. The names of the letters, as the child pronounces them individually, give very little clue to the sound that is to be given to the word formed by them. Thus, the letters *h i t*, as the child pronounces them individually—*aitch, eye, tee*—would naturally spell to him some such word as *achite*, not *hit* at all. And as for the labor and difficulty of writing, a mother who is impatient at the slow progress of her children in the attainment of the art would be aided very much in obtaining a just idea of the difficulties which they experience by sitting upon a chair and at a table both much too high for her, and trying to copy Chinese characters by means of a hair-pencil, and with her left hand—the work to be closely inspected every day by a stern Chinaman of whom she stands in awe, and all the minutest deviations from the copy pointed out to her attention with an air of dissatisfaction and reproval!

Effect of Ridicule.

There is, perhaps, no one cause which exerts a greater influence in chilling the interest that children naturally feel in the acquisition of knowledge, than the depression and discouragement which result from having their mistakes and errors—for a large portion of which they are in no sense to blame—made subjects of censure or ridicule. The effect is still more decided in the case of girls than in that of boys, the gentler sex being naturally so much more sensitive. I have found in many cases, especially in respect to girls who are far enough advanced to have had a tolerably full experience of the usual influences of schools, that the fear of making mistakes, and of being "thought stupid," has had more effect in hindering and retarding progress, by repressing the natural ardor of the pupil, and destroying all alacrity and courage in the efforts to advance, than all other causes combined.

Stupidity.

How ungenerous, and even cruel, it is to reproach or ridicule a child for stupidity, is evident when we reflect that any supposed inferiority in his mental organization can not, by any possibility, be *his* fault. The question what degree of natural intelligence he shall be endowed with, in comparison with other children, is determined, not by himself, but by his

Creator, and depends, probably, upon conditions of organization in his cerebral system as much beyond his control as any thing abnormal in the features of his face, or blindness, or deafness, or any other physical disadvantage. The child who shows any indications of inferiority to others in any of these respects should be the object of his parent's or his teacher's special tenderness and care. If he is near-sighted, give him, at school, a seat as convenient as possible to the blackboard or the map. If he is hard of hearing, place him near the teacher; and for reasons precisely analogous, if you suspect him to be of inferior capacity, help him gently and tenderly in every possible way. Do every thing in your power to encourage him, and to conceal his deficiencies both from others and from himself, so far as these objects can be attained consistently with the general good of the family or of the school.

And, at all events, let those who have in any way the charge of children keep the distinction well defined in their minds between the faults which result from evil intentions, or deliberate and willful neglect of known duty, and those which, whatever the inconvenience they may occasion, are in part or in whole the results of mental or physical immaturity. In all our dealings, whether with plants, or animals, or with the human soul, we ought, in our training, to act very gently in respect to all that pertains to the embryo condition.

CHAPTER XIV.

THE ACTIVITY OF CHILDREN.

In order rightly to understand the true nature of that extraordinary activity which is so noticeable in all children that are in a state of health, so as to be able to deal with it on the right principles and in a proper manner, it is necessary to turn our attention somewhat carefully to certain scientific truths in respect to the nature and action of force in general which are now abundantly established, and which throw great light on the true character of that peculiar form of it which is so characteristic of childhood, and is, indeed, so abundantly developed by the vital functions of almost all young animals. One of the fundamental principles of this system of scientific truth is that which is called the persistence of force.

The Persistence of Force.

By the persistence of force is meant the principle—one now established with so much certainty as to command the assent of every thinking man who examines the subject—that in the ordinary course of nature no force is either ever originated or ever destroyed, but only changed in form. In other words, that all existing forces are but the continuation or prolongation of other forces preceding them, either of the same or other forms, but precisely equivalent in amount; and that no force can terminate its action in any other way than by being transmuted into some other force, either of the same or of some other form; but still, again, precisely equivalent in amount.

It was formerly believed that a force might under certain circumstances be *originated*—created, as it were—and hence the attempts to contrive machines for perpetual motion—that is, machines for the *production* of force. This idea is now wholly renounced by all well-informed men as utterly impossible in the nature of things. All that human mechanism can do is to provide modes for using advantageously a force previously existing, without the possibility of either increasing or diminishing it. No existing force can be destroyed. The only changes possible are changes of direction, changes in the relation of intensity to quantity, and changes of form.

The cases in which a force is apparently increased or diminished, as well as those in which it seems to disappear, are all found, on examination, to be illusive. For example, the apparent increase of a man's power by the use of a lever is really no increase at all. It is true that, by pressing upon the outer arm with his own weight, he can cause the much greater weight of the stone to rise; but then it will rise only a very little way in comparison with the distance through which his own weight descends. His own weight must, in fact, descend through a distance as much greater than that by which the stone ascends, as the weight of the stone is greater than his weight. In other words, so far as the balance of the forces is concerned, the whole amount of the *downward motion* consists of the smaller weight descending through a greater distance, which will be equal to the whole amount of that of the larger one ascending through a smaller distance; and, to produce a preponderance, the whole amount of the downward force must be somewhat greater. Thus the lever only *gathers* or *concentrates* force, as it were, but does not at all increase it.

It is so with all the other contrivances for managing force for the accomplishment of particular purposes. None of them, increase the force, but only alter its form and character, with a view to its better adaptation to the purpose in view.

Nor can any force be extinguished. When a bullet strikes against a solid wall, the force of its movement, which seems to disappear, is not lost; it is converted into heat—the temperature of both the bullet and of that part of the wall on which it impinges being raised by the concussion. And it is found that the amount of the heat which is thus produced is always in exact proportion to the quantity of mechanical motion which is stopped; this quantity depending on the weight of the bullet, and on the velocity with which it was moving. And it has been ascertained, moreover, by the most careful, patient, and many times repeated experiments and calculations, that the quantity of this heat is exactly the same with that which, through the medium of steam, or by any other mode of applying it, may be made to produce the same quantity of mechanical motion that was extinguished in the bullet. Thus the force was not destroyed, but only converted into another form.

And if we should follow out the natural effects of this heat into which the motion of the bullet was transferred, we should find it rarefying the air around the place of concussion, and thus lifting the whole mass of the atmosphere above it, and producing currents of the nature of wind, and through these producing other effects, thus going on forever; the force changing its form, but neither increasing or diminishing its quantity through a series of changes without end.

The Arrest and temporary Reservation of Force.

Now, although it is thus impossible that any force should be destroyed, or in any way cease to exist in one form without setting in action a precisely equal amount in some other form, it may, as it were, pass into a condition of *restraint*, and remain thus suspended and latent for an indefinite period—ready, however, to break into action again the moment that the restraint is removed. Thus a perfectly elastic spring may be bent by a certain force, and retained in the bent position a long time. But the moment that it is released it will unbend itself, exercising in so doing precisely the degree of force expended in bending it. In the same manner air may be compressed in an air-gun, and held thus, with the force, as it were, imprisoned, for any length of time, until at last, when the detent is released by the trigger, the elastic force comes into action, exercising in its action a power precisely the same as that with which it was compressed.

Force or power may be thus, as it were, stored up in a countless variety of ways, and reserved for future action; and, when finally released, the whole amount may be set free at once, so as to expend itself in a single impulse, as in case of the arrow or the bullet; or it may be partially restrained, so as to expend itself gradually, as in the case of a clock or watch. In either case the total amount expended will be precisely the same—namely, the exact equivalent of that which was placed in store.

Vegetable and Animal Life.

There are a vast number of mechanical contrivances in use among men for thus putting force in store, as it were, and then using it more or less gradually, as may be required. And nature, moreover, does this on a scale so stupendous as to render all human contrivances for this purpose utterly insignificant in comparison. The great agent which nature employs in this work is vegetation. Indeed, it may truly be said that the great function of vegetable life, in all the infinitude of forms and characters which it assumes, is to *receive and store up force* derived from the emanations of the sun.

Animal life, on the other hand, exists and fulfills its functions by the *expenditure* of this force. Animals receive vegetable productions containing these reserves of force into their systems, which systems contain arrangements for liberating the force, and employing it for the purposes it is intended to subserve in the animal economy.

The manner in which these processes are performed is in general terms as follows: The vegetable absorbs from the earth and from the air substances existing in their natural condition—that is, united according to their strongest affinities. These substances are chiefly water, containing various mineral salts in solution, from the ground, and carbonic acid from the air. These substances, after undergoing certain changes in the vessels of the plant, are exposed to the influence of the rays of the sun in the leaves. By the power of these rays—including the calorific, the luminous, and the actinic—the natural affinities by which the above-mentioned substances were united are overcome, and they are formed into new combinations, in which they are united by very weak affinities. Of course, they have a strong tendency to break away from the new unions, and fall back into the old. But, by some mysterious and incomprehensible means, the sun has power to lock them, so to speak, in their new forms, so as to require a special condition of things for the releasing of them. Thus they form a reserve of force, which can be held in restraint until the conditions required for their release are realized.

The process can be illustrated more particularly by a single case. Water, one of the substances absorbed by plants, is composed of oxygen and hydrogen, which are united by an affinity of prodigious force. It is the same with carbon and oxygen, in a compound called carbonic acid, which is also one of the principal substances absorbed by plants from the air. Now the heat and other emanations from the sun, acting upon these substances in the leaves, forces the hydrogen and the carbon away from their strong bond of union with oxygen, and sets the oxygen free, and then combines the carbon and hydrogen into a sort of unwilling union with each other—a union from which they are always ready and eager to break away, that they may return to their union with the object of their former and much stronger attachment—namely, oxygen; though they are so locked, by some mysterious means, that they can not break away except when certain conditions necessary to their release are realized.

Hydrocarbons.

The substances thus formed by a weak union of carbon with hydrogen are called hydrocarbons. They comprise nearly all the highly inflammable vegetable substances. Their being combustible means simply that they have a great disposition to resume their union with oxygen—combustion being nothing other than a more or less violent return of a substance to a union with oxygen or some other such substance, usually one from which it had formerly been separated by force—giving out again by its return, in the form of heat, the force by which the original separation had been effected.

A compound formed thus of substances united by very weak affinities, so that they are always ready to separate from each other and form new unions under the influence of stronger affinities, is said to be in a state of *unstable equilibrium.* It is the function of vegetable life to create these unstable combinations by means of the force derived from the sun; and the combinations, when formed, of course hold the force which formed them in reserve, ready to make itself manifest whenever it is released. Animals receive these substances into their systems in their food. A portion of them they retain, re-arranging the components in some cases so as to form new compounds, but still unstable. These they use in constructing the tissues of the animal system, and some they reserve for future use. As fast as they require the heat and the force which are stored in them they expend, them, thus recovering the force which was absorbed in the formation of them, and which now, on being released, re-appears in the three forms of *animal heat, muscular motion,* and *cerebral* or *nervous energy*.

There are other modes besides the processes of animal life by which the reserved force laid up by the vegetable process in these unstable compounds may be released. In many cases it releases itself under ordinary exposures to the oxygen of the atmosphere. A log of wood—which is composed chiefly of carbon and hydrogen in an unstable union—lying upon the ground will gradually *decay*, as we term it—that is, its elements will separate from each other, and form new unions with the elements of the surrounding air, thus returning to their normal condition. They give out, in so doing, a low degree of heat, which, being protracted through a course of years, makes up, in the end, the precise equivalent of that expended by the sun in forming the wood—that is, the power expended in the formation of the wood is all released in the dissolution of it.

This process may be greatly accelerated by heat. If a portion of the wood is raised in temperature to a certain point, the elements begin to combine with the oxygen near, with so much violence as to release the reserved power with great rapidity. And as this force re-appears in the form of heat, the next portions of the wood are at once raised to the right temperature to allow the process of reoxidation to go on rapidly with them. This is the process of combustion. Observations and experiments on decaying wood have been made, showing that the amount of heat developed by the combustion of a mass of wood, though much more intense for a time, is the same in *amount* as that which is set free by the slower process of re-oxidation by gradual decay; both being the equivalent of the amount absorbed by the leaves from the sun, in the process of deoxidizing the carbon and hydrogen when the wood was formed.

The force imprisoned in these unstable compounds may be held in reserve for an unlimited period, so long as all opportunity is denied them of returning the elements that compose them to their original combinations. Such a case occurs when large beds of vegetable substances are buried under layers of sediment which subsequently become stone, and thus shut the hydrocarbonaceous compounds beneath them from all access to oxygen. The beds of coal thus formed retain their reserved force for periods of immense duration; and when at length the material thus protected is brought to the surface, and made to give up its treasured power, it manifests its efficiency in driving machinery, propelling trains, heating furnaces, or diffusing warmth and comfort around the family fireside. In all these cases the heat and power developed from the coal is heat and power derived originally from the sun, and now set free, after having lain dormant thousands and perhaps millions of years.

This simple case of the formation of hydrocarbons from the elements furnished by carbonic acid and water is only adduced as an illustration of the general principle. The modes by which the power of the sun actually takes effect in the decomposition of stable compounds, and the formation of unstable ones from the elements thus obtained, are innumerable, and the processes as well as the combinations that result are extremely complicated. These processes include not only the first formation of the unstable compounds in the leaf, but also an endless series of modifications and re-arrangements which they subsequently undergo, as well in the other organs of the plant as in those of the animal when they are finally introduced into an animal system. In all, however, the general result is substantially the same—namely, the forcing of elements into unnatural combinations, so to speak, by the power of the sun acting through the instrumentality of vegetation, in order that they may subsequently, in the animal system, give out that power again by the effort they make to release themselves from the coercion imposed upon them, and to return to the natural unions in which they can find again stability and repose.

One of the chief elements employed in the formation of these weakly-combined substances is *nitrogen*—its compounds being designated as nitrogenous substances, and noted, as a class, for the facility with which they are decomposed. Nitrogen is, in fact, the great *weak-holder* of nature. Young students in chemistry, when they learn that nitrogen is distinguished by the weakness of its affinities for other elements, and its consequent great *inertness* as a chemical agent, are often astonished to find that its compounds—such as nitric acid, nitre, which gives its explosive character to gunpowder, nitro-glycerine, gun-cotton, and various other explosive substances which it helps to form—are among the most remarkable in nature for the violence and intensity of their action, and for the extent to which the principle of vitality avails itself of them as magazines of *force*, upon which to draw in the fulfillment of its various functions.

186 *GENTLE MEASURES.*

But this is really just what should be expected. It is the very *weakness of the hold* which nitrogen maintains upon the elements combined with it that facilitates their release, and affords them the opportunity to seize with so much avidity and violence on those for which they have a strong attraction.

It is as if a huntsman should conduct a pack of ferocious dogs into a field occupied by a flock of sheep, quietly grazing, holding the dogs securely by very strong leashes. The quiet and repose of the field might not be seriously disturbed; but if, on the other hand, a child comes in, leading the dogs by threads which they can easily sunder, a scene of the greatest violence and confusion would ensue.

In the same manner, when nitrogen, holding the particles of oxygen with which it is combined in the compounds above named by a very feeble control, brings them into the presence of other substances for which they have a very strong affinity, they release themselves at once from their weak custodian, and rush into the combinations which their nature demands with so much avidity as to produce combustions, deflagrations, and explosions of the most violent character.

The force which the elements display in these reunions is always—and this is one aspect of the great discovery of modern times in respect to the *persistence* or *constancy* of force which has already been referred to—precisely the same in amount as that which was required for dissevering them from their original combinations with such substances at some previous time. The *processes of vegetation* are the chief means employed for effecting the original separations, by the power of the sun, and for forming the unstable compounds by which this power is held in reserve. The *animal system*, on the other hand, takes in these compounds, remodels them so far as is required to adapt them to its structure, assimilates them, and then, as occasion requires quires, it releases the concealed force, which then manifests itself in the forms of *animal heat*, of *muscular motion*, and of *cerebral and nervous power*.

In what way, and to what extent, the knowledge of these truths should influence us in the management and training of children in respect to their extraordinary activity, is the question we have next to consider.

Practical Applications of these Principles.

If we watch a bird for a little while hopping along upon the ground, and up and down between the ground and the branches of a tree, we shall at first be surprised at his incessant activity, and next, if we reflect a little, at the utter aimlessness and uselessness of it. He runs a little way along the path; then he hops up upon a twig, then down again upon the ground; then "makes believe" peck at something which he imagines or pretends that he sees in the grass; then, canting his head to one side and upward, the branch of a tree there happens to strike his eye, upon which he at once flies up to it. Perching himself upon it for the moment, he utters a burst of joyous song, and then, instantly afterwards, down he comes upon the ground again, runs along, stops, runs along a little farther, stops again, looks around him a moment, as if wondering what to do next, and then flies off out of our field of view. If we could follow, and had patience to watch him so long, we should find him continuing this incessantly changing but never-ceasing activity all the day long.

We sometimes imagine that the bird's movements are to be explained by supposing that he is engaged in the search for food in these evolutions. But when we reflect how small a quantity of food his little crop will contain, we shall be at once convinced that a large proportion of his apparent pecking for food is only make-believe, and that he moves thus incessantly not so much on account of the end he seeks to attain by it, as on account of the very pleasure of the motion. He hops about and pecks, not for the love of any thing he expects to find, but just for the love of hopping and pecking.

The real explanation is that the food which he has taken is delivering up, within his system, the force stored in it that was received originally from the beams of the sun, while the plant which produced it was growing. This force must have an outlet, and it finds this outlet in the incessant activity of the bird's muscles and brain. The various objects which attract his attention without, *invite* the force to expend itself in *certain special directions*; but the impelling cause is within, and not without; and were there nothing without to serve as objects for its action, the necessity of its action would be none the less imperious. The lion, when imprisoned in his cage, walks to and fro continuously, if there is room for him to take two steps and turn; and if there is not room for this, he moves his head incessantly from side to side. The force within him, which his vital organs are setting at liberty from its imprisonment in his food, must in some way find issue.

Mothers do not often stop to speculate upon, and may even, perhaps, seldom observe the restless and incessant activity of birds, but that of their children forces itself upon their attention by its effects in disturbing their own quiet avocations and pleasures; and they often wonder what can be the inducement which leads to such a perpetual succession of movements made apparently without motive or end. And, not perceiving any possible inducement to account for it, they are apt to consider this restless activity so causeless and unreasonable as to make it a fault for which the child is to be censured or punished, or which they are to attempt to cure by means of artificial restraints. They would not attempt such repressions as this if they were aware that all this muscular and mental energy of action in the child is only the outward manifestation of an inward force developed in a manner wholly independent of its will—a force, too, which must spend itself in some way or other, and that, if not allowed to do this in its own way, by impelling the limbs and members to outward action, it will do so by destroying the delicate mechanism within. We see this in the case of men who are doomed for long periods to solitary confinement. The force derived from their food, and released within their systems by the vital processes, being cut off by the silence and solitude of the dungeon from all usual and natural outlets, begins to work mischief within, by disorganizing the cerebral and other vital organs, and producing insanity and death.

Common Mistake.

We make a great mistake when we imagine that children are influenced in their activity mainly by a desire for the objects which they attain by it. It is not the ends attained, but the pleasurable feeling which the action of the internal force, issuing by its natural channels, affords them, and the sense of power which accompanies the action. An end which presents itself to be attained invites this force to act in one direction rather than another, but it is the action, and not the end, in which the charm resides.

Give a child a bow and arrow, and send him out into the yard to try it, and if he does not happen to see any thing to shoot at, he will shoot at random into the air. But if there is any object which will serve as a mark in sight, it seems to have the effect of drawing his aim towards it. He shoots at the vane on the barn, at an apple on a tree, a knot in a fence—any thing which will serve the purpose of a mark. This is not because he has any end to accomplish in hitting the vane, the apple, or the knot, but only because there is an impulse within him leading him to shoot, and if there happens to be any thing to shoot at, it gives that impulse a direction.

It is precisely the same with the incessant muscular activity of a child. He comes into a room and sits down in the first seat that he sees. Then he jumps up and runs to another, then to another, until he has tried all the seats in the room. This is not because he particularly wishes to try the seats. He wishes to *move*, and the seats happen to be at hand, and they simply give direction to the impulse. If he were out of doors, the same office would be fulfilled by a fence which he might climb over, instead of going through an open gate close by; or a wall that he could walk upon with difficulty, instead of going, without difficulty, along a path at the foot of it; or a pole which he could try to climb, when there was no motive for climbing it but a desire to make muscular exertion; or a steep bank where he can scramble up, when there is nothing that he wishes for on the top of it.

In other words, the things that children do are not done for the sake of the things, but for the sake of the *doing*.

Parents very often do not understand this, and are accordingly continually asking such foolish questions as, "George, what do you wish to climb over that fence for, when there is a gate all open close by?" "James, what good do you expect to get by climbing up that tree, when you know there is nothing on it, not even a bird's nest?" and, "Lucy, what makes you keep jumping up all the time and running about to different places? Why can't you, when you get a good seat, sit still in it?"

The children, if they understood the philosophy of the case, might answer, "We don't climb over the fence at all because we wish to be on the other side of it; or scramble up the bank for the sake of any thing that is on the top of it; or run about to different places because we wish to be in the places particularly. It is the internal force that is in us working itself off, and it works itself off in the ways that come most readily to hand."

Various Modes in which the Reserved Force reappears.

The force thus stored in the food and liberated within the system by the vital processes, finds scope for action in several different ways, prominent among which are, First, in the production of animal heat; Secondly, in muscular contractions and the motions of the limbs and members resulting from them; and Thirdly, in mental phenomena connected with the action of the brain and the nerves. This last branch of the subject is yet enveloped in great mystery; but the proof seems to be decisive that the nervous system of man comprises organs which are actively exercised in the performance of mental operations, and that in this exercise they consume important portions of the vital force. If, for example, a child is actually engaged at play, and we direct him to take a seat and sit still, he will find it very difficult to do so. The inward force will soon begin to struggle within him to find an issue. But if, while he is so sitting, we begin to relate to him some very surprising or exciting story, to occupy his *mind*, he will become motionless, and very likely remain so until the story is ended. It is supposed that in such cases the force is drawn off, so to speak, through the cerebral organs which it is employed in keeping in play, as the instruments by which the emotions and ideas which the story awakens in the mind are evolved. This part of the subject, as has already been remarked, is full of mystery; but the general fact that a portion of the force derived from the food is expended in actions of the brain and nervous system seems well established.

Indeed, the whole subject of the reception and the storing up of force from the sun by the processes of vegetable and animal life, and the subsequent liberation of it in the fulfillment of the various functions of the animal system, is full of difficulties and mysteries. It is only a very simple view of the *general principle* which is presented in these articles. In nature the operations are not simple at all. They are involved in endless complications which are yet only to a very limited extent unravelled. The general principle is, however, well established; and if understood, even as a general principle, by parents and teachers, it will greatly modify their action in dealing with the incessant restlessness and activity of the young. It will teach them, among other things, the following practical rules:

Practical Rules.

1. Never find fault with children for their incapacity to keep still. You may stop the supply of force, if you will, by refusing to give them food; but if you continue the supply, you must not complain of its manifesting itself in action. After giving your boy his breakfast, to find fault with him for being incessantly in motion when his system has absorbed it, is simply to find fault with him for being healthy and happy. To give children food and then to restrain the resulting activity, is conduct very analogous to that of the engineer who should lock the action of his engine, turn all the stop-cocks, and shut down the safety-valve, while he still went on all the time putting in coal under the boiler. The least that he could expect would be a great hissing and fizzling at all the joints of his machine; and it would be only by means of such a degree of looseness in the joints as would allow of the escape of the imprisoned force in this way that could prevent the repression ending in a frightful catastrophe.

Now, nine-tenths of the whispering and playing of children in school, and of the noise, the rudeness, and the petty mischief of children at home, is just this hissing and fizzling of an imprisoned power, and nothing more.

In a word, we must favor and promote, by every means in our power, the activity of children, not censure and repress it. We may endeavor to turn it aside from wrong channels—that is, to prevent its manifesting itself in ways injurious to them or annoying to others. We must not, however, attempt to divert it from these channels by damming it up, but by opening other channels that will draw it away in better directions.

2. In encouraging the activity of children, and in guiding the direction of it in their hours of play, we must not expect to make it available for useful results, other than that of promoting their own physical development and health. At least, we can do this only in a very limited degree. Almost all useful results require for their attainment a long

continuance of efforts of the same kind—that is, expenditure of the vital force by the continued action of the same organs. Now, it is a principle of nature that while the organs of an animal system are in process of formation and growth, they can exercise their power only for a very brief period at a time without exhaustion. This necessitates on the part of all young animals incessant changes of action, or alternations of action and repose. A farmer of forty years of age, whose organs are well developed and mature, will chop wood all day without excessive fatigue. Then, when he comes home at night, he will sit for three hours in the evening upon the settle by his fireside, *thinking*—his mind occupied, perhaps, upon the details of the management of his farm, or upon his plans for the following day. The vital force thus expends itself for many successive hours through his muscles, and then, while his muscles are at rest, it finds its egress for several other hours through the brain. But in the *child* the mode of action must change every few minutes. He is made tired with five minutes' labor. He is satisfied with five minutes' rest. He will ride his rocking-horse, if alone, a short time, and then he comes to you to ask you to tell him a story. While listening to the story, his muscles are resting, and the force is spending its strength in working the mechanism of the brain. If you make your story too long, the brain, in turn, becomes fatigued, and he feels instinctively impelled to divert the vital force again into muscular action.

If, instead of being alone with his rocking-horse, he has company there, he will *seem* to continue his bodily effort a long time; but he does not really do so, for he stops continually, to talk with his companion, thus allowing his muscles to rest for a brief period, during which the vital force expends its strength in carrying on trains of thought and emotion through the brain.

He is not to be blamed for this seeming capriciousness. These frequent changes in the mode of action are a necessity, and this necessity evidently unfits him for any kind of monotonous or continued exertion— the only kind which, in ordinary cases, can be made conducive to any useful results.

3. Parents at home and teachers at school must recognize these

physiological laws, relating to the action of the young, and make their plans and arrangements conform to them. The periods of confinement to any one mode of action in the very young, and especially mental action, must be short; and they must alternate frequently with other modes. That rapid succession of bodily movements and of mental ideas, and the emotions mingling and alternating with them, which constitutes what children call play, must be regarded not simply as an indulgence, but as a necessity for them. The play must be considered as essential as the study, and that not merely for the very young but for all, up to the age of maturity. For older pupils, in the best institutions of the country, some suitable provision is made for this want; but the mothers of young children at home are often at a loss by what means to effect this purpose, and many are very imperfectly aware of the desirableness, and even the necessity, of doing this. As for the means of accomplishing the object—that is, providing channels for the complete expenditure of this force in the safest and most agreeable manner for the child, and the least inconvenient and troublesome for others, much must depend upon the tact, the ingenuity, and the discretion of the mother. It will, however, be a great point gained for her when she once fully comprehends that the *tendency* to incessant activity, and even to turbulence and noise, on the part of her child, only shows that he is all right in his vital machinery, and that this exuberance of energy is something to be pleased with and directed, not denounced and restrained.

CHAPTER XV.

THE IMAGINATION IN CHILDREN.

The reader may, perhaps, recollect that in the last chapter there was an intimation that a portion of the force which was produced, or rather liberated and brought into action, by the consumption of food in the vital system, expended itself in the development of thoughts, emotions, and other forms of mental action, through the organization of the brain and of the nerves.

Expenditure of Force through the Brain.

The whole subject of the expenditure of material force in maintaining those forms of mental action which are carried on through the medium of bodily organs, it must be admitted, is involved in great obscurity; for it is only a glimmering of light which science has yet been able to throw into this field. It is, however, becoming the settled opinion, among all well-informed persons, that the soul, during the time of its connection with a material system in this life, performs many of those functions which we class as mental, through the medium, or instrumentality, in some mysterious way, of material organs, just as we all know is the case with the sensations—that is, the impressions made through the organs of sense; and that the maintaining of these mental organs, so to speak, in action, involves a certain expenditure of some form of physical force, the source of this force being in the food that is consumed in the nourishment of the body.

There is certainly no apparent reason why there should be any antecedent presumption against the supposition that the soul performs the act of remembering or of conceiving an imaginary scene through the instrumentality of a bodily organ, more than that it should receive a sensation of light or of sound through such a channel. The question of the independent existence and the immateriality of the thinking and feeling principle, which takes cognizance of these thoughts and sensations, is not at all affected by any inquiries into the nature of the instrumentality by means of which, in a particular stage of its existence, it performs these functions.

Phenomena explained by this Principle.

This truth, if it be indeed a truth, throws great light on what would be otherwise quite inexplicable in the playful activity of the mental faculties of children. The curious fantasies, imaginings, and make-believes—the pleasure of listening to marvellous and impossible tales, and of hearing odd and unpronounceable words or combination of words —the love of acting, and of disguises—of the impersonation of inanimate objects—of seeing things as they are not, and of creating and giving reality to what has no existence except in their own minds—are all the gambollings and frolics, so to speak, of the embryo faculties just becoming conscious of their existence, and affording, like the muscles of motion, so many different issues for the internal force derived from the food. Thus the action of the mind of a child, in holding an imaginary conversation with a doll, or in inventing or in relating an impossible fairy story, or in converting a switch on which he pretends to be riding into a prancing horse, is precisely analogous to that of the muscles of the lamb, or the calf, or any other young animal in its gambols—that is, it is the result of the force which the vital functions are continually developing within the system, and which flows and must flow continually out through whatever channels are open to it; and in thus flowing, sets all the various systems of machinery into play, each in its own appropriate manner.

In any other view of the subject than this, many of the phenomena of childhood would be still more wonderful and inexplicable than they are. One would have supposed, for example, that the imagination—being, as is commonly thought, one of the most exalted and refined of the mental faculties of man—would be one of the latest, in the order of time, to manifest itself in the development of the mind; instead of which it is, in fact, one of the earliest. Children live, in a great measure, from the earliest age in an ideal world—their pains and their pleasures, their joys and their fears being, to a vast extent, the concomitants of phantasms and illusions having often the slightest bond of connection with the realities around them. The realities themselves, moreover, often have far greater influence over them by what they suggest than by what they are.

Indeed, the younger the child is, within reasonable limits, the more susceptible he seems to be to the power of the imagination, and the more easily his mind and heart are reached and influenced through this avenue. At a very early period the realities of actual existence and the phantasms of the mind seem inseparably mingled, and it is only after much experience and a considerable development of his powers, that the line of distinction between them becomes defined. The power of investing an elongated bag of bran with the attributes and qualities of a thinking being, so as to make it an object of solicitude and affection, which would seem to imply a high exercise of one of the most refined and exalted of the human faculties, does not come, as we might have expected, at the end of a long period of progress and development, but springs into existence, as it were, at once, in the very earliest years. The progress and development are required to enable the child to perceive that the rude and shapeless doll is *not* a living and lovable thing. This mingling of the real and imaginary worlds shows itself to the close observer in a thousand curious ways.

The true explanation of the phenomenon seems to be that the various embryo faculties are brought into action by the vital force at first in a very irregular, intermingled, and capricious manner, just as the muscles are in the endless and objectless play of the limbs and members. They develop themselves and grow by this very action, and we ought not only to indulge, but to cherish the action in all its beautiful manifestations by every means in our power. These mental organs, so to speak—that is, the organs of the brain, through which, while its connection with the body continues, the mind performs its mental functions—grow and thrive, as the muscles do, by being reasonably kept in exercise.

It is evident, from these facts, that the parent should be pleased with, and should encourage the exercise of these embryo powers in his children; and both father and mother may be greatly aided in their efforts to devise means for reaching and influencing their hearts by means of them, and especially through the action of the imagination, which will be found, when properly employed, to be capable of exercising an almost magical power of imparting great attractiveness and giving great effect to lessons of instruction which, in their simple form, would be dull, tiresome, and ineffective. Precisely what is meant by this will be shown more clearly by some examples.

Methods exemplified.

One of the simplest and easiest modes by which a mother can avail herself of the vivid imagination of the child in amusing and entertaining him, is by holding conversations with representations of persons, or even of animals, in the pictures which she shows him. Thus, in the case, for example, of a picture which she is showing to her child sitting in her lap —the picture containing, we will suppose, a representation of a little girl with books under her arm—she may say,

"My little girl, where are you going?—I am going" (speaking now in a somewhat altered voice, to represent the voice of the little girl) "to school.—Ah! you are going to school. You don't look quite old enough to go to school. Who sits next to you at school?—George Williams.—George Williams? Is he a good boy?—Yes, he's a very good boy.—I am glad you have a good boy, and one that is kind to you, to sit by you. That must be very pleasant." And so on, as long as the child is interested in listening.

Or, "What is your name, my little girl?—My name is Lucy.—That's a pretty name! And where do you live?—I live in that house under the trees.—Ah! I see the house. And where is your room in that house?—My room is the one where you see the window open.—I see it. What have you got in your room?—I have a bed, and a table by the window; and I keep my doll there. I have got a cradle for my doll, and a little trunk to keep her clothes in. And I have got—" The mother may go on in this way, and describe a great number and variety of objects in the room, such as are calculated to interest and please the little listener.

It is the pleasurable exercise of some dawning faculty or faculties acting through embryo organs of the brain, by which the mind can picture to itself, more or less vividly, unreal scenes, which is the source of the enjoyment in such cases as this.

A child may be still more interested, perhaps, by imaginary conversations of this kind with pictures of animals, and by varying the form of them in such a way as to call a new set of mental faculties into play; as, for example,

"Here is a picture of a squirrel. I'll ask him where he lives. 'Bunny! bunny! stop a minute; I want to speak to you. I want you to tell me where you live.—I live in my hole.—Where is your hole?—It is under that big log that you see back in the woods.' Yes" (speaking now to the child), "I see the log. Do you see it? Touch it with your finger. Yes, that must be it. But I don't see any hole. 'Bunny' (assuming now the tone of speaking again to the squirrel), 'I don't see your hole.—No, I did not mean that any body should see it. I made it in a hidden place in the ground, so as to have it out of sight.—I wish I could see it, and I wish more that I could look down into it and see what is there. What is there *in* your hole, bunny?—My nest is there, and my little bunnies.—How many little bunnies have you got?'"—And so on, to any extent that you desire.

It is obvious that conversations of this kind may be made the means of conveying, indirectly, a great deal of instruction to young children on a great variety of subjects; and lessons of duty may be inculcated thus in a very effective manner, and by a method which is at the same time easy and agreeable for the mother, and extremely attractive to the child.

This may seem a very simple thing, and it is really very simple; but any mother who has never resorted to this method of amusing and instructing her child will be surprised to find what an easy and inexhaustible resource for her it may become. Children are always coming to ask for stories, and the mother often has no story at hand, and her mind is too much preoccupied to invent one. Here is a ready resort in every such emergency.

"Very well," replies the mother to such a request, "I'll tell you a story; but I must have a picture to my story. Find me a picture in some book."

The child brings a picture, no matter what. There is no possible picture that will not suggest to a person possessed of ordinary ingenuity an endless number of talks to interest and amuse the child. To take an extreme case, suppose the picture is a rude pencil drawing of a post, and nothing besides. You can imagine a boy hidden behind the post, and you can call to him, and finally obtain an answer from him, and have a long talk with him about his play and who he is hiding from, and what other way he has of playing with his friend. Or you can talk with the post directly. Ask him where he came from, who put him in the ground, and what he was put in the ground for, and what kind of a tree he was when he was a part of a tree growing in the woods; and, following the subject out, the conversation may be the means of not only amusing the child for the moment, but also of gratifying his curiosity, and imparting a great amount of useful information to him which will materially aid in the development of his powers.

Or you may ask the post whether he has any relatives, and he may reply that he has a great many cousins. He has some cousins that live in the city, and they are called lamp-posts, and their business is to hold lamps to light people along the streets; and he has some other cousins who stand in a long row and hold up the telegraph-wire to carry messages from one part of the world to another; and so on without end. If all this may done by means of a rude representation of a simple post, it may easily be seen that no picture which the child can possibly bring can fail to serve as a subject for such conversations.

Some mothers may, perhaps, think it must require a great deal of ingenuity and skill to carry out these ideas effectively in practice, and that is true; or rather, it is true that there is in it scope for the exercise of a great deal of ingenuity and skill, and even of genius, for those who possess these qualities; but the degree of ingenuity required for a commencement in this method is very small, and that necessary for complete success in it is very easily acquired.

Personification of Inanimate Objects.

It will at once occur to the mother that any inanimate object may be personified in this way and addressed as a living and intelligent being. Your child is sick, I will suppose, and is somewhat feverish and fretful. In adjusting his dress you prick him a little with a pin, and the pain and annoyance acting on his morbid sensibilities bring out expressions of irritation and ill-humor. Now you may, if you please, tell him that he must not be so impatient, that you did not mean to hurt him, that he must not mind a little prick, and the like, and you will meet with the ordinary success that attends such admonitions. Or, in the spirit of the foregoing suggestions, you may say,

"Did the pin prick you? I'll catch the little rogue, and hear what he has to say for himself. Ah, here he is—I've caught him! I'll hold him fast. Lie still in my lap, and we will hear what he has to say.

"'Look up here, my little prickler, and tell me what your name is.—My name is pin.—Ah, your name is pin, is it? How bright you are! How came you to be so bright?—Oh, they brightened me when they made me. —Indeed! And how did they make you?—They made me in a machine.

—In a machine? That's very curious! How did they make you in the machine? Tell us all about it!—They made me out of wire. First the machine cut off a piece of the wire long enough to make me, and then I was carried around to different parts of the machine to have different things done to me. I went first to one part to get straightened. Don't you see how straight I am?—Yes, you are very straight indeed.—Then I went to another part of the machine and had my head put on; and then I went to another part and had my point sharpened; and then I was polished, and covered all over with a beautiful silvering, to make me bright and white.'"

And so on indefinitely. The mother may continue the talk as long as the child is interested, by letting the pin give an account of the various adventures that happened to it in the course of its life, and finally call it to account for pricking a poor little sick child.

Any mother can judge whether such a mode of treating the case, or the more usual one of gravely exhorting the child to patience and good-humor, when sick, is likely to be most effectual in soothing the nervous irritation of the little patient, and restoring its mind to a condition of calmness and repose.

The mother who reads these suggestions in a cursory manner, and contents herself with saying that they are very good, but makes no resolute and persevering effort to acquire for herself the ability to avail herself of them, will have no idea of the immense practical value of them as a means of aiding her in her work, and in promoting the happiness of her children. But if she will make the attempt, she will most certainly find enough encouragement in her first effort to induce her to persevere.

She must, moreover, not only originate, herself, modes of amusing the imagination of her children, but must fall in with and aid those which *they* originate. If your little daughter is playing with her doll, look up from your work and say a few words to the doll or the child in a grave and serious manner, assuming that the doll is a living and sentient being. If your boy is playing horses in the garden while you are there attending to your flowers, ask him with all gravity what he values his horse at, and whether he wishes to sell him. Ask him whether he ever bites, or breaks out of his pasture; and give him some advice about not driving him too fast up hill, and not giving him oats when he is warm. He will at once enter into such a conversation in the most serious manner, and the pleasure of his play will be greatly increased by your joining with him in maintaining the illusion.

There is a still more important advantage than the temporary increase to your children's happiness by acting on this principle. By thus joining with them, even for a few moments, in their play, you establish a closer bond of sympathy between your own heart and theirs, and attach them to you more strongly than you can do by any other means. Indeed, in many cases the most important moral lessons can be conveyed in connection with these illusions of children, and in a way not only more agreeable but far more effective than by any other method.

Influence without Claim to Authority.

Acting through the imagination of children—if the art of doing so is once understood—will prove at once an invaluable and an inexhaustible resource for all those classes of persons who are placed in situations requiring them to exercise an influence over children without having any proper authority over them; such, for example, as uncles and aunts, older brothers and sisters, and even visitors residing more or less permanently in a family, and desirous, from a wish to do good, of promoting the welfare and the improvement of the younger members of it. It often happens that such a visitor, without any actual right of authority, acquires a greater influence over the minds of the children than the parents themselves; and many a mother, who, with all her threatenings and scoldings, and even punishments, can not make herself obeyed, is surprised at the absolute ascendency which some inmate residing in the family acquires over them by means so silent, gentle, and unpretending, that they seem mysterious and almost magical. "What is the secret of it?" asks the mother sometimes in such a case. "You never punish the children, and you never scold them, and yet they obey you a great deal more readily and certainly than they do me."

There are a great many different means which may be employed in combination with each other for acquiring this kind of ascendency, and among them the use which may be made of the power of the imagination in the young is one of the most important.

The Intermediation of the Dolls again.

A young teacher, for example, in returning from school some day, finds the children of the family in which she resides, who have been playing with their dolls in the yard, engaged in some angry dispute. The first impulse with many persons in such a case might be to sit down with the children upon the seat where they were playing, and remonstrate with them, though in a very kind and gentle manner, on the wrongfulness and folly of such disputings, to show them that the thing in question is not worth disputing about, that angry feelings are uncomfortable and unhappy feelings, and that it is, consequently, not only a sin, but a folly to indulge in them.

Now such a remonstrance, if given in a kind and gentle manner, will undoubtedly do good. The children will be somewhat less likely to become involved in such a dispute immediately after it than before, and in process of time, and through many repetitions of such counsels, the fault may be gradually cured. Still, at the time, it will make the children uncomfortable, by producing in their minds a certain degree of irritation. They will be very apt to listen in silence, and with a morose and sullen air; and if they do not call the admonition a scolding, on account of the kind and gentle tones in which it is delivered, they will be very apt to consider it much in that light.

Suppose, however, that, instead of dealing with the case in this matter-of-fact and naked way, the teacher calls the imagination of the children to her aid, and administers her admonition and reproof indirectly, through the dolls. She takes the dolls in her hand, asks their names, and inquires which of the two girls is the mother of each. The dolls' names are Bella and Araminta, and the mothers' are Lucy and Mary.

"But I might have asked Araminta herself," she adds; and, so saying, she holds the doll before her, and enters into a long imaginary conversation with her, more or less spirited and original, according to the talent and ingenuity of the young lady, but, in any conceivable case, enough so to completely absorb the attention of the children and fully to occupy their minds. She asks each of them her name, and inquires of each which of the girls is her mother, and makes first one of them, and then the other, point to her mother in giving her answer. By this time the illusion is completely established in the children's minds of regarding their dolls as living beings, responsible to mothers for their conduct and behavior; and the young lady can go on and give her admonitions and instructions in respect to the sin and folly of quarrelling to them—the children listening. And it will be found that by this management the impression upon the minds of the children will be far greater and more effective than if the counsels were addressed directly to them; while, at the same time, though they may even take the form of very severe reproof, they will produce no sullenness or vexation in the minds of those for whom they are really intended. Indeed, the very reason why the admonition thus given will be so much more effective is the fact that it does *not* tend in any degree to awaken resentment and vexation, but associates the lesson which the teacher wishes to convey with amusement and pleasure.

"You are very pretty"—she says, we will suppose, addressing the dolls—"and you look very amiable. I suppose you *are* very amiable."

Then, turning to the children, she asks, in a confidential undertone, "Do they ever get into disputes and quarrels?"

"*Sometimes,*" says one of the children, entering at once into the idea of the teacher.

"Ah!" the teacher exclaims, turning again to the dolls. "I hear that you dispute and quarrel sometimes, and I am very sorry for it. That is very foolish. It is only silly little children that we expect will dispute and quarrel. I should not have supposed it possible in the case of such young ladies as you. It is a great deal better to be yielding and kind. If one of you says something that the other thinks is not true, let it pass without contradiction; it is foolish to dispute about it. And so if one has any thing that the other wants, it is generally much better to wait for it than to quarrel. It is hateful to quarrel. Besides, it spoils your beauty. When children are quarrelling they look like little furies."

The teacher may go on in this way, and give a long moral lecture to the dolls in a tone of mock gravity, and the children will listen to it with the most profound attention; and it will have a far greater influence upon them than the same admonitions addressed directly to *them*.

So effectually, in fact, will this element of play in the transaction open their hearts to the reception of good counsel, that even direct admonitions to *them* will be admitted with it, if the same guise is maintained; for the teacher may add, in conclusion, addressing now the children themselves with the same mock solemnity:

"That is a very bad fault of your children—very bad, indeed. And it is one that you will find very hard to correct. You must give them a great deal of good counsel on the subject, and, above all, you must be careful to set them a good example yourselves. Children always imitate what they see in their mothers, whether it is good or bad. If you are always amiable and kind to one another, they will be so too."

The thoughtful mother, in following out the suggestions here given, will see at once how the interest which the children take in their dolls, and the sense of reality which they feel in respect to all their dealings with them, opens before her a boundless field in respect to modes of reaching and influencing their minds and hearts.

The Ball itself made to teach Carefulness.

There is literally no end to the modes by which persons having the charge of young children can avail themselves of their vivid imaginative powers in inculcating moral lessons or influencing their conduct. A boy, we will suppose, has a new ball. Just as he is going out to play with it his father takes it from him to examine it, and, after turning it round and looking at it attentively on every side, holds it up to his ear. The boy asks what his father is doing. "I am listening to hear what he says." "And what does he say, father?" "He says that you won't have him to play with long." "Why not?" "I will ask him, why not?" (holding the ball again to his ear). "What does he say, father?" "He says he is going to run away from you and hide. He says you will go to play near some building, and he means, when you throw him or knock him, to fly against the windows and break the glass, and then people will take your ball away from you." "But I won't play near any windows." "He says, at any rate you will play near some building, and when you knock him he means to fly up to the roof and get behind a chimney, or roll down into the gutter where you can't get him." "But, father, I am not going to play near any building at all." "Then you will play in some place where there are holes in the ground, or thickets of bushes near, where he can hide." "No, father, I mean to look well over the ground, and not play in any place where there is any danger at all." "Well, we shall see; but the little rogue is determined to hide somewhere." The boy takes his ball and goes out to play with it, far more effectually cautioned than he could have been by any direct admonition.

The Teacher and the Tough Logs

A teacher who was engaged in a district school in the country, where the arrangement was for the older boys to saw and split the wood for the fire, on coming one day, at the recess, to see how the work was going on, found that the boys had laid one rather hard-looking log aside. They could not split that log, they said.

"Yes," said the teacher, looking at the log, "I don't wonder. I know that log. I saw him before. His name is Old Gnarly. He says he has no idea of coming open for a parcel of boys, even if they *have* got beetle and wedges. It takes a man, he says, to split *him*."

The boys stood looking at the log with a very grave expression of countenance as they heard these words.

"Is that what he says?" asked one of them. "Let's try him again, Joe."

"It will do no good," said the teacher, "for he won't come open, if he can possibly help it. And *there's* another fellow (pointing). His name is Slivertwist. If you get a crack in him, you will find him full of twisted splinters that he holds himself together with. The only way is to cut them through with a sharp axe. But he holds on so tight with them that I don't believe you can get him open. He says he never gives up to boys."

So saying, the teacher went away. It is scarcely necessary to say to any one who knows boys that the teacher was called out not long afterwards to see that Old Gnarly and Old Slivertwist were both split up fine—the boys standing around the heaps of well-prepared fire-wood which they had afforded, and regarding them with an air of exultation and triumph.

Muscles reinvigorated through the Action of the Mind.

An older sister has been taking a walk, with little Johnny, four years old, as her companion. On their return, when within half a mile of home, Johnny, tired of gathering flowers and chasing butterflies, comes to his sister, with a fatigued and languid air, and says he can not walk any farther, and wants to be carried.

"I can't carry you very well," she says, "but I will tell you what we will do; we will stop at the first tavern we come to and rest. Do you see that large flat stone out there at the turn of the road? That is the tavern, and you shall be my courier. A courier is a man that goes forward as fast as he can on his horse, and tells the tavern-keeper that the traveller is coming, and orders supper. So you may gallop on as fast as you can go, and, when you get to the tavern, tell the tavern-keeper that the princess is coming—I am the princess—and that he must get ready an excellent supper."

The boy will gallop on and wait at the stone. When his sister arrives she may sit and rest with him a moment, entertaining him by imagining conversations with the inn-keeper, and then resume their walk.

"Now," she may say, "I must send my courier to the post-office with a letter. Do you see that fence away forward? That fence is the post-office. We will play that one of the cracks between the boards is the letter-box. Take this letter (handing him any little scrap of paper which she has taken from her pocket and folded to represent a letter) and put it in the letter-box, and speak to the postmaster through the crack, and tell him to send the letter as soon as he can."

Under such management as this, unless the child's exhaustion is very great, his sense of it will disappear, and he will accomplish the walk not only without any more complaining, but with a great feeling of pleasure. The nature of the action in such a case seems to be that the vital force, when, in its direct and ordinary passage to the muscles through the nerves, it has exhausted the resources of that mode of transmission, receives in some mysterious way a reinforcement to its strength in passing round, by a new channel, through the organs of intelligence and imagination.

These trivial instances are only given as examples to show how infinitely varied are the applications which may be made of this principle of appealing to the imagination of children, and what a variety of effects may be produced through its instrumentality by a parent or teacher who once takes pains to make himself possessed of it. But each one must make himself possessed of it by his own practice and experience. No general instructions can do any thing more than to offer the suggestion, and to show how a beginning is to be made.

CHAPTER XVI.

TRUTH AND FALSEHOOD.

The duty of telling the truth seems to us, until we have devoted special consideration to the subject, the most simple thing in the world, both to understand and to perform; and when we find young children disregarding it we are surprised and shocked, and often imagine that it indicates something peculiar and abnormal in the moral sense of the offender. A little reflection, however, will show us how very different the state of the case really is. What do we mean by the obligation resting upon us to tell the truth? It is simply, in general terms, that it is our duty to make our statements correspond with the realities which they purport to express. This is, no doubt, our duty, as a general rule, but there are so many exceptions to this rule, and the principles on which the admissibility of the exceptions depend are so complicated and so abstruse, that it is wonderful that children learn to make the necessary distinctions as soon as they do.

Natural Guidance to the Duty of telling the Truth.

The child, when he first acquires the art of using and understanding language, is filled with wonder and pleasure to find that he can represent external objects that he observes, and also ideas passing through his mind, by means of sounds formed by his organs of speech. Such sounds, he finds, have both these powers—that is, they can represent realities or fancies. Thus, when he utters the sounds *I see a bird*, they may denote either a mere conception in his mind, or an outward actuality. How is he possibly to know, by any instinct, or intuition, or moral sense when it is right for him to use them as representations of a mere idea, and when it is wrong for him to use them, unless they correspond with some actual reality?

The fact that vivid images or conceptions may be awakened in his mind by the mere hearing of certain sounds made by himself or another is something strange and wonderful to him; and though he comes to his consciousness of this susceptibility by degrees, it is still, while he is acquiring it, and extending the scope and range of it, a source of continual pleasure to him. The necessity of any correspondence of these words, and of the images which they excite, with actual realities, is a necessity which arises from the relations of man to man in the social state, and he has no means whatever of knowing any thing about it except by instruction.

There is not only no ground for expecting that children should perceive any such necessity either by any kind of instinct, or intuition, or embryo moral sense, or by any reasoning process of which his incipient powers are capable; but even if he should by either of these means be inclined to entertain such an idea, his mind would soon be utterly confused in regard to it by what he observes constantly taking place around him in respect to the use of language by others whose conduct, much more than their precepts, he is accustomed to follow as his guide.

A very nice Distinction.

A mother, for example, takes her little son, four or five years old, into her lap to amuse him with a story. She begins: "When I was a little boy I lived by myself. All the bread and cheese I got I laid upon the shelf," and so on to the end. The mother's object is accomplished. The boy is amused. He is greatly interested and pleased by the wonderful phenomenon taking place within him of curious images awakened in his mind by means of sounds entering his ear—images of a little boy living alone, of his reaching up to put bread and cheese upon a shelf, and finally of his attempting to wheel a little wife home—the story ending with the breaking and downfall of the wheelbarrow, wife and all. He does not reflect philosophically upon the subject, but the principal element of the pleasure afforded him is the wonderful phenomenon of the formation of such vivid and strange images in his mind by means of the mere sound of his mother's voice.

He knows at once, if any half-formed reflections arise in his mind at all, that what his mother has told him is not true—that is, that the words and images which they awaken in his mind had no actual realities corresponding with them. He knows, in the first place, that his mother never was a boy, and does not suppose that she ever lived by herself, and laid up her bread and cheese upon a shelf. The whole story, he understands, if he exercises any thought about it whatever—wheelbarrow catastrophe and all—consists only of words which his mother speaks to him to give him pleasure.

By-and-by his mother gives him a piece of cake, and he goes out into the garden to play. His sister is there and asks him to give her a piece of his cake. He hesitates. He thinks of the request long enough to form a distinct image in his mind of giving her half of it, but finally concludes not to do so, and eats it all himself.

When at length he comes in, his mother accidentally asks him some question about the cake, and he says he gave half of it to his sister. His mother seems much pleased. He knew that she would be pleased. He said it, in fact, on purpose to please her. The words represented no actual reality, but only a thought passing through his mind, and he spoke, in a certain sense, for the purpose of giving his mother pleasure. The case corresponds in all these particulars with that of his mother's statement in respect to her being once a little boy and living by herself. Those words were spoken by her to give him pleasure, and he said what he did to give her pleasure. To give her pleasure! the reader will perhaps say, with some surprise, thinking that to assign such a motive as that is not, by any means, putting a fair and proper construction upon the boy's act. His design was, it will be said, to shield himself from censure, or to procure undeserved praise. And it is, no doubt, true that, on a nice analysis of the motives of the act, such as we, in our maturity, can easily make, we shall find that design obscurely mingled with them. But the child does not analyze. He can not. He does not look forward to ultimate ends, or look for the hidden springs that lie concealed among the complicated combinations of impulses which animate him. In the case that we are supposing, all that we can reasonably believe to be present to his mind is a kind of instinctive feeling that for him to say that he ate the cake all himself would bring a frown, or at least a look of pain and distress, to his mother's face, and perhaps words of displeasure for him; while, if he says that he gave half to his sister, she will look pleased and happy. This is as far as he sees. And he may be of such an age, and his mental organs may be in so embryonic a condition, that it is as far as he ought to be expected to look; so that, as the case presents itself to his mind in respect to the impulse which at the moment prompts him to act, he said what he did from a desire to give his mother pleasure, and not pain. As to the secret motive, which might have been his ultimate end, *that* lay too deeply concealed for him to be conscious of it. And we ourselves too often act from the influence of hidden impulses of selfishness, the existence of which we are wholly unconscious of, to judge him too harshly for his blindness.

At length, by-and-by, when his sister conies in, and the untruth is discovered, the boy is astonished and bewildered by being called to account in a very solemn manner by his mother on account of the awful wickedness of having told a lie!

How the Child sees it.

Now I am very ready to admit that, notwithstanding the apparent resemblance between these two cases, this resemblance is only apparent and superficial; but the question is, whether it is not sufficient to cause such a child to confound them, and to be excusable, until he has been enlightened by appropriate instruction, for not clearly distinguishing the cases where words must be held strictly to conform to actual realities, from those where it is perfectly right and proper that they should only represent images or conceptions of the mind.

A father, playing with his children, says, "Now I am a bear, and am going to growl." So he growls. Then he says, "Now I am a dog, and am going to bark." He is not a bear, and he is not a dog, and the children know it. His words, therefore, even to the apprehension of the children, express an untruth, in the sense that they do not correspond with any actual reality. It is not a wrongful untruth. The children understand perfectly well that in such a case as this it is not in any sense wrong to say what is not true. But how are they to know what kind of untruths are right, and what kind are wrong, until they are taught what the distinction is and upon what it depends.

Unfortunately many parents confuse the ideas, or rather the moral sense of their children, in a much more vital manner by untruths of a different kind from this—as, for example, when a mother, in the presence of her children, expresses a feeling of vexation and annoyance at seeing a certain visitor coming to make a call, and then, when the visitor enters the room, receives her with pretended pleasure, and says, out of politeness, that she is very glad to see her. Sometimes a father will join with his children, when peculiar circumstances seem, as he thinks, to require it, in concealing something from their mother, or deceiving her in regard to it by misrepresentations or positive untruths. Sometimes even the mother will do this in reference to the father. Of course such management as this must necessarily have the effect of bringing up the children to the idea that deceiving by untruths is a justifiable resort in certain cases—a doctrine which, though entertained by many well-meaning persons, strikes a fatal blow at all confidence in the veracity of men; for whenever we know of any persons that they entertain this idea, it is never afterwards safe to trust in what they say, since we never can know that the case in hand is not, for some reason unknown to us, one of those which justify a resort to falsehood.

But to return to the case of the children that are under the training of parents who will not themselves, under any circumstances, falsify their word—that is, will never utter words that do not represent actual reality in any of the wrongful ways. Such children can not be expected to know of themselves, or to learn without instruction, what the wrongful ways are, and they never do learn until they have made many failures. Many, it is true, learn when they are very young. Many evince a remarkable tenderness of conscience in respect to this as well as to all their other duties, so fast as they are taught them. And some become so faithful and scrupulous in respect to truth, at so early an age, that their parents quite forget the progressive steps by which they advanced at the beginning. We find many a mother who will say of her boy that he never told an untruth, but we do not find any man who will say of himself, that when he was a boy he never told one.

Imaginings and Rememberings easily mistaken for each other.

But besides the complicated character of the general subject, as it presents itself to the minds of children—that is, the intricacy to them of the question when there must be a strict correspondence between the words spoken and an actual reality, and when they may rightly represent mere images or fancies of the mind—there is another great difficulty in their way, one that is very little considered and often, indeed, not at all understood by parents—and that is, that in the earliest years the distinction between realities and mere fancies of the mind is very indistinctly drawn. Even in our minds the two things are often confounded. We often have to pause and think in order to decide whether a mental perception of which we are conscious is a remembrance of a reality, or a revival of some image formed at some previous time, perhaps remote, by a vivid description which we have read or heard, or even by our own fancy. "Is that really so, or did I dream it?" How often is such a question heard. And persons have been known to certify honestly, in courts of justice, to facts which they think they personally witnessed, but which were really pictured in their minds in other ways. The picture was so distinct and vivid that they lost, in time, the power of distinguishing it from other and, perhaps, similar pictures which had been made by their witnessing the corresponding realities.

Indeed, instead of being surprised that these different origins of present mental images are sometimes confounded, it is actually wonderful that they can generally be so clearly distinguished; and we can not explain, even to ourselves, what the difference is by which we do distinguish them.

For example, we can call up to our minds the picture of a house burning and a fireman going up by a ladder to rescue some person appearing at the window. Now the image, in such a case, may have had several different modes of origin. 1. We may have actually witnessed such a scene the evening before. 2. Some one may have given us a vivid description of it. 3. We may have fancied it in writing a tale, and 4. We may have dreamed it. Here are four different prototypes of a picture which is now renewed, and there is something in the present copy which enables us, in most cases, to determine at once what the real prototype was. That is, there is something in the picture which now arises in our mind as a renewal or repetition of the picture made the day before, which makes us immediately cognizant of the cause of the original picture— that is, whether it came from a reality that we witnessed, or from a verbal or written description by another person, or whether it was a fanciful creation of our own mind while awake, or a dream. And it is extremely difficult for us to discover precisely what it is, in the present mental picture, which gives us this information in respect to the origin of its prototype. It is very easy to say, "Oh, we *remember*." But remember is only a word. We can only mean by it, in such a case as this, that there is some *latent difference* between the several images made upon our minds to-day of things seen, heard of, fancied, or dreamed yesterday, by which we distinguish each from all the others. But the most acute metaphysicians—men who are accustomed to the closest scrutiny of the movements and the mode of action of their minds—find it very difficult to discover what this difference is.

The Result in the Case of Children.

Now, in the case of young children, the faculties of perception and consciousness and the power of recognizing the distinguishing characteristics of the different perceptions and sensations of their minds are all immature, and distinctions which even to mature minds are not so clear but that they are often confounded, for them form a bewildering maze. Their minds are occupied with a mingled and blended though beautiful combination of sensations, conceptions, fancies, and remembrances, which they do not attempt to separate from each other, and their vocal organs are animated by a constant impulse to exercise themselves with any utterances which the incessant and playful gambollings of their faculties frame. In other words, the vital force liberated by the digestion of the food seeks an issue now in this way and now in that, through every variety of mental and bodily action. Of course, to arrange and systematize these actions, to establish the true relations between all these various faculties and powers, and to regulate the obligations and duties by which the exercise of them should be limited and controlled, is a work of time, and is to be effected, not by the operation of any instinct or early intuition, but by a course of development—effected mainly by the progress of growth and experience, though it is to be aided and guided by assiduous but gentle training and instruction.

If these views are correct, we can safely draw from them the following conclusions.

Practical Conclusions.

1. We must not expect from children that they will from the beginning understand and feel the obligation to speak the truth, any more than we look for a recognition, on their part, of the various other principles of duty which arise from the relations of man to man in the social state. We do not expect that two babies creeping upon the floor towards the same plaything should each feel instinctively impelled to grant the other the use of it half of the time. Children must be taught to tell the truth, just as they must be taught the principles of justice and equal rights. They generally get taught by experience—that is, by the rough treatment and hard knocks which they bring upon themselves by their violation of these principles. But the faithful parent can aid them in acquiring the necessary knowledge in a far easier and more agreeable manner by appropriate instruction.

2. The mother must not be distressed or too much troubled when she finds that her children, while very young are prone to fall into deviations from the truth, but only to be made to feel more impressed with the necessity of renewing her own efforts to teach them the duty, and to train them to the performance of it.

3. She must not be too stern or severe in punishing the deviations from truth in very young children, or in expressing the displeasure which they awaken in her mind. It is instruction, not expressions of anger or vindictive punishment, that is required in most cases. Explain to them the evils that would result if we could not believe what people say, and tell them stories of truth-loving children on the one hand, and of false and deceitful children on the other. And, above all, notice, with indications of approval and pleasure, when the child speaks the truth under circumstances which might have tempted him to deviate from it. One instance of this kind, in which you show that you observe and are pleased by his truthfulness, will do more to awaken in his heart a genuine love for the truth than ten reprovals, or even punishments, incurred by the violation of it. And in the same spirit we must make use of the religious considerations which are appropriate to this subject—that is, we must encourage the child with the approval of his heavenly Father, when he resists the temptation to deviate from the truth, instead of frightening him, when he falls, by terrible denunciations of the anger of God against liars; denunciations which, however well-deserved in the cases to which they are intended to apply, are not designed for children in whose minds the necessary discriminations, as pointed out in this chapter, are yet scarcely formed.

Danger of confounding Deceitfulness and Falsehood.

4. Do not confound the criminality of deceitfulness by acts with falsehood by words, by telling the child, when he resorts to any artifice or deception in order to gain his ends, that it is as bad to deceive as to lie. It is not as bad, by any means. There is a marked line of distinction to be drawn between falsifying one's word and all other forms of deception, for there is such a sacredness in the spoken word, that the violation of it is in general far more reprehensible than the attempt to accomplish the

same end by mere action. If a man has lost a leg, it may be perfectly right for him to wear a wooden one which is so perfectly made as to deceive people—and even to wear it, too, with the *intent* to deceive people by leading them to suppose that both his legs are genuine—while it would be wrong; for him to assert in words that this limb was not an artificial one. It is right to put a chalk egg in a hen's nest to deceive the hen, when, if the hen could understand language, and if we were to suppose hens "to have any rights that we are bound to respect," it would be wrong to *tell* her that it was a real egg. It would be right for a person, when his house was entered by a robber at night, to point an empty gun at the robber to frighten him away by leading him to think that the gun was loaded; but it would be wrong, as I think—though I am aware that many persons would think differently—for him to say in words that the gun was loaded, and that he would fire unless the robber went away. These cases show that there is a great difference between deceiving by false appearances, which is sometimes right, and doing it by false statements, which, as I think, is always wrong. There is a special and inviolable sacredness, which every lover of the truth should attach to his spoken word.

5. We must not allow the leniency with which, according to the views here presented, we are to regard the violations of truth by young persons, while their mental faculties and their powers of discrimination are yet imperfectly developed, to lead us to lower the standard of right in their minds, so as to allow them to imbibe the idea that we think that falsehood is, after all, no great sin, and still less, to suppose that we consider it sometimes, in extreme cases, allowable. We may, indeed, say, "The truth is not to be spoken at all times," but to make the aphorism complete we must add, that *falsehood* is to be spoken *never*. There is no other possible ground for absolute confidence in the word of any man except the conviction that his principle is, that it is *never, under any circumstances, or to accomplish any purpose whatever,* right for him to falsify it.

A different opinion, I am aware, prevails very extensively among mankind, and especially among the continental nations of Europe, where it seems to be very generally believed that in those cases in which falsehood will on the whole be conducive of greater good than the truth it is allowable to employ it. But it is easy to see that, so far as we know that those around us hold to this philosophy, all reasonable ground for confidence in their statements is taken away; for we never can know, in respect to any statement which they make, that the case is not one of those in which, for reasons not manifest to us, they think it is expedient —that is, conducive in some way to good—to state what is not true.

While, therefore, we must allow children a reasonable time to bring their minds to a full sense of the obligation of making their words always conform to what is true, instead of shaping them so as best to attain their purposes for the time being—which is the course to which their earliest natural instincts prompt them—and must deal gently and leniently with their incipient failures, we must do all in our power to bring them forward as fast as possible to the adoption of the very highest standard as their rule of duty in this respect; inculcating it upon them, by example as well as by precept, that we can not innocently, under any circumstances, to escape any evil, or to gain any end, falsify our word. For there is no evil so great, and no end to be attained so valuable, as to justify the adoption of a principle which destroys all foundation for confidence between man and man.

CHAPTER XVII.

JUDGMENT AND REASONING.

It is a very unreasonable thing for parents to expect young children to be reasonable. Being reasonable in one's conduct or wishes implies the taking into account of those bearings and relations of an act which are more remote and less obvious, in contradistinction from being governed exclusively by those which are immediate and near. Now, it is not reasonable to expect children to be influenced by these remote considerations, simply because in them the faculties by which they are brought forward into the mind and invested with the attributes of reality are not yet developed. These faculties are all in a nascent or formative state, and it is as idle to expect them, while thus immature, to fulfill their functions for any practical purpose, as it would be to expect a baby to expend the strength of its little arms in performing any useful labor.

Progress of Mental Development.

The mother sometimes, when she looks upon her infant lying in her arms, and observes the intentness with which he seems to gaze upon objects in the room—upon the bright light of the window or of the lamp, or upon the pictures on the wall—wonders what he is thinking of. The truth probably is that he is not thinking at all; he is simply *seeing*—that is to say, the light from external objects is entering his eyes and producing images upon his sensorium, and that is all. He *sees* only. There might have been a similar image of the light in his mind the day before, but the reproduction of the former image which constitutes memory does not probably take place at all in his case if he is very young, so that there is not present to his mind, in connection with the present image, any reproduction of the former one. Still less does he make any mental comparison between the two. The mother, as she sees the light of to-day, may remember the one of yesterday, and mentally compare the two; may have many *thoughts* awakened in her mind by the sensation and the recollection—such as, this is from a new kind of oil, and gives a brighter light than the other; that she will use this kind of oil in all her lamps, and will recommend it to her friends, and so on indefinitely. But the child has none of these thoughts and can have none; for neither have the faculties been developed within him by which they are conceived, nor has he had the experience of the previous sensations to form the materials for framing them. He is conscious of the present sensations, and that is all.

As he advances, however, in his experience of sensations, and as his mental powers gradually begin to be unfolded, what may be called *thoughts* arise, consisting at first, probably, of recollections of past sensations entering into his consciousness in connection with the present ones. These combinations, and the mental acts of various kinds which are excited by them, multiply as he advances towards maturity; but the images produced by present realities are infinitely more vivid and have a very much greater power over him than those which memory brings up from the past, or that his fancy can anticipate in the future.

This state of things, though there is, of course, a gradual advancement in the relative influence of what the mind can conceive, as compared with that which the senses make real, continues substantially the same through all the period of childhood and youth. In other words, the organs of sense and of those mental faculties which are directly occupied with the sensations, are the earliest to be developed, as we might naturally suppose would be the case; and, by consequence, the sensible properties of objects and the direct and immediate effects of any action, are those which have a controlling influence over the volitions of the mind during all the earlier periods of its development. The *reason*, on the other hand, which, as applied to the practical affairs of life, has for its function the bringing in of the more remote bearings and relations of a fact, or the indirect and less obvious results of an action, is very slowly developed. It is precisely on this account that the period of immaturity in the human species is so long protracted in comparison with that of the inferior animals. The lives of these animals are regulated by the cognizance simply of the sensible properties of objects, and by the immediate results of their acts, and they accordingly become mature as soon as their senses and their bodily organs are brought completely into action. But man, who is to be governed by his reason—that is, by much more far-reaching and comprehensive views of what concerns him—requires a much longer period to fit him for independent action, since he must wait for the development of those higher faculties which are necessary for the attainment of these extended views; and during this period he must depend upon the reason of his parents instead of being governed by his own.

Practical Effect of these Truths.

The true course, then, for parents to pursue is not to expect too much from the ability of their children to see what is right and proper for them, but to decide all important questions themselves, using their own experience and their own power of foresight as their guide. They are, indeed, to cultivate and train the reasoning and reflective powers of their children, but are not to expect them in early life to be sufficiently developed and strengthened to bear any heavy strain, or to justify the placing of any serious reliance upon them. They must, in a word, treat the reason and the judgment of their children as the farmer treats the strength of his colt, which he exercises and, to a certain extent, employs, but never puts upon it any serious burden.

It results from this view of the case that it is not wise for a parent to resort to arguing or reasoning with a child, as a substitute for authority, or even as an aid to make up for a deficiency of authority, in regard to what it is necessary that the child should do. No doubt it is a good plan sometimes to let the child decide for himself, but when you pretend to allow him to decide let him do it really. When you go out with him to take a walk, if it is so nearly immaterial which way you go that you are willing that he should determine the question, then lay the case before him, giving him the advantages and disadvantages of the different ways, and let him decide; and then act according to his decision. But if you have determined in your own mind which way to go, simply announce your determination; and if you give reasons at all, do not give them in such a way as to convey the idea to his mind that his obligation to submit is to rest partly on his seeing the force of them. For every parent will find that this principle is a sound one and one of fundamental importance in the successful management of children—namely, that it is much easier for a child to do what he does not like to do as an act of simple submission to superior authority, than for him to bring himself to an accordance with the decision by hearing and considering the reasons. In other words, it is much easier for him to obey your decision than to bring himself to the same decision against his own will.

In serious Cases no Reliance to be placed on the Reason of the Child.

In all those cases, therefore, in which the parent can not safely allow the children really to decide, such as the question of going to school, going to church, taking medicine, remaining indoors on account of indisposition or of the weather, making visits, choice of playmates and companions, and a great many others which it would not be safe actually to allow them to decide, it is true kindness to them to spare their minds the painful perplexity of a conflict. Decide for them. Do not say, "Oh, I would not do this or that"—whatever it may be—"because"—and then go on to assign reasons thought of perhaps at the moment to meet the emergency, and indeed generally false; but, "Yes, I don't wonder that you would like to do it. I should like it if I were you. But it can not be done." When there is medicine to be taken, do not put the child in misery for half an hour while you resort to all sorts of arguments, and perhaps artifices, to bring him to a willingness to take it; but simply present it to him, saying, "It is something very disagreeable, I know, but it must be taken;" and if it is refused, allow of no delay, but at once, though without any appearance of displeasure, and in the gentlest-manner possible, force it down. Then, after the excitement of the affair has passed away, and you have your little patient in your lap, and he is in good-humor—this is all, of course, on the supposition that he is not very sick—say to him, "You would not take your medicine a little while ago, and we had to force it down: I hope it did not hurt you much."

The child will probably make some fretful answer.

"It is not surprising that you did not like to take it. All children, while they are too young to be reasonable, and all animals, such as horses and cows, when they are sick, are very unwilling to take their medicine, and we often have to force it down. You will, perhaps, refuse to take yours a good many times yet before you are old enough to see that it is a great deal easier to take it willingly than it is to have it forced down."

And then go on and tell him some amusing story of the difficulty some people had in forcing medicine down the throat of a sick horse, who did not know enough to take it like a man.

The idea is—for this case is only meant as an illustration of a general principle—that the comfort and enjoyment of children, as well as the easy and successful working of parental government, is greatly promoted by deciding for the children at once, and placing their action on the simple ground of obedience to authority in all those cases where the *decision can not really and honestly be* left to the children themselves.

To listen reluctantly to the persistent arguments of children in favor of their being allowed to do what we are sure that we shall decide in the end that it is not best for them to do, and to meet them with counter arguments which, if they are not actually false, as they are very apt to be in such a case, are utterly powerless, from the incapacity of the children to appreciate them, on account of their being blinded by their wishes, is not to strengthen the reasoning powers, but to confuse and bewilder them, and impede their development.

Mode of Dealing with the Reason of a Child.

The effect, however, will be excellent of calling into exercise the reason and the judgment of the child in cases where the conclusion which he arrives at can be safely allowed to determine his action. You can help him in such cases by giving him any information that he desires, but do not embarrass him, and interfere with his exercising his own judgment by obtruding advice. Allow him in this way to lay out his own garden, to plan the course of a walk or a ride, and to decide upon the expenditure of his own pocket-money, within certain restrictions in respect to such things as would be dangerous or hurtful to himself, or annoying to others. As he grows older you can give him the charge of the minor arrangements on a journey, such as taking care of a certain number of the parcels carried in the hand, choosing a seat in the car, selecting and engaging a hand on arriving at the place of destination. Commit such things to his charge only so fast as you can really intrust him with power to act, and then, with slight and not obtrusive supervision on your part, leave the responsibility with him, noticing encouragingly whatever of fidelity and success you observe, and taking little notice—generally in fact, none at all—of such errors and failures as result simply from inexperience and immaturity.

In a word, make no attempt to seek support from his judgment, or by convincing his reason, in important cases, where his feelings or wishes are involved, but in all such cases rest your decisions solely upon your own authority. But then, on the other hand, in unimportant cases, where no serious evil can result whichever of the various possible courses are taken, call his judgment into exercise, and abide by its decisions. Give him the responsibility if he likes to take it, but with the responsibility give him the power.

Substantially the same principles as explained above, in their application to the exercise of the judgment, apply to the cultivation of the reasoning powers—that is to say, in the act of arguing, or drawing conclusions from premises. Nothing can be more unprofitable and useless, to say nothing of its irritating and vexatious effect, than maintaining an argument with a child—or with any body else, in fact—to convince him against his will. Arguing very soon degenerates, in such a case, into an irritating and utterly useless dispute. The difference of opinion which gives occasion for such discussions arises generally from the fact that the child sees only certain of the more obvious and immediate relations and bearings of the subject in question, which is, in fact, all that can be reasonably expected of him, and forms his opinion from these alone. The parent, on the other hand, takes a wider view, and includes among the premises on which his conclusion is founded considerations which have never been brought to the attention of the child. The proper course, therefore, for him to pursue in order to bring the child's mind into harmony with his own, is not to ridicule the boy's reasoning, or chide him for taking so short-sighted a view of the subject, or to tell him it is very foolish for him to talk as he does, or silence him by a dogmatic decision, delivered in a dictatorial and overbearing manner, all of which is too often found to characterize the discussions between parents and children, but calmly and quietly to present to him the considerations bearing upon the question which he has not yet seen. To this end, and to bring the mind of the child into that listening and willing state without which all arguments and even all attempts at instruction are wasted, we must listen candidly to what he says himself, put the best construction upon it, give it its full force; see it, in a word, as nearly as possible as *he* sees it, and let him know that we do so. Then he will be much more ready to receive any additional considerations which we may present to his mind, as things that must also be taken into account in forming a final judgment on the question.

A boy, for example, who is full of health and increasing vigor, and in whom, of course, those organs on which the consciousness of strength and the impulses of courage depend are in the course of rapid and healthy development, in reading to his mother a story in which a thief that came into a back store-room of a house in the evening, with a bag, to steal meal, was detected by the owner and frightened away, looks up from his book and says, in a very valiant manner,

"If I had been there, and had a gun, I would have shot him on the spot."

The Rough Mode of Treatment.

Now, if the mother wishes to confuse and bewilder, and to crush down, so to speak, the reasoning faculties of her child, she may say,

"Nonsense, George! It is of no use for you to talk big in that way. You would not dare to fire a gun in such a case, still less, to shoot a man. The first thing you would do would be to run away and hide. And then, besides, it would be very wicked for you to kill a man in that way. You would be very likely to get yourself hung for murder. Besides, the Bible says that we must not resist evil; so you should not talk so coolly about shooting a man."

The poor boy would be overpowered by such a rebuke as this, and perhaps silenced. The incipient and half-formed ideas in his mind in respect to the right of self-defense, the virtue of courage, the sanctity of life, the nature and the limits of the doctrine of non-resistance, would be all thrown together into a jumble of hopeless confusion in his mind, and the only result would be his muttering to himself, after a moment of bewilderment and vexation, "I *would* shoot him, anyhow." Such treatment would not only fail to convince him that his idea was wrong, but would effectually close his heart against any such conviction.

The Gentle Mode of Treatment.

But let the mother first see and recognize those bearings and relations of the question which the boy sees—that is, those which are the most direct and immediate—and allow them their full force, and she establishes a sympathy between his mind and hers, and prepares the way for his being led by her to taking into the account other considerations which, though of greater importance, are not so obvious, and which it would be wholly unreasonable to expect that the boy would see himself, since they do not come within the range of observation that could be reached spontaneously by the unaided faculties of such a child. Suppose the mother says, in reply to her boy's boastful declaration that he would shoot the robber,

"There would be a certain degree of justice in that, no doubt."

"Yes," rejoins the boy, "it would be no more than he deserved."

"When a man engages in the commission of a crime," adds the mother, "he runs the risk of all the perils that he exposes himself to, from the efforts of people to defend their property, and perhaps their lives; so that, perhaps, *he* would have no right to complain if people did shoot at him."

"Not a bit of right," says the boy.

"But then there are some other things to be considered," says the mother, "which, though they do not show that it would be unjust towards him, might make it bad for *us* to shoot him."

"What things?" asks the boy.

The mother having candidly admitted whatever there was of truth in the boy's view of the subject, and thus placed herself, as it were, side by side with him, he is prepared to see and admit what she is going to point out to his observation—not as something directly antagonistic to what he has said, but as something additional, something which is *also* to be taken into the account.

"In the first place," continues the mother, "there would be the body to be disposed of, if you were to shoot him. How should we manage about that?"

It would make a great difference in such a case in respect to the danger of putting the boy's mind into a state of antagonism against his mother's presentation of the case, whether she says, "How shall *we* manage about that?" or, "How will *you* manage about that?"

"Oh," replies the boy, "we would send to where he lives, and let his people come and take him away; or, if he was in a city, we would call in the police."

"That would be a good plan," says his mother. "We would call in the police, if there were any police at hand. But then there would be the blood all over the carpet and the floor."

"There would not be any carpet on the floor in a store-room," says the boy.

"True," replies the mother; "you are right there; so that there would not be, after all, any great trouble about the blood. But the man might not be killed outright, and it might be some time before the policemen would come, and we should see him all that time writhing and struggling in dreadful convulsions, which would fix horrid impressions upon our minds, that would haunt us for a long time afterwards."

The mother could then go on to explain that, if the man had a wife and children, any one who had killed the husband and father would pity them as long as he lived, and could never see them or hear them spoken of without feeling pain, and even some degree of self-reproach; although, so far as the man himself was concerned, it might be that no injustice had been done. After the excitement was over, too, he would begin to make excuses for the man, thinking that perhaps he was poor, and his children were suffering for bread, and it was on their account that he was tempted to steal, and this, though it would not justify, might in some degree palliate the act for which he was slain; or that he had been badly brought up, having never received any proper instruction, but had been trained and taught from his boyhood to pilfer and steal.

These and many analogous considerations might be presented to the child, going to show that, whatever the rule of strict justice in respect to the criminal may enjoin, it is not right to take the life of a wrong-doer merely to prevent the commission of a minor offense. The law of the land recognizes this principle, and does not justify the taking of life except in extreme cases, such as those of imminent personal danger.

A friendly conversation of this kind, carried on, not in a spirit of antagonism to what the boy has said, but in the form of presenting information novel to him in respect to considerations which were to be taken into the account in addition to those which he had himself perceived, will have a great effect not only in modifying his opinion in this case, but also in impressing him with the general idea that, before adopting a decisive opinion on any subject, we must take care to acquaint ourselves not merely with the most direct and obvious relations of it, but must look farther into its bearings and results, so that our conclusion may have a solid foundation by reposing upon as many as possible of the considerations which ought really to affect it. Thus, by avoiding all appearance of antagonism, we secure a ready reception for the truths we offer, and cultivate the reasoning powers at the same time.

General Principles.

The principles, then, which are meant to be illustrated and enforced in this chapter are these:

1. That the mental faculties of children on which the exercise of judgment and of the power of reasoning depend are not among those which are the earliest developed, and they do not attain, in the first years of life, to such a degree of strength or maturity as to justify placing any serious reliance upon them for the conduct of life.

2. Parents should, accordingly, not put them to any serious test, or impose any heavy burden upon them; but should rely solely on their own authority, as the expression of their own judgment, and not upon their ability to convince the judgment of the child, in important cases, or in those where its inclinations or its feelings are concerned.

3. But they may greatly promote the healthy development of these faculties on the part of their children, by bringing to their view the less obvious bearings and relations of various acts and occurrences on which judgment is to be passed, in cases where their feelings and inclinations are not specially concerned—doing this either in the form of explaining their own parental principles of management, or practically, by intrusting them with responsibility, and giving them a degree of actual power

commensurate with it, in cases where it is safe to do so; and,

4. They may enlarge the range of the children's ideas, and accustom them to take wider views of the various subjects which occupy their attention, by discussing with them the principles involved in the several cases; but such discussions must be conducted in a calm, gentle, and considerate manner, the parent looking always upon what the child says in the most favorable light, putting the best construction upon it, and admitting its force, and then presenting such additional views as ought also to be taken into account, with moderate earnestness, and in an unobtrusive manner, thus taking short and easy steps himself in order to accommodate his own rate of progress to the still imperfectly developed capabilities of the child.

In a word, it is with the unfolding of the mental faculties of the young as it is with the development of their muscles and the improvement of their bodily powers; and just as the way to teach a child to walk is not to drag him along hurriedly and forcibly by the arm faster than he can himself form the necessary steps, but to go slowly, accommodating your movements to those which are natural to him, and encouraging him by letting him perceive that his own efforts produce appreciable and useful results—so, in cultivating any of their thinking and reasoning powers, we must not put at the outset too heavy a burden upon them, but must call them gently into action, within the limits prescribed by the degree of maturity to which they have attained, standing a little aside, as it were, in doing so, and encouraging them to do the work themselves, instead of taking it out of their hands and doing it for them.

CHAPTER XVIII.

WISHES AND REQUESTS.

In respect to the course to be pursued in relation to the requests and wishes of children, the following general rules result from the principles inculcated in the chapter on Judgment and Reasoning, or, at least, are in perfect accordance with them—namely:

Absolute Authority in Cases of vital Importance.

1. In respect to all those questions in the decision of which their permanent and essential welfare are involved, such as those relating to their health, the company they keep, the formation of their characters, the progress of their education, and the like, the parent should establish and maintain in the minds of the children from their earliest years, a distinct understanding that the decision of all such questions is reserved for his own or her own exclusive jurisdiction. While on any of the details connected with these questions the feelings and wishes of the child ought to be ascertained, and, so far as possible, taken into the account, the course to be pursued should not, in general, be discussed with the child, nor should their objections be replied to in any form. The parent should simply take such objections as the judge takes the papers in a case which has been tried before him, and reserve his decision. The principles by which the parent is governed in the course which he pursues, and the reasons for them, may be made the subject of very free conversation, and may be fully explained, provided that care is taken that this is never done when any practical question is pending, such as would give the explanations of the parent the aspect of persuasions, employed to supply the deficiency of authority too weak to enforce obedience to a command. It is an excellent thing to have children see and appreciate the reasonableness of their parents' commands, provided that this reasonableness is shown to them in such a way that they are not led to imagine that their being able to see it is in any sense a condition precedent of obedience.

Great Indulgence in Cases not of vital Importance.

2. The authority of the parent being thus fully established in regard to all those things which, being of paramount importance in respect to the child's present and future welfare, ought to be regulated by the comparative far-seeing wisdom of the parent, with little regard to the evanescent fancies of the child, it is on every account best, in respect to all other things, to allow to the children the largest possible indulgence. The largest indulgence for them in their occupations, their plays, and even in their caprices and the freaks of their fancy, means *freedom of action* for their unfolding powers of body and mind; and freedom of action for these powers means the most rapid and healthy development

of them.

The rule is, in a word, that, after all that is essential for their health, the formation of their characters, and their progress in study is secured, by being brought under the dominion of absolute parental authority, in respect to what remains the children are to be indulged and allowed to have their own way as much as possible. When, in their plays, they come to you for permission to do a particular thing, do not consider whether or not it seems to you that you would like to do it yourself, but only whether there is any *real and substantial objection to their doing it.*

The Hearing to come before the Decision, not after it.

The courts of justice adopt what seems to be a very sensible and a very excellent mode of proceeding, though it is exactly the contrary to the one which many parents pursue, and that is, they hear the case *first*, and decide afterwards. A great many parents seem to prefer to decide first, and then hear—that is to say, when the children come to them with any request or proposal, they answer at once with a refusal more or less decided, and then allow themselves to be led into a long discussion on the subject, if discussion that may be called which consists chiefly of simple persistence and importunity on one side, and a gradually relaxing resistance on the other, until a reluctant consent is finally obtained.

Now, just as it is an excellent way to develop and strengthen the muscles of a child's arms, for his father to hold the two ends of his cane in his hands while the child grasps it by the middle, and then for them to pull against each other, about the yard, until, finally, the child is allowed to get the cane away; so the way to cherish and confirm the habit of "teasing" in children is to maintain a discussion with them for a time in respect to some request which is at first denied, and then finally, after a protracted and gradually weakening resistance, to allow them to gain the victory and carry their point. On the other hand, an absolutely certain way of preventing any such habit from being formed, and of effectually breaking it up when it is formed, is the simple process of hearing first, and deciding afterwards.

When, therefore, children come with any request, or express any wish, in cases where no serious interests are involved, in deciding upon the answer to be given, the mother should, in general, simply ask herself, not Is it wise? Will they succeed in it? Will they enjoy it? Would I like to do it if I were they?—but simply, Is there any harm or danger in it? If not, readily and cordially consent. But do not announce your decision till *after* you have heard all that they have to say, if you intend to hear what they have to say at all.

If there are any objections to what the children propose which affect the question in relation to it as a means of *amusement for them*, you may state them in the way of information for them, *after* you have given your consent. In that way you present the difficulties as subjects for their consideration, and not as objections on your part to their plan. But, however serious the difficulties may be in the way of the children's accomplishing the object which they have in view, they constitute no objection to their making the attempt, provided that their plans involve no serious harm or damage to themselves, or to any other person or interest.

The Wrong Way.

Two boys, for example, William and James, who have been playing in the yard with their little sister Lucy, come in to their mother with a plan for a fish-pond. They wish for permission to dig a hole in a corner of the yard and fill it with water, and then to get some fish out of the brook to put into it.

The mother, on hearing the proposal, says at once, without waiting for any explanations,

"Oh no, I would not do that. It is a very foolish plan. You will only get yourselves all muddy. Besides, you can't catch any fishes to put into it, and if you do, they won't live. And then the grass is so thick that you could not get it up to make your hole."

But William says that they can dig the grass up with their little spades. They had tried it, and found that they could do so.

And James says that they have already tried catching the fishes, and found that they could do it by means of a long-handled dipper; and Lucy says that they will all be very careful not to get themselves wet and muddy.

"But you'll get your feet wet standing on the edge of the brook," says the mother. "You can't help it."

"No, mother," replies James, "there is a large flat stone that we can stand upon, and so keep our feet perfectly dry. See!"

So saying, he shows his own feet, which are quite dry.

Thus the discussion goes on; the objections made—being, as usual in such cases, half of them imaginary ones, brought forward only for effect—are one after another disposed of, or at least set aside, until at length the mother, as if beaten off her ground after a contest, gives a reluctant and hesitating consent, and the children go away to commence their work only half pleased, and separated in heart and affection, for the time being, from their mother by not finding in her, as they think, any sympathy with them, or disposition to aid them in their pleasures.

They have, however, by their mother's management of the case, received an excellent lesson in arguing and teasing. They have found by it, what they have undoubtedly often found on similar occasions before, that their mother's first decision is not at all to be taken as a final one; that they have only to persevere in replying to her objections and answering her arguments, and especially in persisting in their importunity, and they will be pretty sure to gain their end at last.

This mode of management, also, has the effect of fixing the position of their mother in their minds as one of antagonism to them in respect to their childish pleasures.

The Right Way.

If in such a case as this the mother wishes to avoid these evils, the way is plain. She must first consider the proposal herself, and come to her own decision in regard to it. Before coming to a decision, she may, if she has leisure and opportunity, make additional inquiries in respect to the details of the plan; or, if she is otherwise occupied, she may consider them for a moment in her own mind. If the objections are decisive, she should not state them at the time, unless she specially wishes them not to have a fair hearing; for when children have a plan in mind which they are eager to carry out, their very eagerness entirely incapacitates them for properly appreciating any objections which may be offered to it. It is on every account better, therefore—as a general rule—not to offer any such objections at the time, but simply to give your decision.

On the other hand, if there is no serious evil to be apprehended in allowing children to attempt to carry any particular plan they form into effect, the foolishness of it, in a practical point of view, or even the impossibility of success in accomplishing the object proposed, constitute no valid objection to it; for children amuse themselves as much, and sometimes learn as much, and promote as effectually the development of their powers and faculties, by their failures as by their successes.

In the case supposed, then, the mother, in order to manage it right, would first consider for a moment whether there was any decisive objection to the plan. This would depend, perhaps, upon the manner in which the children were dressed at the time, or upon the amount of injury that would be done to the yard; and this question would in its turn depend, in many cases, on the comparative value set by the mother upon the beauty of her yard, and the health, development, and happiness of her children. But supposing that she sees—which she can do in most instances at a glance—that there can no serious harm be done by the experiment, but only that it is a foolish plan so far as the attainment of the object is concerned, and utterly hopeless of success, which, considering that the real end to be attained is the healthy development of the children's powers by the agreeable exercise of them in useless as well as in useful labors, is no objection at all, then she should answer at once, "Yes, you can do that if you like; and perhaps I can help you about planning the work."

After saying this, any pointing out of obstacles and difficulties on her part does not present itself to their minds in the light of opposition to their plan, but of aid in helping it forward, and so places her, in their view, *on their side*, instead of in antagonism to them.

"What do you propose to do with the earth that you take out of the hole?" she asks.

The children had, perhaps, not thought of that.

"How would it do," continues the mother, "to put it in your wheelbarrow and let it stay there, so that in case your plan should not succeed—and men, in any thing that they undertake, always consider it wise to take into account the possibility that they may not succeed—you can easily bring it all back and fill up the hole again."

The children think that would be a very good plan.

"And how are you going to fill your hole with water when you get it dug out?" asks the mother.

They were going to carry the water from the pump in a pail.

"And how are you going to prevent spilling the water over upon your trousers and into your shoes while carrying it?"

"Oh, we will be very careful," replied William.

"How would it do only to fill the pail half full each time," suggests the mother. "You would have to go more times, it is true, but that would be better than getting splashed with water."

The boys think that that would be a very good plan.

In this manner the various difficulties to be anticipated may be brought to the notice of the children, while, they and their mother being in harmony and sympathy with each other—and not in opposition—in the consideration of them, she can bring them forward without any difficulty, and make them the means of teaching the children many useful lessons of prudence and precaution.

Capriciousness in Play.

The mother, then, after warning the children that they must expect to encounter many unexpected difficulties in their undertaking, and telling them that they must not be too much disappointed if they should find that they could not succeed, dismisses them to their work. They proceed to dig the hole, putting the materials in the wheelbarrow, and then fill up the hole with water brought in half pailfuls at a time from the pump; but are somewhat disappointed to find that the water soaks away pretty rapidly into the ground, and that, moreover, it is so turbid, and the surface is so covered with little leaves, sticks, and dust, as to make it appear very doubtful whether they would be able to see the fishes if they were to succeed in catching any to put in. However, they take their long-handled dipper and proceed towards the brook. On the way they stop to gather some flowers that grow near the path that leads through the field, when the idea suddenly enters Lucy's head that it would be better to make a garden than a fish-pond; flowers, as she says, being so much prettier than fishes. So they all go back to their mother and explain the change of their plan. They ask for leave to dig up a place which they had found where the ground was loose and sandy, and easy to dig, and to set out flowers in it which they had found in the field already in bloom. "We are going to give up the fish-pond," they say in conclusion, "because flowers are so much prettier than fishes."

The mother, instead of finding fault with them for being so capricious and changeable in their plans, says, "I think you are right. Fishes look pretty enough when they are swimming in the brook, but flowers are much prettier to transport and take care of. But first go and fill up the hole you made for the pond with the earth that is in the wheelbarrow; and when you have made your garden and moved the flowers into it, I advise you to get the watering-pot and give them a good watering."

It may be said that children ought to be brought up in habits of steadiness and perseverance in what they undertake, and that this kind of indulgence in their capriciousness would have a very bad tendency in this respect. The answer is, that there are times and seasons for all the different kinds of lessons which children have to learn, and that when in their hours of recreation they are amusing themselves in play, lessons in perseverance and system are out of place. The object to be sought for *then* is the exercise and growth of their bodily organs and members, the development of their fancy and imagination, and their powers of observation of nature. The work of training them to habits of system and of steady perseverance in serious pursuits, which, though it is a work that ought by no means to be neglected, is not the appropriate work of such a time.

Summary of Results.

The general rules for the government of the parent in his treatment of his children's requests and wishes are these: In all matters of essential importance he is to decide himself and simply announce his decision, without giving any reasons *for the purpose of justifying it*, or for *inducing submission to it*.

And in all matters not of essential importance he is to allow the children the greatest possible freedom of action.

And the rule for children is that they are always to obey the command the first time it is given, without question, and to take the first answer to any request without any objection or demurring whatever.

It is very easy to see how smoothly and happily the affairs of domestic government would go on if these rules were established and obeyed. All that is required on the part of parents for their complete establishment is, first, a clear comprehension of them, and then a calm, quiet, and gentle, but still inflexible firmness in maintaining them. Unfortunately, however, such qualities as these, simple as they seem, are the most rare. If, instead of gentle but firm consistency and steadiness of action, ardent, impulsive, and capricious energy and violence were required, it would be comparatively easy to find them. How seldom do we see a mother's management of her children regulated by a calm, quiet, gentle, and considerate decision that thinks before it speaks in all important matters, and when it speaks, is firm; and yet, which readily and gladly accords to the children every liberty and indulgence which can do themselves or others no harm. And on the other hand, how often do we see foolish laxity and indulgence in yielding to importunity in cases of vital importance, alternating with vexatious thwartings, rebuffs, and refusals in respect to desires and wishes the gratification of which could do no injury at all.

CHAPTER XIX.

CHILDREN'S QUESTIONS.

The disposition to ask questions, which is so universal and so strong a characteristic of childhood, is the open door which presents to the mother the readiest and most easy access possible to the mind and heart of her child. The opportunities and facilities thus afforded to her would be the source of the greatest pleasure to herself, and of the greatest benefit to her child, if she understood better how to avail herself of them. I propose, in this chapter, to give some explanations and general directions for the guidance of mothers, of older brothers and sisters, and of teachers—of all persons, in fact, who may, from time to time, have young children under their care or in their society. I have no doubt that some of my rules will strike parents, at first view, as paradoxical and, perhaps, almost absurd; but I hope that on more mature reflection they will be found to be reasonable and just.

The Curiosity of Children not a Fault.

1. The curiosity of children is not a fault, and therefore we must never censure them for asking questions, or lead them to think that we consider the disposition to do so a fault on their part; but, on the other hand, this disposition is to be encouraged as much as possible.

We must remember that a child, when his powers of observation begin to be developed, finds every thing around him full of mystery and wonder. Why some things are hard and some are soft—why some things will roll and some will not—why he is not hurt when he falls on the sofa, and is hurt when he falls on the floor—why a chair will tumble over when he climbs up by the rounds of it, while yet the steps of the stairs remain firm and can be ascended without danger—why one thing is black, and another red, and another green—why water will all go away of itself from his hands or his dress, while mud will not—why he can dig in the ground, but can not dig in a floor—all is a mystery, and the little adventurer is in a continual state of curiosity and wonder, not only to learn the meaning of all these things, but also of desire to extend his observations, and find out more and more of the astonishing phenomena that are exhibited around him. The good feeling of the mother, or of any intelligent friend who is willing to aid him in his efforts, is, of course, invaluable to him as a means of promoting his advancement in knowledge and of developing his powers.

Remember, therefore, that the disposition of a child to ask questions is not a fault, but only an indication of his increasing mental activity, and of his desire to avail himself of the only means within his reach of advancing his knowledge and of enlarging the scope of his intelligence in respect to the strange and wonderful phenomena constantly observable around him.

Sometimes, perhaps, a Source of Inconvenience.

Of course there will be times when it is inconvenient for the parent to attend to the questions of the child, and when he must, consequently, be debarred of the pleasure and privilege of asking them; but even at such times as these the disposition to ask them must not be attributed to him as a fault. Never tell him that he is "a little tease"—that "you are tired to death of answering his questions"—that he is "a chatter-box that would weary the patience of Job;" or that, if he will "sit still for half an hour, without speaking a word, you will give him a reward." If you are going to be engaged, and so can not attend to him, say to him that you *wish* you could talk with him, and answer the questions, but that you are going to be busy and can not do it; and then, after providing him with some other means of occupation, require him to be silent: though even then you ought to relieve the tedium of silence for him by stopping every ten or fifteen minutes from your reading, or your letter-writing, or the planning of your work, or whatever your employment may be, and giving your attention to him for a minute or two, and affording him an opportunity to relieve the pressure on his mind by a little conversation.

Answers to be short and simple.

2. Give generally to children's questions the shortest and simplest answers possible.

One reason why parents find the questions of children so fatiguing to them, is that *they attempt too much* in their answers. If they would give the right kind of answers, they would find the work of replying very easy, and in most of their avocations it would occasion them very little interruption. These short and simple answers are all that a child requires. A full and detailed explanation of any thing they ask about is as tiresome for them to listen to as it is for the mother to frame and give; while a short and simple reply which advances them one step in their knowledge of the subject is perfectly easy for the mother to give, and is, at the same time, all that they wish to receive.

For example, let us suppose that the father and mother are taking a ride on a summer afternoon after a shower, with little Johnny sitting upon the seat between them in the chaise. The parents are engaged in conversation with each other, we will suppose, and would not like to be interrupted. Johnny presently spies a rainbow on a cloud in the east, and, after uttering an exclamation of delight, asks his mother what made the rainbow. She hears the question, and her mind, glancing for a moment at the difficulty of giving an intelligible explanation of so grand a phenomenon to such a child, experiences an obscure sensation of perplexity and annoyance, but not quite enough to take off her attention from her conversation; so she goes on and takes no notice of Johnny's inquiry. Johnny, accordingly, soon repeats it, "Mother! mother! what makes the rainbow?"

At length her attention is forced to the subject, and she either tells Johnny that she can't explain it to him—that he is not old enough to understand it; or, perhaps, scolds him for interrupting her with so many teasing questions.

In another such case, the mother, on hearing the question, pauses long enough to look kindly and with a smile of encouragement upon her face towards Johnny, and to say simply, "The sun," and then goes on with her conversation. Johnny says "Oh!" in a tone of satisfaction. It is a new and grand idea to him that the sun makes the rainbow, and it is enough to fill his mind with contemplation for several minutes, during which his parents go on without interruption in their talk. Presently Johnny asks again,

"Mother, *how* does the sun make the rainbow?"

His mother answers in the same way as before, "By shining on the cloud:" and, leaving that additional idea for Johnny to reflect upon and receive fully into his mind, turns again to her husband and resumes her conversation with him after a scarcely perceptible interruption.

Johnny, after having reflected in silence some minutes, during which he has looked at the sun and at the rainbow, and observed that the cloud on which the arch is formed is exactly opposite to the sun, and fully exposed to his beams, is prepared for another step, and asks,

"Mother, how does the sun make a rainbow by shining on the cloud?"

His mother replies that it shines on millions of little drops of rain in the cloud, and makes them of all colors, like drops of dew on the ground, and all the colors together make the rainbow.

Here are images presented to Johnny's mind enough to occupy his thoughts for a considerable interval, when perhaps he will have another question still, to be answered by an equally short and simple reply; though, probably, by this time his curiosity will have become satisfied in respect to his subject of inquiry, and his attention will have been arrested by some other object.

To answer the child's questions in this way is so easy, and the pauses which the answers lead to on the part of the questioner are usually so long, that very little serious interruption is occasioned by them to any of the ordinary pursuits in which a mother is engaged; and the little interruption which is caused is greatly overbalanced by the pleasure which the mother will experience in witnessing the gratification and improvement of the child, if she really loves him, and is seriously interested in the development of his thinking and reasoning powers.

Answers should attempt to communicate but little Instruction.

3. The answers which are given to children should not only be short and simple in form, but each one should be studiously designed to communicate as small an amount of information as possible.

This may seem, at first view, a strange idea, but the import of it simply is that, in giving the child his intellectual nourishment, you must act as you do in respect to his bodily food—that is, divide what he is to receive into small portions, and administer a little at a time. If you give him too much at once in either case, you are in danger of choking him.

For example, Johnny asks some morning in the early winter, when the first snow is falling, and he has been watching it for some time from the window in wonder and delight, "Mother, what makes it snow?" Now, if the mother imagines that she must give any thing like a full answer to the question, her attention must be distracted from her work to enable her to frame it; and if she does not give up the attempt altogether, and rebuke the boy for teasing her with "so many silly questions," she perhaps suspends her work, and, after a moment's perplexing thought, she says the vapor of the water from the rivers and seas and damp ground rises into the air, and there at last congeals into flakes of snow, and these fall through the air to the ground.

The boy listens and attempts to understand the explanation, but he is bewildered and lost in the endeavor to take in at once this extended and complicated process—one which is, moreover, not only extended and complicated, but which is composed of elements all of which are entirely new to him.

If the mother, however, should act on the principle of communicating as small a portion of the information required as it is possible to give in one answer, Johnny's inquiry would lead, probably, to a conversation somewhat like the following, the answers on the part of the mother being so short and simple as to require no perceptible thought on her part, and so occasioning no serious interruption to her work, unless it should be something requiring special attention.

"Mother," asks Johnny, "what makes it snow?"

"It is the snow-flakes coming down out of the sky," says his mother. "Watch them!"

"Oh!" says Johnny, uttering the child's little exclamation of satisfaction. He looks at the flakes as they fall, catching one after another with his eye, and following it in its meandering descent. He will, perhaps, occupy himself several minutes in silence and profound attention, in bringing fully to his mind the idea that a snow-storm consists of a mass of descending flakes of snow falling through the air. To us, who are familiar with this fact, it seems nothing to observe this, but to him the analyzing of the phenomenon, which before he had looked upon as one grand spectacle filling the whole sky, and only making an impression on his mind by its general effect, and resolving it into its elemental parts of individual flakes fluttering down through the air, is a great step. It is a step which exercises his nascent powers of observation and reflection very deeply, and gives him full occupation for quite a little interval of time. At length, when he has familiarized himself with this idea, he asks again, perhaps,

"Where do the flakes come from, mother?"

"Out of the sky."

"Oh!" says Johnny again, for the moment entirely satisfied.

One might at first think that these words would be almost unmeaning, or, at least, that they would give the little questioner no real information. But they do give him information that is both important and novel. They advance him one step in his inquiry. Out of the sky means, to him, from a great height. The words give him to understand that the flakes are not formed where they first come into his view, but that they descend from a higher region. After reflecting on this idea a moment, he asks, we will suppose,

"How high in the sky, mother?"

Now, perhaps, a mother might think that there was no possible answer to be given to such a question as this except that "she does not know;" inasmuch as few persons have any accurate ideas of the elevation in the atmosphere at which snow-clouds usually form. But this accurate information is not what the child requires. If the mother possessed it, it would be useless for her to attempt to communicate it to him. In the sense in which he asks the question she *does* understand it, and can give him a perfectly satisfactory answer.

"How high is it in the sky, mother, to where the snow comes from?" asks the child.

"Oh, *very* high—higher than the top of the house," replies the mother.

"As high as the top of the chimney?"

"Yes, higher than that."

"As high as the moon?"

"No, not so high as the moon."

"How high is it then, mother?"

"About as high as birds can fly."

"Oh!" says Johnny, perfectly satisfied.

The answer is somewhat indefinite, it is true, but its indefiniteness is the chief element in the value of it. A definite and precise answer, even if one of that character were ready at hand, would be utterly inappropriate to the occasion.

An Answer may even be good which gives no Information at all.

4. It is not even always necessary that an answer to a child's question should convey *any information at all*. A little conversation on the subject of the inquiry, giving the child an opportunity *to hear and to use language* in respect to it, is often all that is required.

It must be remembered that the power to express thoughts, or to represent external objects by language, is a new power to young children, and, like all other new powers, the mere exercise of it gives great pleasure. If a person in full health and vigor were suddenly to acquire the art of flying, he would take great pleasure in moving, by means of his wings, through the air from one high point to another, not because he had any object in visiting those high points, but because it would give him pleasure to find that he could do so, and to exercise his newly acquired power. So with children in their talk. They talk often, perhaps generally, for the sake of the *pleasure of talking*, not for the sake of what they have to say. So, if you will only talk with them and allow them to talk to you about any thing that interests them, they are pleased, whether you communicate to them any new information or not. This single thought, once fully understood by a mother, will save her a great deal of trouble in answering the incessant questions of her children. The only essential thing in many cases is to *say something* in reply to the question, no matter whether what you say communicates any information or not.

If a child asks, for instance, what makes the stars shine so, and his mother answers, "Because they are so bright," he will be very likely to be as well satisfied as if she attempted to give a philosophical explanation of the phenomenon. So, if he asks what makes him see himself in the looking-glass, she may answer, "You see an *image* of yourself there. They call it an image. Hold up a book and see if you can see an image of that in the glass too." He is pleased and satisfied. Nor are such answers useless, as might at first be supposed. They give the child practice in the use of language, and, if properly managed, they may be made the means of greatly extending his knowledge of language and, by necessary consequence, of the ideas and realities which language represents.

"Father," says Mary, as she is walking with her father in the garden, "what makes some roses white and some red?" "It is very curious, is it not?" says her father. "Yes, father, it is very curious indeed. What makes it so?" "There must be *some* cause for it" says her father. "And the apples that grow on some trees are sweet, and on others they are sour. That is curious too." "Yes, very curious indeed," says Mary. "The *leaves* of trees seem to be always green," continues her father, "though the flowers are of various colors." "Yes, father," says Mary. "Except," adds her father, "when they turn yellow, and red, and brown, in the fall of the year."

A conversation like this, without attempting any thing like an answer to the question with which it commenced, is as satisfactory to the child, and perhaps as useful in developing its powers and increasing its knowledge of language, as any attempt to explain the phenomenon would be; and the knowledge of this will make it easy for the mother to dispose of many a question which might seriously interrupt her if she conceived it necessary either to attempt a satisfactory explanation of the difficulty, or not to answer it at all.

Be always ready to say "I don't know."

5. The mother should be always ready and willing to say "I don't know," in answer to children's questions.

Parents and teachers are very often somewhat averse to this, lest, by often confessing their own ignorance, they should lower themselves in the estimation of their pupils or their children. So they feel bound to give some kind of an explanation to every difficulty, in hopes that it may satisfy the inquirer, though it does not satisfy themselves. But this is a great mistake. The sooner that pupils and children understand that the field of knowledge is utterly boundless, and that it is only a very small portion of it that their superiors in age and attainment have yet explored, the better for all concerned. The kind of superiority, in the estimation of children, which it is chiefly desirable to attain, consists in their always finding that the explanation which we give, whenever we attempt any, is *clear, fair,* and *satisfactory,* not in our being always ready to offer an explanation, whether satisfactory or not.

Questions on Religious Subjects.

The considerations presented in this chapter relate chiefly to the questions which children ask in respect to what they observe taking place around them in external nature. There is another class of questions and difficulties which they raise—namely, those that relate to religious and moral subjects; and to these I have not intended now to refer. The inquiries which children make on these subjects arise, in a great measure, from the false and puerile conceptions which they are so apt to form in respect to spiritual things, and from which they deduce all sorts of absurdities. The false conceptions in which their difficulties originate are due partly to errors and imperfections in our modes of teaching them on these subjects, and partly to the immaturity of their powers, which incapacitates them from clearly comprehending any elements of thought that lie beyond the direct cognizance of the senses. We shall, however, have occasion to refer to this subject in another chapter.

In respect, however, to all that class of questions which children ask in relation to the visible world around them, the principles here explained may render the mother some aid in her intercourse with the little learners under her charge, if she clearly understands and intelligently applies them. And she will find the practice of holding frequent conversations with them, in these ways, a source of great pleasure to her, as well as of unspeakable advantage to them. Indeed, the conversation of a kind and intelligent mother is far the most valuable and important means of education for a child during many years of its early life. A boy whose mother is pleased to have him near her, who likes to hear and answer his questions, to watch the gradual development of his thinking and reasoning powers, and to enlarge and extend his knowledge of language —thus necessarily and of course expanding the range and scope of his ideas—will find that though his studies, strictly so called—that is, his learning to read, and the committing to memory lessons from books— may be deferred, yet, when he finally commences them he will go at once to the head of his classes at school, through the superior strength and ampler development which his mental powers will have attained.

CHAPTER XX.

THE USE OF MONEY.

The money question in the management and training of children has a distinct bearing on the subjects of some of the preceding chapters. It is extremely important, first, in respect to opportunities which are afforded in connection with the use of money for cultivating and developing the qualities of sound judgment and of practical wisdom; and then, in the second place, the true course to be pursued with them in respect to money forms a special point to be considered in its bearing upon the subject of the proper mode of dealing with their wishes and requests.

Evil Results of a very Common Method.

If a parent wishes to eradicate from the mind of his boy all feelings of delicacy and manly pride, to train him to the habit of obtaining what he wants by importunity or servility, and to prevent his having any means of acquiring any practical knowledge of the right use of money, any principles of economy, or any of that forethought and thrift so essential to sure prosperity in future life, the best way to accomplish these ends would seem to be to have no system in supplying him with money in his boyish days, but to give it to him only when he asks for it, and in quantities determined only by the frequency and importunity of his calls.

Of course under such a system the boy has no inducement to take care of his money, to form any plans of expenditure, to make any calculations, to practise self-denial to-day for the sake of a greater good to-morrow. The source of supply from which he draws money, fitful and uncertain as it may be in what it yields to him, he considers unlimited; and as the amount which he can draw from it does not depend at all upon his frugality, his foresight, or upon any incipient financial skill that he may exercise, but solely upon his adroitness in coaxing, or his persistence in importunity, it is the group of bad qualities, and not the good, which such management tends to foster. The effect of such a system is, in other words, not to encourage the development and growth of those qualities on which thrift and forehandedness in the management of his affairs in future life, and, in consequence, his success and prosperity, depend; but, on the contrary, to cherish the growth of all the mean and ignoble propensities of human nature by accustoming him, so far as relates to this subject, to gain his ends by the arts of a sycophant, or by rude pertinacity.

Not that this system always produces these results. It may be, and perhaps generally is, greatly modified by other influences acting upon the mind of the child at the same time, as well as by the natural tendencies of the boy's character, and by the character and general influence upon him of his father and mother in other respects. It can not be denied, however, that the above is the tendency of a system which makes a boy's income of spending-money a matter of mere chance, on which no calculations can be founded, except so far as he can increase it by adroit manoeuvring or by asking for it directly, with more or less of urgency or persistence, as the case may require; that is to say, by precisely those means which are the most ignoble and most generally despised by honorably-minded men as means for the attainment of any human end.

Now one of the most important parts of the education of both girls and boys, whether they are to inherit riches, or to enjoy a moderate income from the fruits of their own industry, or to spend their lives in extreme poverty, is to teach them the proper management and use of money. And this may be very effectually done by giving them a fixed and definite income to manage, and then throwing upon them the responsibility of the management of it, with such a degree of guidance, encouragement, and aid as a parent can easily render.

Objection to the Plan of a regular Allowance.

There are no parents among those who will be likely to read this book of resources so limited that they will not, from time to time, allow their children *some* amount of spending-money in a year. All that is necessary, therefore, is to appropriate to them this amount and pay it to them, or credit them with it, in a business-like and regular manner. It is true that by this system the children will soon begin to regard their monthly or weekly allowance as their due; and the parent will lose the pleasure, if it is any pleasure to him or her, of having the money which they give them regarded in each case as a present, and received with a sense of obligation. This is sometimes considered an objection to this plan. "When I furnish my children with money," says the parent, "as a gratification, I wish to have the pleasure of *giving* it to them. Whereas, on this proposed plan of paying it to them regularly at stated intervals, they will come to consider each payment as simply the payment of a debt. I wish them to consider it as a gratuity on my part, so that it may awaken gratitude and renew their love for me."

There is some seeming force in this objection, though it is true that the adoption of the plan of a systematic appropriation, as here recommended, does not prevent the making of presents of money, or of any thing else, to the children, whenever either parent desires to do so. Still the plan will not generally be adopted, except by parents in whose minds the laying of permanent foundations for their children's welfare and happiness through life, by training them from their earliest years to habits of forecast and thrift, and the exercise of judgment and skill in the management of money, is entirely paramount to any petty sentimental gratification to themselves, while the children are young.

Two Methods.

In case the parent—it may be either the father or the mother—decides to adopt the plan of appropriating systematically and regularly a certain sum to be at the disposal of the child, there are two modes by which the business may be transacted—one by paying over the money itself in the amounts and at the stated periods determined upon, and the other by opening an account with the child, and giving him credit from time to time for the amount due, charging on the other side the amounts which he draws.

1. *Paying the money.* This is the simplest plan. If it is adopted, the money must be ready and be paid at the appointed time with the utmost exactitude and certainty. Having made the arrangement with a child that he is to have a certain sum—six cents, twelve cents, twenty-five cents, or more, as the case may be—every Saturday night, the mother—if it is the

mother who has charge of the execution of the plan—must consider it a sacred debt, and must be *always* ready. She can not expect that her children will learn regularity, punctuality, and system in the management of their money affairs, if she sets them the example of laxity and forgetfulness in fulfilling her engagements, and offering excuses for non-payment when the time comes, instead of having the money ready when it is due. The money, when paid, should not, in general, be carried by the children about the person, but they should be provided with a purse or other safe receptacle, which, however, should be entirely in their custody, and so exposed to all the accidents to which any carelessness in the custody would expose it. The mother must remember that the very object of the plan is to have the children learn by experience to take care of money themselves, and that she defeats that object by virtually relieving them of this care. It should, therefore, be paid to them with the greatest punctuality, especially at the first introduction of the system, and with the distinct understanding that the charge and care of keeping it devolves entirely upon them from the time of its passing into their hands.

2. *Opening an account.* The second plan, and one that will prove much the most satisfactory in its working—though many mothers will shrink from it on the ground that it would make them a great deal of trouble—is to keep an account. For this purpose a small book should be made, with as many leaves as there are children, so that for each account there can be two pages. The book should be ruled for accounts, and the name of each child should be entered at the head of the two pages appropriated to his account. Then, from time to time, the amount of his allowance that has fallen due should be entered on the credit side, and any payment made to him on the other.

The plan of keeping an account in this way obviates the necessity of paying money at stated times, for the account will show at any time how much is due.

There are some advantages in each of these modes. Much depends on the age of the children, and still more upon the facilities which the father or mother have at hand for making entries in writing. To a man of business, accustomed to accounts, who could have a book made small enough to go into his wallet, or to a mother who is systematic in her habits, and has in her work-table or her secretary facilities for writing at any time, the plan of opening an account will be found much the best. It will afford an opportunity of giving the children a great deal of useful knowledge in respect to account-keeping—or, rather, by habituating them from an early age to the management of their affairs in this systematic manner, will train them from the beginning to habits of system and exactness. A very perceptible effect in this direction will be produced on the minds of children, even while they have not yet learned to read, and so can not understand at all the written record made of their pecuniary transactions. They will, at any rate, understand that a written record is made; they will take a certain pride and pleasure in it, and impressions will be produced which may have an effect upon their habits of accuracy and system in their pecuniary transactions through all future life.

Interest on Balances.

One great advantage of the plan of having an account over that of paying cash at stated times is, that it affords an opportunity for the father or mother to allow interest for any balances left from time to time in their hands, so as to initiate the children into a knowledge of the nature and the advantages of productive investments, and familiarize them with the idea that money reserved has within it a principle of increase. The interest allowed should be altogether greater than the regular rate, so as to make the advantage of it in the case of such small sums appreciable to the children—but not too great. Some judgment and discretion must be exercised on this as on all other points connected with the system.

The arrangements for the keeping of an account being made, and the account opened, there is, of course, no necessity, as in the case of payments made simply in cash, that the business should be transacted at stated times. At any time when convenient, the entry may be made of the amount which has become due since the time of the last entry. And when, from time to time, the child wishes for money, the parent will look at his account and see if there is a balance to his credit. If there is, the child will be entitled to receive whatever he desires up to the amount of the balance. Once in a month, or at any other times when convenient, the account can be settled, and the balance, with the accrued interest, carried to a new account.

All this, instead of being a trouble, will only be a source of interest and pleasure to the parent, as well as to the children themselves, and, without occupying any sensible portion of time, will be the means of gradually communicating a great deal of very useful instruction.

Employment of the Money.

It will have a great effect in "training up children in the way in which they should go," in respect to the employment of money, if a rule is made for them that a certain portion, one-quarter or one-half, for example, of all the money which comes into their possession, both from their regular allowance and from gratuities, is to be laid aside as a permanent investment, and an account at some Savings Bank be opened, or some other formal mode of placing it be adopted—the bank-book or other documentary evidence of the amount so laid up to be deposited among the child's treasures.

In respect to the other portion of the money—namely, that which is to be employed by the children themselves as spending-money, the disbursement of it should be left *entirely at their discretion,* subject only to the restriction that they are not to buy any thing that will be injurious or dangerous to themselves, or a means of disturbance or annoyance to others. The mother may give them any information or any counsel in regard to the employment of their money, provided she does not do it in the form of expressing any *wish,* on her part, in regard to it. For the very object of the whole plan is to bring out into action, and thus to develop and strengthen, the judgment and discretion of the child; and just as children can not learn to walk by always being carried, so they can not learn to be good managers without having the responsibility of actual management, on a scale adapted to their years, thrown really upon them. If a boy wishes to buy a bow and arrow, it may in some cases be right not to give him permission to do it, on account of the danger accompanying the use of such a plaything. But if he wishes to buy a kite which the mother is satisfied is too large for him to manage, or if she thinks there are so many trees about the house that he can not prevent its getting entangled in them, she must not object to it on that account. She can explain these dangers to the boy, if he is inclined to listen, but not in a way to show that she herself wishes him not to buy the kite. "Those are the difficulties which you may meet with," she may say, "but you may buy the kite if you think best."

Then when he meets with the difficulties, when he finds that he can not manage the kite, or that he loses it among the trees, she must not triumph over him, and say, "I told you how it would be. You would not take my advice, and now you see how it is." On the contrary, she must help him, and try to alleviate his disappointment, saying, "Never mind. It is a loss, certainly. But you did what you thought was best at the time, and we all meet with losses sometimes, even when we have done what we thought was best. You will make a great many other mistakes, probably, hereafter in spending money, and meet with losses; and this one will give you an opportunity of learning to bear them like a man."

The most implicit Faith to be kept with Children in Money Transactions.

I will not say that a father, if he is a man of business, ought to be as jealous of his credit with his children as he is of his credit at the bank; but I think, if he takes a right view of the subject, he will be extremely sensitive in respect to both. If he is a man of high and honorable sentiments, and especially if he looks forward to future years when his children shall have arrived at maturity, or shall be approaching towards it, and sees how important and how delicate the pecuniary relations between himself and them may be at that time, he will feel the importance of beginning by establishing, at the very commencement, not only by means of precept, but by example, a habit of precise, systematic, and scrupulous exactitude in the fulfillment of every pecuniary obligation. It is not necessary that he should do any thing mean or small in his dealings with them in order to accomplish this end. He may be as liberal and as generous with them in many ways as he pleases, but he must keep his accounts with them correctly. He must always, without any demurring or any excuse, be ready to fulfill his engagements, and teach them to fulfill theirs.

Possible Range of Transactions between Parents and Children.

The parent, after having initiated his children into the regular transaction of business by his mode of managing their allowance-fund, may very advantageously extend the benefits of the system by engaging with them from time to time in other affairs, to be regulated in a business-like and systematic manner. For example, if one of his boys has been reserving a portion of his spending-money as a watch-fund, and has already half enough for the purchase, the father may offer to lend him the balance and take a mortgage of the watch, to stand until the boy shall have taken it up out of future savings; and he can make out a mortgage-deed expressing in a few and simple words the fact that the watch is pledged to him as security for the sum advanced, and is not to become the absolute property of the boy till the money for which it is pledged is paid. In the course of years, a great number of transactions in this way may take place between the father or mother and their boy, each of which will not only be a source of interest and enjoyment to both parties, but will afford the best possible means of imparting, not only to the child directly interested in them, but to the other children, a practical knowledge of financial transactions, and of forming in them the habit of conducting all their affairs in a systematic and business-like manner.

The number and variety of such transactions in which the modes of doing business among men may be imitated with children, greatly to their enjoyment and interest, is endless. I could cite an instance when what was called a bank was in operation for many years among a certain number of children, with excellent effect. One was appointed president, another cashier, another paying-teller. There was a ledger under the charge of the cashier, with a list of stockholders, and the number of shares held by each, which was in proportion to the respective ages of the children. The bank building was a little toy secretary, something in the form of a safe, into which there mysteriously appeared, from time to time, small sums of money; the stockholders being as ignorant of the source from which the profits of the bank were derived as most stockholders probably are in the case of larger and more serious institutions. Once in six months, or at other periods, the money was counted, a dividend was declared, and the stockholders were paid in a regular and business-like manner.

The effect of such methods as these is not only to make the years of childhood pass more pleasantly, but also to prepare them to enter, when the time comes, upon the serious business of life with some considerable portion of that practical wisdom in the management of money which is often, when it is deferred to a later period, acquired only by bitter experience and through much suffering.

Indeed, any parent who appreciates and fully enters into the views presented in this chapter will find, in ordinary cases, that his children make so much progress in business capacity that he can extend the system so as to embrace subjects of real and serious importance before the children arrive at maturity. A boy, for instance, who has been trained in this way will be found competent, by the time that he is ten or twelve years old, to take the contract for furnishing himself with caps, or boots and shoes, and, a few years later, with all his clothing, at a specified annual sum. The sum fixed upon in the case of caps, for example, should be intermediate between that which the caps of a boy of ordinary heedlessness would cost, and that which would be sufficient with special care, so that both the father and the son could make money, as it were, by the transaction. Of course, to manage such a system successfully, so that it could afterwards be extended to other classes of expenses, requires tact, skill, system, patience, and steadiness on the part of the father or mother who should attempt it; but when the parent possesses these qualities, the time and attention that would be required would be as nothing compared with the trouble, the vexation, the endless dissatisfaction on both sides, that attend upon the ordinary methods of supplying children's wants—to say nothing of the incalculable benefit to the boy himself of such a training, as a part of his preparation for future life.

Evil Results to be feared.

Nor is it merely upon the children themselves, and that after they enter upon the responsibilities of active life, that the evils resulting from their having had no practical training in youth in respect to pecuniary responsibilities and obligations, that evil consequences will fall. The great cities are full of wealthy men whose lives are rendered miserable by the recklessness in respect to money which is displayed by their sons and daughters as they advance towards maturity, and by the utter want, on their part, of all sense of delicacy, and of obligation or of responsibility of any kind towards their parents in respect to their pecuniary transactions. Of course this must, in a vast number of cases, be the result when the boy is brought up from infancy with the idea that the only limit to his supply of money is his ingenuity in devising modes of putting a pressure upon his father. Fifteen or twenty years spent in managing his affairs on this principle must, of course, produce the fruit naturally to be expected from such seed.

The great Difficulty.

It would seem, perhaps, at first view, from what has been said in this chapter, that it would be a very simple and easy thing to train up children thus to correct ideas and habits in respect to the use of money; and it would be so—for the principles involved seem to be very plain and simple—were it not that the *qualities which it requires in the parent* are just those which are most rare. Deliberateness in forming the plan, calmness and quietness in proposing it, inflexible but mild and gentle firmness in carrying it out, perfect honesty in allowing the children to exercise the power and responsibility promised them, and an indulgent spirit in relation to the faults and errors into which they fall in the exercise of it—these and other such qualities are not very easily found. To make an arrangement with a child that he is to receive a certain sum every Saturday, and then after two or three weeks to forget it, and when the boy comes to call for it, to say, petulantly, "Oh, don't come to bother me about that now—I am busy; and besides, I have not got the money now;" or, when a boy has spent all his allowance on the first two or three days of the week, and comes to beg importunately for more, to say, "It was very wrong in you to spend all your money at once, and I have a great mind not to give you any more. I will, however, do it just this time, but I shall not again, you may depend;" or, to borrow money in some sudden emergency out of the fund which a child has accumulated for a special purpose, and then to forget or neglect to repay it—to manage loosely and capriciously in any such ways as these will be sure to make the attempt a total failure; that is to say, such management will be sure to be a failure in respect to teaching the boy to act on right principles in the management of money, and training him to habits of exactness and faithfulness in the fulfillment of his obligations. But in making him a thoughtless, wasteful, teasing, and selfish boy while he remains a boy, and fixing him, when he comes to manhood, in the class of those who are utterly untrustworthy, faithless in the performance of their promises, and wholly unscrupulous in respect to the means by which they obtain money, it may very probably turn out to be a splendid success.

CHAPTER XXI.

CORPORAL PUNISHMENT.

It might, perhaps, be thought that, in a book which professes to show how an efficient government can be established and maintained by *gentle measures*, the subject of corporal punishment could have no place. It seems important, however, that there should be here introduced a brief though distinct presentation of the light in which, in a philosophical point of view, this instrumentality is to be regarded.

The Teachings of Scripture.

The resort to corporal punishment in the training of children seems to be spoken of in many passages contained in the Scriptures as of fundamental necessity. But there can be no doubt that the word *rod*, as used in those passages, is used simply as the emblem of parental authority. This is in accordance with the ordinary custom of Hebrew writers in those days, and with the idiom of their language, by which a single visible or tangible object was employed as the representative or expression of a general idea—as, for example, the sword is used as the emblem of magisterial authority, and the sun and the rain, which are spoken of as being sent with their genial and fertilizing power upon the evil and the good, denote not specially and exclusively those agencies, but all the beneficent influences of nature which they are employed to represent. The injunctions, therefore, of Solomon in respect to the use of the rod are undoubtedly to be understood as simply enjoining upon parents the necessity of bringing up their children *in complete subjection* to their authority. No one can imagine that he could wish the rod to be used when complete subjection to the parental authority could be secured by more gentle means. And how this is to be done it is the object precisely of this book to show.

In this sense, therefore—and it is undoubtedly the true sense—namely, that children must be *governed by the authority of the parent*, the passages in question express a great and most essential truth. It is sometimes said that children must be governed by reason, and this is true, but it is the reason of their parents, and not their own which must hold the control. If children were endowed with the capacity of seeing what is best for them, and with sufficient self-control to pursue what is best against the counter-influences of their animal instincts and propensities, there would be no necessity that the period of subjection to parental authority should be extended over so many years. But so long as their powers are yet too immature to be safely relied upon, they must, of necessity, be subject to the parental will; and the sooner and the more perfectly they are made to understand this, and to yield a willing submission to the necessity, the better it will be, not only for their parents, but also for themselves.

The parental authority must, therefore, be established—by gentle means, if possible—but it must by all means be established, and be firmly maintained. If you can not govern your child without corporal punishment, it is better to resort to it than not to govern him at all. Taking a wide view of the field, I think there may be several cases in which a resort to the infliction of physical pain as the only available means of establishing authority may be the only alternative. There are three cases of this kind that are to be specially considered.

Possible Cases in which it is the only Alternative.—Savages.

1. In savage or half-civilized life, and even, perhaps, in so rude a state of society as must have existed in some parts of Judea when the Proverbs of Solomon were written, it is conceivable that many parents, owing to their

own ignorance, and low animal condition, would have no other means at their command for establishing their authority over their children than scoldings and blows. It must be so among savages. And it is certainly better, if the mother knows no other way of inducing her boy to keep within her sight, that she should whip him when he runs away, than that he should be bitten by serpents or devoured by bears. She *must* establish her authority in some way, and if this is the best that she is capable of pursuing, she must use it.

Teachers whose Tasks surpass their Skill.

2. A teacher, in entering upon the charge of a large school of boys made unruly by previous mismanagement, may, perhaps, possibly find himself unable to establish submission to his authority without this resource. It is true that if it is so, it is due, in a certain sense, to want of skill on the teacher's part; for there are men, and women too, who will take any company of boys that you can give them, and, by a certain skill, or tact, or knowledge of human nature, or other qualities which seem sometimes to other persons almost magical, will have them all completely under subjection in a week, and that without violence, without scolding, almost without even a frown. The time may, perhaps, come when every teacher, to be considered qualified for his work, must possess this skill. Indeed, the world is evidently making great and rapid progress in this direction. The methods of instruction and the modes by which the teacher gains and holds his influence over his pupils have been wonderfully improved in recent times, so that where there was one teacher, fifty years ago, who was really beloved by his pupils, we have fifty now. In Dr. Johnson's time, which was about a hundred and fifty years ago, it would seem that there was no other mode but that of violent coercion recognized as worthy to be relied upon in imparting instruction, for he said that he knew of no way by which Latin could be taught to boys in his day but "by having it flogged into them."

From such a state of things to that which prevails at the present day there has been an astonishing change. And now, whether a teacher is able to manage an average school of boys without physical force is simply a question of tact, knowledge of the right principles, and skill in applying them on his part. It is, perhaps, yet too soon to expect that all teachers can possess, or can acquire, these qualifications to such a degree as to make it safe to forbid the infliction of bodily pain in any case, but the time for it is rapidly approaching, and in some parts of the country it has, perhaps, already arrived. Until that time comes, every teacher who finds himself under the necessity of beating a boy's body in order to attain certain moral or intellectual ends ought to understand that the reason is the incompleteness of his understanding and skill in dealing directly with his mind; though for this incompleteness he may not himself be personally at all to blame.

Children spoiled by Neglect and Mismanagement.

3. I am even willing to admit that one or more boys in a family may reach such a condition of rudeness and insubordination, in consequence of neglect or mismanagement on the part of their parents in their early years, and the present clumsiness and incapacity of the father in dealing with the susceptibilities and impulses of the human soul, that the question will lie between keeping them within some kind of subordination by bodily punishment or not controlling them at all. If a father has been so engrossed in his business that he has neglected his children, has never established any common bond of sympathy between himself and them, has taken no interest in their enjoyments, nor brought them by moral means to an habitual subjection to his will; and if their mother is a weak, irresolute woman, occupying herself with the pursuits and pleasures of fashionable society, and leaving her children to the management of servants, the children will, of course, in general, grow up exacting, turbulent, and ungovernable; and when, with advancing maturity, their increasing strength and vigor makes this turbulence and disorder intolerable in the house, and there is, as of course there usually will be in such a case, no proper knowledge and skill in the management of the young on the part of either parent to remedy the evil by gentle measures, the only alternative in many cases may be either a resort to violent punishment, or the sending away of the unmanageable subjects to school. The latter part of the alternative is the best, and, fortunately, it is the one generally adopted. But where it can not be adopted, it is certainly better that the boys should be governed by the rod than to grow up under

no government at all.

Gentle Measures effectual where Rightfully and Faithfully employed.

However it may be with respect to the exceptional cases above enumerated, and perhaps some others, there can, I think, be no doubt that parents who should train their children from the beginning on the principles explained in this volume, and upon others analogous to them, would never, in any case, have to strike a blow. They would accomplish the end enjoined by the precepts of Solomon, namely, the complete subjection of their children to their authority, by improved methods not known in his day, or, at least, not so fully developed that they could then be relied upon. They who imagine that parents are bound to use the rod as the instrumentality, because the Scriptures speak of the rod as the means of establishing parental authority best known in those days, instead of employing the more effective methods which the progress of improvement has developed and made available at the present day, ought, in order to be consistent, to insist on the retention of the harp in religious worship, because David enjoins it upon believers to "praise the Lord with harp:" to "sing unto him with psaltery, and an instrument of ten strings." The truth is, that what we are to look at in such injunctions is the end that is to be attained, which is, in this last case, the impressive and reverential exaltation of Almighty God in our minds by the acts of public worship; and if, with the improvements in musical instruments which have been made in modern times, we can do this more satisfactorily by employing in the place of a psaltery or a harp of ten strings an organ of ten or a hundred stops, we are bound to make the substitution. In a word, we must look at the end and not at the means, remembering that in questions of Scripture interpretation the "letter killeth, the spirit maketh alive."

Protracted Contests with Obstinacy.

It seems to me, though I am aware that many excellent persons think differently, that it is never wise for the parent to allow himself to be drawn into a contest with a child in attempting to compel him to do something that from ill-temper or obstinacy he refuses to do. If the attempt is successful, and the child yields under a moderate severity of coercion, it is all very well. But there is something mysterious and unaccountable in the strength of the obstinacy sometimes manifested in such cases, and the degree of endurance which it will often inspire, even in children of the most tender age. We observe the same inexplicable fixedness sometimes in the lower animals—in the horse, for example; which is the more unaccountable from the fact that we can not suppose, in his case, that peculiar combination of intelligence and ill-temper which we generally consider the sustaining power of the protracted obstinacy on the part of the child. The degree of persistence which is manifested by children in contests of this kind is something wonderful, and can not easily be explained by any of the ordinary theories in respect to the influence of motives on the human mind. A state of cerebral excitement and exaltation is not unfrequently produced which seems akin to insanity, and instances have been known in which a child has suffered itself to be beaten to death rather than yield obedience to a very simple command. And in vast numbers of instances, the parent, after a protracted contest, gives up in despair, and is compelled to invent some plausible pretext for bringing it to an end.

Indeed, when we reflect upon the subject, we see what a difficult task we undertake in such contests—it being nothing less than that of *forcing the formation of a volition* in a human mind. We can easily control the bodily movements and actions of another person by means of an external coercion that we can apply, and we have various indirect means of *inducing* volitions; but in these contests we seem to come up squarely to the work of attempting, by outward force, to compel the *forming of a volition* in the mind; and it is not surprising that this should, at least sometimes, prove a very difficult undertaking.

No Necessity for these Contests.

There seems to be no necessity that a parent or teacher should ever become involved in struggles of this kind in maintaining his authority. The way to avoid them, as it seems to me, is, when a child refuses out of obstinacy to do what is required of him, to impose the proper punishment or penalty for the refusal, and let that close the transaction. Do not attempt to enforce his compliance by continuing the punishment until he yields. A child, for example, going out to play, wishes for his blue cap. His mother chooses that he shall wear his gray one. She hangs the blue cap up in its place, and gives him the gray one. He declares that he will not wear it, and throws it down upon the floor. The temptation now is for the mother, indignant, to punish him, and then to order him to take up the cap which he had thrown down, and to feel that it is her duty, in case he refuses, to persist in the punishment until she conquers his will, and compels him to take it up and put it upon his head.

But instead of this, a safer and a better course, it seems to me, is to avoid a contest altogether by considering the offense complete, and the transaction on his part finished by the single act of rebellion against her authority. She may take the cap up from the floor herself and put it in its place, and then simply consider what punishment is proper for the wrong already done. Perhaps she forbids the boy to go out at all. Perhaps she reserves the punishment, and sends him to bed an hour earlier that night. The age of the boy, or some other circumstances connected with the case, may be such as to demand a severer treatment still. At any rate, she limits the transaction to the single act of disobedience and rebellion already committed, without giving an opportunity for a repetition of it by renewing the command, and inflicts for it the proper punishment, and that is the end of the affair.

And so a boy in reciting a lesson will not repeat certain words after his mother. She enters into no controversy with him, but shuts the book and puts it away. He, knowing his mother's usual mode of management in such cases, and being sure that some penalty, privation, or punishment will sooner or later follow, relents, and tells his mother that he will say the words if she will try him again.

"No, my son," she should reply, "the opportunity is past. You should have done your duty at the right time. You have disobeyed me, and I must take time to consider what to do."

If, at the proper time, in such a case, when all the excitement of the affair is over, a penalty or punishment apportioned to the fault, or some other appropriate measures in relation to it, are *certain to come*, and if this method is always pursued in a calm and quiet manner but with inflexible firmness in act, the spirit of rebellion will be much more effectually subdued than by any protracted struggles at the time, though ending in victory however complete.

But all this is a digression, though it seemed proper to allude to the subject of these contests here, since it is on these occasions, perhaps, that parents are most frequently led, or, as they think, irresistibly impelled, to the infliction of bodily punishments as the last resort, when they would, in general, be strongly inclined to avoid them.

The Infliction of Pain sometimes the speediest Remedy.

There are, moreover, some cases, perhaps, in the ordinary exigencies of domestic life, as the world goes, when some personal infliction is the *shortest* way of disposing of a case of discipline, and may appear, for the time being, to be the most effectual. A slap is very quickly given, and a mother may often think that she has not time for a more gentle mode of managing the case, even though she may admit that if she had the time at her command the gentle mode would be the best. And it is, indeed, doubtless true that the principles of management advocated in this work are such as require that the parents should devote some time and attention, and, still more essentially, some *heart* to the work; and they who do not consider the welfare and happiness of their children in future life, and their own happiness in connection with them as they advance towards their declining years, as of sufficient importance to call for the bestowment of this time and attention, will doubtless often resort to more summary methods in their discipline than those here recommended.

The Sting that it leaves behind.

Indeed, the great objection, after all, to the occasional resort to the infliction of bodily pain in extreme cases is, as it seems to me, the sting which it leaves behind; not that, which it leaves in the heart of the child who may suffer it—for that soon passes away—but in the heart of the parent who inflicts it. The one is, or may be, very evanescent; the other may very long remain; and what is worse, the anguish of it may be revived and made very poignant in future years.

This consideration makes it specially imperative on every parent never, for any cause, to inflict punishment by violence when himself under the influence of any irritation or anger awakened by the offense. For though the anger which the fault of the child naturally awakens in you carries you through the act of punishing well enough, it soon afterwards passes away, while the memory of it remains, and in after years, like any other sin, it may come back to exact a painful retribution. When the little loved one who now puts you out of patience with her heedlessness, her inconsiderateness, and, perhaps, by worse faults and failings—all, however, faults which may very possibly, in part or in whole, be the result of the immature and undeveloped condition of her mental or bodily powers—falls sick and dies, and you follow her as she is borne away, and with a bursting heart see her laid in her little grave, it will be a great comfort to you then to reflect that you did all in your power, by means of the gentlest measures at your command, to train her to truth and duty, that you never lost patience with her, and that she never felt from your hand any thing but gentle assistance or a loving caress.

And your boy—now so ardent and impulsive, and often, perhaps, noisy, troublesome, and rude, from the exuberant action of his growing powers—when these powers shall have received their full development, and he has passed from your control to his place in the world as a man, and he comes back from time to time to the maternal home in grateful remembrance of his obligations to his mother, bringing with him tokens of his affection and love, you will think with pain of the occasions when you subjected him to the torture of the rod under the impulse of irritation or anger, or to accomplish the ends of discipline which might have been attained in other ways. Time, as you then look back over the long interval of years which have elapsed, will greatly soften the recollection of the fault, but it will greatly aggravate that of the pain which was made the retribution of it. You will say to yourself, it is true, I did it for the best. If I had not done it, my son would perhaps not be what he is. He, if he remembers the transaction, will doubtless say so too; but there will be none the less for both a certain sting in the recollection, and you will wish that the same end could have been accomplished by gentler means.

The substance of it is that children must, at all events, be governed. The proper authority over them *must be* maintained; but it is a great deal better to secure this end by gentle measures, if the parent have or can acquire the skill to employ them.

CHAPTER XXII.

GRATITUDE IN CHILDREN.

Mothers are very often pained at what seems to them the ingratitude of their children. They long, above all things, for their love. They do every thing in their power—I mean, of course, that some mothers do—to win it. They make every sacrifice, and give every possible evidence of affection; but they seem to fail entirely of bringing out any of those evidences of gratitude and affection in return which, if they could only witness them, would fill their hearts with gladness and joy. But the only feeling which their children manifest towards them seems to be a selfish one. They come to them when in trouble, they even fly to them eagerly when in danger, and they consider their parents the chief resource for procuring nearly all their means of gratification. But they think little, as it often seems, of the mother's comfort and enjoyment in return, and seldom or never do any thing voluntarily to give her pleasure.

It would be a great exaggeration to say that this is always the feeling of the mother in respect to her children. I only mean that this is sometimes, and I might probably say very often, the case.

Two Forms of Love.

Now there are two distinct forms which the feeling of love may assume in the mature mind, both of which are gratifying to the object of it, though they are very different, and indeed in some sense exactly the opposite of each other. There is the *receiving* and the *bestowing* love. It is true that the two forms are often conjoined, or rather they often exist in intimate combination with each other; but in their nature they are essentially distinct. A young lady, for example, may feel a strong attachment for the gentleman to whom she is engaged—or a wife for her husband—in the sense of liking to receive kindness and attention from him more than from any other man. She may be specially pleased when he invites her to ride with him, or makes her presents, or shows in any way that he thinks of her and seeks her happiness—more so than she would be to receive the same attentions from any other person. This is love. It may be very genuine love; but it is love in the form of taking special pleasure in the kindness and favor bestowed by the object of it. Yet it is none the less true, as most persons have had occasion to learn from their own experience, that this kind of love may be very strong without being accompanied by any corresponding desire on the part of the person manifesting it to make sacrifices of her own ease and comfort in order to give happiness to the object of her love in return.

In the same manner a gentleman may feel a strong sentiment of love for a lady, which shall take the form of enjoying her society, of being happy when he is near her, and greatly pleased at her making sacrifices for his sake, or manifesting in any way a strong attachment for him. There *may be* also united with this the other form of love—namely, that which would lead him to deny himself and make sacrifices *for her*. But the two, though they may often—perhaps generally—exist together, are in their nature so essentially different that they may be entirely separated, and we may have one in its full strength while there is very little of the other. You may love a person in the sense of taking greater pleasure in receiving attentions and favors from him than from all the world beside, while yet you seldom think of making efforts to promote his comfort and happiness in any thing in which you are not yourself personally concerned. On the other hand, you may love him with the kind of affection which renders it the greatest pleasure of your life to make sacrifices and endure self-denial to promote his welfare in any way.

In some cases these two forms are in fact entirely separated, and one or the other can exist entirely distinct from the other—as in the case of the kind feelings of a good man towards the poor and miserable. It is quite possible to feel a very strong interest in such objects, and to be willing to put ourselves to considerable inconvenience to make them comfortable and happy, and to take great pleasure in learning that our efforts have been effectual, without feeling any love for them at all in the other form —that is, any desire to have them with us, to receive attentions and kindness from them, and to enjoy their society.

On the other hand, in the love of a young child for his mother the case is reversed. The love of the child consists chiefly in liking to be with his mother, in going to her rather than to any one else for relief from pain or for comfort in sorrow, and is accompanied with very few and very faint desires to make efforts, or to submit to privations, or to make sacrifices, for the promotion of her good.

Order of their Development.

Now the qualities and characteristics of the soul on which the capacity for these two forms of love depend seem to be very different, and they advance in development and come to maturity at different periods of life; so that the mother, in feeling dejected and sad because she can not awaken in the mind of her child the gratitude and the consideration for her comfort and happiness which she desires, is simply looking for a certain kind of fruit at the wrong time. You have one of the forms of love for you on the part of the child now while he is young. In due time, when he arrives at maturity, if you will wait patiently, you will assuredly have the other. Now he runs to you in every emergency. He asks you for every thing that he wants. He can find comfort nowhere else but in your arms, when he is in distress or in suffering from pain, disappointment, or sorrow. But he will not make any effort to be still when you are sick, or to avoid interrupting you when you are busy; and insists, perhaps, on your carrying him when he is tired, without seeming to think or care whether you may not be tired too. But in due time all this will be changed. Twenty years hence he will conceal all his troubles from you instead of coming with them to you for comfort. He will be off in the world engaged in his pursuits, no longer bound closely to your side. But he will think all the time of your comfort and happiness. He will bring you presents, and pay you innumerable attentions to cheer your heart in your declining years. He will not run to you when he has hurt himself; but if any thing happens to *you*, he will leave every thing to hasten to your relief, and bring with him all the comforts and means of enjoyment for you that his resources can command. The time will thus come when you will have his love to your heart's content, in the second form. You must be satisfied, while he is so young, with the first form of it, which is all that his powers and faculties in their present stage are capable of developing.

The truth of the case seems to be that the faculties of the human mind—or I should perhaps rather say, the susceptibilities of the soul—like the instincts of animals, are developed in the order in which they are required for the good of the subject of them.

Indeed, it is very interesting and curious to observe how striking the analogy in the order of development, in respect to the nature of the bond of attachment which binds the offspring to the parent, runs through all those ranks of the animal creation in which the young for a time depend upon the mother for food or for protection. The chickens in any moment of alarm run to the hen; and the lamb, the calf, and the colt to their respective mothers; but none of them would feel the least inclination to come to the rescue of the parent if the parent was in danger. With the mother herself it is exactly the reverse. Her heart—if we can speak of the seat of the maternal affections of such creatures as a heart—is filled with desires to bestow good upon her offspring, without a desire, or even a thought, of receiving any good from them in return.

There is this difference, however, between the race of man and those of the inferior animals—namely, that in his case the instinct, or at least a natural desire which is in some respects analogous to an instinct, prompting him to repay to his parents the benefits which he received from them in youth, comes in due time; while in that of the lower animals it seems never to come at all. The little birds, after opening their mouths so wide every time the mother comes to the nest during all the weeks while their wings are growing, fly away when they are grown, without the least care or concern for the anxiety and distress of the mother occasioned by their imprudent flights; and once away and free, never come back, so far as we know, to make any return to their mother for watching over them, sheltering them with her body, and working so indefatigably to provide them with food during the helpless period of their infancy—and still less to seek and protect and feed her in her old age. But the boy, reckless as he sometimes seems in his boyhood, insensible apparently to his obligations to his mother, and little mindful of her wishes or of her feelings—his affection for her showing itself mainly in his readiness to go to her with all his wants, and in all his troubles and sorrows—will begin, when he has arrived at maturity and no longer needs her aid, to remember with gratitude the past aid that she has rendered him. The current of affection in his heart will turn and flow the other way. Instead of wishing to receive, he will now only wish to give. If she is in want, he will do all he can to supply her. If she is in sorrow, he will be happy if he can do any thing to comfort her. He will send her memorials of his gratitude, and objects of comfort and embellishment for her home, and will watch with solicitude and sincere affection over her declining years.

And all this change, if not the result of a new instinct which reaches its development only when the period of maturity arrives, is the unfolding of a sentiment of the heart belonging essentially to the nature of the subject of it as man. It is true that this capacity may, under certain circumstances, be very feebly developed. In some cases, indeed, it would seem that it was scarcely developed at all; but there is a provision for it in the nature of man, while there is no provision for it at all in the sentient principles of the lower animals.

Advancing the Development of the Sentiment of Gratitude.

Now, although parents must not be impatient at the slow appearance of this feeling in their children, and must not be troubled in its not appearing before its time, they can do much by proper efforts to cultivate its growth, and give it an earlier and a more powerful influence over them than it would otherwise manifest. The mode of doing this is the same as in all other cases of the cultivation of moral sentiments in children, and that is by the influence over them of sympathy with those they love. Just as the way to cultivate in the minds of children a feeling of pity for those who are in distress is not to preach it as a duty, but to make them love you, and then show such pity yourself; and the way to make them angry and revengeful in character—if we can conceive of your being actuated by so unnatural a desire—would be often to express violent resentment yourself, with scowling looks and fierce denunciations against those who have offended you; so, to awaken them to sentiments of gratitude for the favors they receive, you must gently lead them to sympathize with you in the gratitude which *you* feel for the favors that *you* receive.

When a child shows some special unwillingness to comply with her mother's desires, her mother may address to her a kind but direct and plain expostulation on the obligations of children to their parents, and the duty incumbent on them of being grateful for their kindness, and to be willing to do what they can in return. Such an address would probably do no good at all. The child would receive it simply as a scolding, no matter how mildly and gently the reproof might be expressed, and would shut her heart against it. It is something which she must stand still and endure, and that is all.

But let the mother say the same things precisely when the child has shown a willingness to make some little sacrifice to aid or to gratify her mother, so that the sentiment expressed may enter her mind in the form of approval and not of condemnation, and the effect will be very different. The sentiments will, at any rate, now not be rejected from the mind, but the way will be open for them to enter, and the conversation will have a good effect, so far as didactic teaching can have effect in such a case.

But now to bring in the element of sympathy as a means of reaching and influencing the mind of the child: The mother, we will suppose, standing at the door some morning before breakfast in spring, with her little daughter, seven or eight years old, by her side, hears a bird singing on a tree near by. She points to the tree, and says, in a half-whisper, "Hark!"

When the sound ceases, she looks to the child with an expression of pleasure upon her countenance, and says,

"Suppose we give that bird some crumbs because he has been singing us such a pretty song."

"Well!" says the child.

"Would you?" asks the mother.

"Yes, mother, I should like to give him some very much. Do you suppose he sang the song for us?"

"I don't *know* that he did," replies the mother. "We don't know exactly what the birds mean by all their singing. They take some pleasure in seeing us, I think, or else they would not come so much around our house; and I don't know but that this bird's song may come from some kind of joy or gladness he felt in seeing us come to the door. At any rate, it will be a pleasure to us to give him some crumbs to pay him for his song."

The child will think so too, and will run off joyfully to bring a piece of bread to form crumbs to be scattered upon the path.

And the whole transaction will have the effect of awakening and cherishing the sentiment of gratitude in her heart. The effect will not be great, it is true, but it will be of the right kind. It will be a drop of water upon the unfolding cotyledons of a seed just peeping up out of the ground, which will percolate below after you have gone away, and give the little roots a new impulse of growth. For when you have left the child seated upon the door-step, occupied in throwing out the crumbs to the bird, her heart will be occupied with the thoughts you have put into it, and the sentiment of gratitude for kindness received will commence its course of development, if it had not commenced it before.

The Case of older Children.

Of course the employment of such an occasion as this of the singing of a little bird and such a conversation in respect to it for cultivating the sentiment of gratitude in the heart, is adapted only to the case of quite a young child. For older children, while the principle is the same, the circumstances and the manner of treating the case must be adapted to a maturer age. Robert, for example—twelve years of age—had been sick, and during his convalescence his sister Mary, two years older than himself, had been very assiduous in her attendance upon him. She had waited upon him at his meals, and brought him books and playthings, from time to time, to amuse him. After he had fully recovered his health, he was sitting in the garden, one sunny morning in the spring, with his mother, and she said,

"How kind Mary was to you while you were sick!"

"Yes," said Robert, "she was very kind indeed."

"If you would like to do something for her in return," continued his mother, "I'll tell you what would be a good plan."

Robert, who, perhaps, without this conversation would not have thought particularly of making any return, said he should like to do something for her very much.

"Then," said his mother, "you might make her a garden. I can mark off a place for a bed for her large enough to hold a number of kinds of flowers, and then you can dig it up, and rake it over, and lay it off into little beds, and sow the seeds. I'll buy the seeds for you. I should like to do something towards making the garden for her, for she helped me a great deal, as well as you, in the care she took of you."

"Well," said Robert, "I'll do it."

"You are well and strong now, so you can do it pretty easily," added the mother; "but still, unless you would like to do it yourself for her sake, I can get the man to do it. But if you would like to do it yourself, I think it would please her very much as an expression of your gratitude and love for her."

"Yes," said Robert, "I should a great deal rather do it myself, and I will begin this very day."

And yet, if his mother had not made the suggestion, he would probably not have thought of making any such return, or even any return at all, for his sister's devoted kindness to him when he was sick. In other words, the sentiment of gratitude was in his heart, or, rather, the capacity for it was there, but it needed a little fostering care to bring it out into action. And the thing to be observed is, that by this fostering care it was not only brought out at the time, but, by being thus brought out and drawn into action, it was strengthened and made-to grow, so as to be ready to come out itself without being called, on the next occasion.-It was like a little plant just coming out of the ground under influences not altogether favorable. It needs a little help and encouragement; and the aid that is given by a few drops of water at the right time will bring it forward and help it to attain soon such a degree of strength and vigor as will make it independent of all external aid.

But there must be consideration, tact, a proper regard to circumstances, and, above all, there must be no secret and selfish ends concealed, on the part of the mother in such cases. You may deluge and destroy your little plant by throwing on the water roughly or rudely; or, in the case of a boy upon whose mind you seem to be endeavoring to produce some moral result, you may really have in view some object of your own—your interest in the moral result being only a pretense.

For instance, Egbert, under circumstances similar to those recited above —in respect to the sickness of the boy, and the kind attentions of his sister—came to his mother one afternoon for permission to go a-fishing with some other boys who had called for him. He was full of excitement and enthusiasm at the idea. But his mother was not willing to allow him to go. The weather was lowering. She thought that he had not yet fully recovered his health; and she was afraid of other dangers. Instead of saying calmly, after a moment's reflection, to show that her answer was a deliberate one, that he could not go, and then quietly and firmly, but without assigning any reasons, adhering to her decision—a course which, though it could not have saved the boy from emotions of disappointment, would be the best for making those feelings as light and as brief in duration as possible—began to argue the case thus;

"Oh no, Egbert, I would not go a-fishing this afternoon, if I were you. I think it is going to rain. Besides, it is a nice cool day to work in the garden, and Lucy would like to have her garden made very much. You know that she was very kind to you when you were sick—how many things she did for you; and preparing her garden for her would be such a nice way of making her a return. I am sure you would not wish to show yourself ungrateful for so much kindness."

Then follows a discussion of some minutes, in which Egbert, in a fretful and teasing tone, persists in urging his desire to go a-fishing. He can make the garden, he says, some other day. His mother finally yields, though with great unwillingness, doing all she can to extract all graciousness and sweetness from her consent, and to spoil the pleasure of the excursion to the boy, by saying as he goes away, that she is sure he ought not to go, and that she shall be uneasy about him all the time that he is gone.

Now it is plain that such management as this, though it takes ostensibly the form of a plea on the part of the mother in favor of a sentiment of gratitude in the heart of the boy, can have no effect in cherishing and bringing forward into life any such sentiment, even if it should be already existent there in a nascent state; but can only tend to make the object of it more selfish and heartless than ever.

Thus the art of cultivating the sentiment of gratitude, as is the case in all other departments of moral training, can not be taught by definite lessons or learned by rote. It demands tact and skill, and, above all, an honest and guileless sincerity. The mother must really look to, and aim for the actual moral effect in the heart of the child, and not merely make formal efforts ostensibly for this end, but really to accomplish some temporary object of her own. Children easily see through all covert intentions of any kind. They sometimes play the hypocrite themselves, but they are always great detectors of hypocrisy in others.

But gentle and cautious efforts of the right kind—such as require no high attainments on the part of the mother, but only the right spirit—will in time work wonderful effects; and the mother who perseveres in them, and who does not expect the fruits too soon, will watch with great interest for the time to arrive when her boy will spontaneously, from the promptings of his own heart, take some real trouble, or submit to some real privation or self-denial, to give pleasure to her. She will then enjoy the double gratification, first, of receiving the pleasure, whatever it may be, that her boy has procured for her, and also the joy of finding that the tender plant which she has watched and watered so long, and which for a time seemed so frail that she almost despaired of its ever coming to any good, is really advanced to the stage of beginning to bear fruit, and giving her an earnest of the abundant fruits which she may confidently expect from it in future years.

CHAPTER XXIII.

RELIGIOUS TRAINING.

It has been my aim in this volume to avoid, as far as possible, all topics involving controversy, and only to present such truths, and to elucidate such principles, as can be easily made to commend themselves to the good sense and the favorable appreciation of all the classes of minds likely to be found among the readers of the work. There are certain very important aspects of the religious question which may be presented, I think, without any serious deviation from this policy.

In what True Piety consists.

Indeed; I think there is far more real than seeming agreement among parents in respect to this subject, or rather a large portion of the apparent difference consists in different modes of expressing in words thoughts and conceptions connected with spiritual things, which from their very nature can not any of them be adequately expressed in language at all; and thus it happens that what are substantially the same ideas are customarily clothed by different classes of persons in very different phraseology, while, on the other hand, the same set of phrases actually represent in different minds very different sets of ideas.

For instance, there is perhaps universal agreement in the idea that some kind of change—a change, too, of a very important character—is implied in the implanting or developing of the spirit of piety in the heart of a child. There is also universal agreement in the fact—often very emphatically asserted in the New Testament—that the essential principles in which true piety consists are those of entire submission in all things to the will of God, and cordial kind feeling towards every man.

There is endless disagreement, and much earnest contention among different denominations of Christians, in respect to the means by which the implanting of these principles is to be secured, and to the modes in which, when implanted, they will manifest themselves; but there is not, so far as would appear, any dissent whatever anywhere from the opinion that the end to be aimed at is the implanting of these principles—that is that it consists in bringing the heart to a state of complete and cordial submission to the authority and to the will of God, and to a sincere regard for the welfare and happiness of every human being.

A Question of Words

There seems, at first view, to be a special difference of opinion in respect to the nature of the process by which these principles come to be implanted or developed in the minds of the young; for all must admit that in early infancy they are not there, or, at least, that they do not appear. *No* one would expect to find in two infants—twin-brothers, we will suppose—creeping on the floor, with one apple between them, that there could be, at that age, any principles of right or justice, or of brotherly love existing in their hearts that could prevent their both crying and quarrelling for it. "True," says one; "but there are germs of those principles which, in time, will be developed." "No," rejoins another," there are no *germs* of them, there are only *capacities* for them, through which, by Divine power, the germs may hereafter be introduced." But when we reflect upon the difficulty of forming any clear and practical idea of the difference between a *germ*—in a bud upon an apple-tree, for instance—which may ultimately produce fruit, and a *capacity* for producing it which may subsequently be developed, and still more, how difficult is it to picture to our minds what is represented by these words in the case of a human soul, it would seem as if the apparent difference in people's opinions on such a point must be less a difference in respect to facts than in respect to the phraseology by which the facts should be represented.

And there would seem to be confirmation of this view in the fact that the great apparent difference among men in regard to their theoretical views of human nature does not seem to produce any marked difference in their action in practically dealing with it. Some parents, it is true, habitually treat their children with gentleness, kindness, and love; others are harsh and severe in all their intercourse with them. But we should find, on investigation, that such differences have very slight connection with the theoretical views of the nature of the human soul which the parents respectively entertain. Parents who in their theories seem to think the worst of the native tendencies of the human heart are often as kind and considerate and loving in their dealings with it as any; while no one would be at all surprised to find another, who is very firm in his belief in the native tendency of childhood to good, showing himself, in practically dealing with the actual conduct of children, fretful, impatient, complaining, and very ready to recognize, in fact, tendencies which in theory he seems to deny. And so, two bank directors, or members of the board of management of any industrial undertaking, when they meet in the street on Sunday, in returning from their respective places of public worship, if they fall into conversation on the moral nature of man, may find, or think they find, that they differ extremely in their views, and may even think each other bigoted or heretical, as the case may be; but yet the next day, when they meet at a session of their board, and come to the work of actually dealing with the conduct and the motives of men, they may find that there is *practically* no difference between them whatever. Or, if there should be any difference, such as would show itself in a greater readiness in one than in the other to place confidence in the promises or to confide in the integrity of men, the difference would, in general, have no perceptible relation whatever to the difference in the theological phraseology which they have been accustomed to hear and to assent to in their respective churches. All which seems to indicate, as has already been said, that the difference in question is rather apparent than real, and that it implies less actual disagreement about the facts of human nature than diversity in the phraseology by which the facts are represented.

Agency of the Divine Spirit.

It may, however, be said that in this respect, if not in any other, there is a radical difference among parents in respect to human nature, in relation to the religious education of children—namely, that some think that the implanting of the right principles of repentance for all wrong-doing, and sincere desires for the future to conform in all things to the will of God, and seek the happiness and welfare of men, can not come except by a special act of Divine intervention, and is utterly beyond the reach—in respect to any actual efficiency—of all human instrumentalities. This is no doubt true; but it is also no less true in respect to all the powers and capacities of the human soul, as well as to those pertaining to moral and religious duty. If the soul itself is the product of the creative agency of God, *all* its powers and faculties must be so, and, consequently, the development of them all—and there certainly can be no reason for making the sentiment of true and genuine piety an exception—must be the work of the same creative power.

But some one may say. There is, however, after all, a difference; for while we all admit that both the original entrance of the embryo soul into existence, and every step of its subsequent progress and development, including the coming into being and into action of all its various faculties and powers, are the work of the Supreme creative power, the commencement of the divine life in the soul is, in a *special and peculiar sense*, the work of the Divine hand.

And this also is doubtless true; at least, there is a certain important truth expressed in that statement. And yet when we attempt to picture to our minds two modes of Divine action, one of which is special and peculiar, and the other is not so, we are very likely to find ourselves bewildered and confused, and we soon perceive that in making such inquiries we are going out of our depth—or, in other words, are attempting to pass beyond the limits which mark the present boundaries of human knowledge.

In view of these thoughts and suggestions, in the truth of which it would seem that all reasonable persons must concur, we may reasonably conclude that all parents who are willing to look simply at the facts, and who are not too much trammelled by the forms of phraseology to which they are accustomed, must agree in admitting the substantial soundness of the following principles relating to the religious education of children.

Order of Development in respect to different Propensities and Powers.

1. We must not expect any perceptible awakening of the moral and religious sentiments too soon, nor feel discouraged and disheartened because they do not earlier appear; for, like all the other higher attributes of the soul, they pertain to a portion of the mental structure which is not early developed. It is the group of purely animal instincts that first show themselves in the young, and those even, as we see in the young of the lower animals, generally appear somewhat in the order in which they are required for the individual's good. Birds just hatched from the egg seem to have, for the first few days, only one instinct ready for action—that of opening their mouths wide at the approach of any thing towards their nest. Even this instinct is so imperfect and immature that it can not distinguish between the coming of their mother and the appearance of the face of a boy peering down upon them, or even the rustling of the leaves around them by a stick. In process of time, as their wings become formed, another instinct begins to appear—that of desiring to use the wings and come forth into the air. The development of this instinct and the growth of the wings advance together. Later still, when the proper period of maturity arrives, other instincts appear as they are required—such as the love of a mate, the desire to construct a nest, and the principle of maternal affection.

Now there is something analogous to this in the order of development to be observed in the progress of the human being through the period of infancy to that of maturity, and we must not look for the development of any power or susceptibility before its time, nor be too much troubled if we find that, in the first two or three years of life, the animal propensities —which are more advanced in respect to the organization which they depend upon—seem sometimes to overpower the higher sentiments and principles, which, so far as the capacity for them exists at all, must be yet in embryo. We must be willing to wait for each to be developed in its own appointed time.

Dependence upon Divine Aid.

2. Any one who is ready to feel and to acknowledge his dependence upon Divine aid for any thing whatever in the growth and preservation of his child, will surely be ready to do so in respect to the work of developing or awakening in his heart the principles of piety, since it must be admitted by all that the human soul is the highest of all the manifestations of Divine power, and that that portion of its structure on which the existence and exercise of the moral and religious sentiments depend is the crowning glory of it. It is right, therefore—I mean right, in the sense of being truly philosophical—that if the parent feels and acknowledges his dependence upon Divine power in any thing, he should specially feel and acknowledge it here; while there is nothing so well adapted as a deep sense of this dependence, and a devout and habitual recognition of it, and reliance upon it, to give earnestness and efficiency to his efforts, and to furnish a solid ground of hope that they will be crowded with success.

The Christian Paradox.

3. The great principle so plainly taught in the Sacred Scriptures—namely, that while we depend upon the exercise of Divine power for the success of all our efforts for our own spiritual improvement or that of others, just as if we could do nothing ourselves, we must do every thing that is possible ourselves, just us if nothing was to be expected from Divine power—may be called the Christian paradox. "Work out your own salvation with fear and trembling, for it is God that worketh in you both to will and to do." It would seem, it might be thought, much more logical to say, "Work out your own salvation, for there is nobody to help you;" or, "It is not necessary to make any effort yourselves, for it is God that worketh in you." It seems strange and paradoxical to say, "*Work out your own* salvation, *for* it is *God that worketh in you* both to will and to do."

But in this, as in all other paradoxes, the difficulty is in the explanation of the theory, and not in the practical working of it. There is in natural philosophy what is called the hydrostatic paradox, which consists in the fact that a small quantity of any liquid—as, for example, the coffee in the nose of the coffee-pot—will balance and sustain a very much larger quantity—as that contained in the body of it—so as to keep the surface of each at the same level. Young students involve themselves sometimes in hopeless entanglements among the steps of the mathematical demonstration showing how this can be, but no housekeeper ever meets with any practical difficulty in making her coffee rest quietly in its place on account of it. The Christian paradox, in the same way, gives rise to a great deal of metaphysical floundering and bewilderment among young theologians in their attempts to vindicate and explain it, but the humble-minded Christian parent finds no difficulty in practice. It comes very easy to him to do all he can, just as if every thing depended upon his efforts, and at the same time to cast all his care upon God, just as if there was nothing at all that he himself could do.

Means must be Right Means.

4. We are apt to imagine—or, at least, to act sometimes as if we imagined—that our dependence upon the Divine aid for what our Saviour, Jesus, designated as the new birth, makes some difference in the obligation on our part to employ such means as are naturally adapted to the end in view. If a gardener, for example, were to pour sand from his watering-pot upon his flowers, in time of drought, instead of water, he might make something like a plausible defense of his action, in reply to a remonstrance, thus: "*I* have no power to make the flowers grow and bloom. The secret processes on which the successful result depends are altogether beyond my reach, and in the hands of God, and he can just as easily bless one kind of instrumentality as another. I am bound to do something, it is true, for I must not be idle and inert; but God, if he chooses to do so, can easily bring out the flowers into beauty and bloom, however imperfect and ill-adapted the instrumentalities I use may be. He can as easily make use, for this purpose, of sand as of water."

Now, although there may be a certain plausibility in this reasoning, such conduct would appear to every one perfectly absurd; and yet many parents seem to act on a similar principle. A mother who is from time to time, during the week, fretful and impatient, evincing no sincere and hearty consideration for the feelings, still less for the substantial welfare and happiness, of those dependent upon her; who shows her insubmission to the will of God, by complaints and repinings at any thing untoward that befalls her; and who evinces a selfish love for her own gratification—her dresses, her personal pleasures, and her fashionable standing; and then, as a means of securing the salvation of her children, is very strict, when Sunday comes, in enforcing upon them the study of their Sunday lessons, or in requiring them to read good books, or in repressing on that day any undue exuberance of their spirits—relying upon the blessing of God upon her endeavors—will be very apt to find, in the end, that she has been watering her delicate flowers with sand.

The means which we use to awaken or impart the feelings of sorrow for sin, submission to God, and cordial good-will to man, in which all true piety consists, must be means that are *appropriate in themselves* to the accomplishment of the end intended. The appliance must be water, and not sand—or rather water *or* sand, with judgment, discrimination, and tact; for the gardener often finds that a judicious mixture of sand with the clayey and clammy soil about the roots of his plants is just what is required. The principle is, that the appliance must be an appropriate one —that is, one indicated by a wise consideration of the circumstances of the case, and of the natural characteristics of the infantile mind.

Power of Sympathy.

5. In respect to religious influence over the minds of children, as in all other departments of early training, the tendency to sympathetic action between the heart of the child and the parent is the great source of the parental influence and power. The principle, "Make a young person love you, and then simply *be* in his presence what you wish him to be," is the secret of success.

The tendency of young children to become what they see those around them whom they love are, seems to be altogether the most universally acting and the most powerful of the influences on which the formation of the character depends; and yet it is remarkable that we have no really appropriate name for it. We call it sometimes sympathy; but the word sympathy is associated more frequently in our minds with the idea of compassionate participation in the sufferings of those we love.

Sometimes we term it a spirit of imitation, but that phrase implies rather a conscious effort to *act* like those whom we love, than that involuntary tendency to *become* like them, which is the real character of the principle in question. The principle is in some respects like what is called *induction* in physical science, which denotes the tendency of a body, which is in any particular magnetic or electric condition, to produce the same condition, and the same direction of polarity, in any similar body placed near it. There is a sort of *moral induction*, which is not exactly sympathy, in the ordinary sense of that word, nor a desire of imitation, nor the power of example, but an immediate, spontaneous, and even unconscious tendency to *become what those around us are*. This tendency is very strong in the young while the opening faculties are in the course of formation and development, and it is immensely strengthened by the influence of love. Whatever, therefore, a mother wishes her child to be—whether a sincere, honest Christian, submissive to God's will and conscientious in the discharge of every duty, or proud, vain, deceitful, hypocritical, and pharisaical—she has only to be either the one or the other herself, and without any special teaching her child will be pretty sure to be a good copy of the model.

Theological Instruction.

6. If the principle above stated is correct, it helps to explain why so little good effect is ordinarily produced by what may be called instruction in theological truth on the minds of the young. Any system of theological truth consists of grand generalizations, which, like all other generalizations, are very interesting, and often very profitable, to mature minds, especially to minds of a certain class; but they are not appreciable by children, and can only in general be received by them as words to be fixed in the memory by rote. Particulars first, generalizations afterwards, is, or ought to be, the order of progress in all acquisition of knowledge. This certainly has been the course pursued by the Divine Spirit in the moral training of the human race. There is very little systematic theology in the Old Testament, and it requires a considerable degree of ingenuity to make out as much as the theologians desire to find even in the teachings of Jesus Christ. It is very well to exercise this ingenuity, and the systematic results which are to be obtained by it may be very

interesting, and very beneficial, to those whose minds are mature enough to enter into and appreciate them. But they are not adapted to the spiritual wants of children, and can only be received by them, if they are received at all, in a dry, formal, mechanical manner. Read, therefore, the stories in the Old Testament, or the parables and discourses of Jesus in the New, without attempting to draw many inferences from them in the way of theoretical belief, but simply to bring out to the mind and heart of the child the moral point intended in each particular case, and the heart of the child will be touched, and he will receive an *element* of instruction which he can arrange and group with others in theological generalization by-and-by, when his faculties have advanced to the generalizing stage.

No repulsive Personal Applications.

7. In reading the Scriptures, and, indeed, in all forms of giving religious counsel or instruction, we must generally beware of presenting the thoughts that we communicate in the form of reproachful personal application. There may be exceptions to this rule, but it is undoubtedly, in general, a sound one. For the work which we have to do, is not to attempt to drive the heart from the wrong to the right by any repellent action which the wrong may be made to exert, but to allure it by an attractive action with which the right may be invested. We must, therefore, present the incidents and instructions of the Word in their alluring aspect—assuming, in a great measure, that our little pupil will feel pleasure with us in the manifestations of the right, and will sympathize with us in disapproval of the wrong. To secure them to our side, in the views which we take, we must show a disposition to *take* them to it by an affectionate sympathy.

Our Saviour set us an excellent example of relying on the superior efficiency of the bond of sympathy and love in its power over the hearts of children, as compared with that of formal theological instruction, in the few glimpses which we have of his mode of dealing with them. When they brought little children to him, he did not begin to expound to them the principles of the government of God, or the theoretical aspects of the way of salvation; but took them *up in his arms and blessed them*, and called the attention of the by standers at the same time to qualities and characteristics which they possessed that he seemed to regard with special affection, and which others must imitate to be fit for the kingdom of God. Of course the children went away pleased and happy from such an interview, and would be made ready by it to receive gladly to their hearts any truths or sentiments which they might subsequently hear attributed to one who was so kind a friend to them.

If, however, instead of this, he had told them—no matter in what kind and gentle tones—that they had very wicked hearts, which must be changed before either God or any good man could truly love them, and that this change could only be produced by a power which they could only understand to be one external to themselves, and that they must earnestly pray for it every day, how different would have been the effect. They would have listened in mute distress, would have been glad to make their escape when the conversation was ended, and would shrink from ever seeing or hearing again one who placed himself in an attitude so uncongenial to them.

And yet all that might be true. They might have had yet only such appetites and propensities developed within them as would, if they continued to hold paramount control over them all their lives, make them selfish, unfeeling, and wicked men; and that they were, in a special though mysterious manner, dependent on the Divine power for bringing into action within them other and nobler principles. And so, if a physician were called in to see a sick child, he might see that it was in desperate danger, and that unless something could be done, and that speedily, to arrest the disease, his little patient would be dead in a few hours; and yet to say that to the poor child, and overwhelm it with terror and distress, would not be a very suitable course of procedure for averting the apprehended result.

Judge not, that ye be not judged.

8. And this leads us to reflect, in the eighth place, that we ought to be very careful, in our conversations with children, and especially in addresses made to them in the Sunday-school, or on any other occasion, not to say any thing to imply that we consider them yet unconverted

sinners. No one can possibly know at how early an age that great change which consists in the first faint enkindling of the Divine life in the soul may begin to take place, nor with what faults, and failings, and yieldings to the influence of the mere animal appetites and passions of childhood it may, for a time, co-exist. We should never, therefore, say any thing to children to imply that, in the great question of their relations to God and the Saviour, we take it for granted that they are on the wrong side. We can not possibly know on which side they really are, and we only dishearten and discourage them, and alienate their hearts from us, and tend to alienate them from all good, by seeming to take it for granted that, while *we* are on the right side, *they* are still upon the wrong. We should, in a word, say *we*, and not *you*, in addressing children on religious subjects, so as to imply that the truths and sentiments which we express are equally important and equally applicable to us as to them, and thus avoid creating that feeling of being judged and condemned beforehand, and without evidence, which is so apt to produce a broad though often invisible gulf of separation in heart between children, on the one hand, and ministers and members of the Church, on the other.

Promised Rewards and threatened Punishments.

9. It is necessary to be extremely moderate and cautious in employing the influence of promised rewards or threatened punishments as a means of promoting early piety. In a religious point of view, as in every other, goodness that is bought is only a pretense of goodness—that is, in reality it is no goodness at all; and as it is true that love casteth out fear, so it is also true that fear casteth out love. Suppose—though it is almost too violent a supposition to be made even for illustration's sake—that the whole Christian world could be suddenly led to believe that there was to be no happiness or suffering at all for them beyond the grave, and that the inducement to be grateful to God for his goodness and submissive to his will, and to be warmly interested in the welfare and happiness of man, were henceforth to rest on the intrinsic excellence of those principles, and to their constituting essentially the highest and noblest development of the moral and spiritual nature of man—how many of the professed disciples of Jesus would abandon their present devotion to the cause of love to God and love to man? Not one, except the hypocrites

and pretenders!

The truth is, that as piety that is genuine and sincere must rest on very different foundations from hope of future reward or fear of future punishment, so this hope and this fear are very unsuitable instrumentalities to be relied on for awakening it. The kind of gratitude to God which we wish to cherish in the mind of a child is not such as would be awakened towards an earthly benefactor by saying—in the case of a present made by an uncle, for instance—"Your uncle has made you a beautiful present. Go and thank him very cordially, and perhaps you will get another." It is rather of a kind which might be induced by saying, "Your uncle, who has been so kind to you in past years, is poor and sick, and can never do any thing more for you now. Would you like to go and sit in his sick-room to show your love for him, and to be ready to help him if he wants any thing?"

True piety, in a word, which consists in entering into and steadily maintaining the right moral and spiritual relations with God and man, marks the highest condition which the possibilities of human nature allow, and must rest in the soul which attains to it on a very different foundation from any thing like hope or fear. That there is a function which it is the province of these motives to fulfill, is abundantly proved by the use that is sometimes made of them in the Scriptures. But the more we reflect upon the subject, the more we shall be convinced, I think, that all such considerations ought to be kept very much in the back-ground in our dealings with children. If a child is sick, and is even likely to die, it is a very serious question whether any warning given to him of his danger will not operate as a hindrance rather than a help, in awakening those feelings which will constitute the best state of preparation for the change. For a sense of gratitude to God for his goodness, and to the Saviour for the sacrifice which he made for his sake, penitence for his sins, and trust in the forgiving mercy of his Maker, are the feelings to be awakened in his bosom; and these, so far as they exist, will lead him to lie quietly, calmly, and submissively in God's hands, without anxiety in respect to what is before him. It is a serious question whether an entire uncertainty as to the time when his death is to come is not more favorable to the awakening of these feelings, than the state of alarm and distress which would be excited by the thought that it was near.

The Reasonableness of Gentle Measures in Religious Training.

The mother may sometimes derive from certain religious considerations the idea that she is bound to look upon the moral delinquencies and dangers which she observes in her children, under an aspect more stern and severe than seems to be here recommended. But a little reflection must convince us that the way to true repentance of, and turning from sin, is not necessarily through the suffering of terror and distress. The Gospel is not an instrumentality for producing terror and distress, even as means to an end. It is an instrumentality for saving us from these ills; and the Divine Spirit, in the hidden and mysterious influence which it exercises in forming, or transforming, the human soul into the image of God, must be as ready, it would seem, to sanction and bless efforts made by a mother to allure her child away from its sins by loving and gentle invitations and encouragements, as any attempts to drive her from them by the agency of terror or pain. It would seem that no one who remembers the way in which Jesus Christ dealt with the children that were brought to him could possibly have any doubt of this.

CHAPTER XXIV.

CONCLUSION.

Any person who has acquired the art of examining and analyzing his own thoughts will generally find that the mental pictures which he forms of the landscapes, or the interiors, in which the scenes are laid of the events or incidents related in any work of fiction which interests him, are modelled more or less closely from prototypes previously existing in his own mind, and generally upon those furnished by the experiences of his childhood. If, for example, he reads an account of transactions represented as taking place in an English palace or castle, he will usually, on a careful scrutiny, find that the basis of his conception of the scene is derived from the arrangement of the rooms of some fine house with which he was familiar in early life. Thus, a great many things which attract our attention, and impress themselves upon our memories in childhood, become the models and prototypes—more or less aggrandized and improved, perhaps—of the conceptions and images which we form in later years.

Nature of the Effect produced by Early Impressions.

Few persons who have not specially reflected on this subject, or examined closely the operations of their own minds, are aware what an extended influence the images thus stored in the mind in childhood have in forming the basis, or furnishing the elements of the mental structures of future life. But the truth, when once understood, shows of what vast importance it is with what images the youthful mind is to be stored. A child who ascends a lofty mountain, under favorable circumstances in his childhood, has his conceptions of all the mountain scenery that he reads of, or hears of through life, modified and aggrandized by the impression made upon his sensorium at this early stage. Take your daughter, who has always, we will suppose, lived in the country, on an excursion with you to the sea-shore, and allow her to witness for an hour, as she sits in silence on the cliff, the surf rolling in incessantly upon the beach, and infinitely the smallest part of the effect is the day's gratification which you have given her. That is comparatively nothing. You have made a life-long change, if not in the very structure, at least in the permanent furnishing of her mind, and performed a work that can never by any possibility be undone. The images which have been awakened in her mind, the emotions connected with them, and the effect of these images and emotions upon her faculties of imagination and conception, will infuse a life into them which will make her, in respect to this aspect of her spiritual nature, a different being as long as she lives.

The Nature and Origin of general Ideas.

It is the same substantially in respect to all those abstract and general ideas on moral or other kindred subjects which constitute the mental furnishing of the adult man, and have so great an influence in the formation of his habits of thought and of his character. They are chiefly formed from combinations of the impressions made in childhood. A person's idea of justice, for instance, or of goodness, is a generalization of the various instances of justice or goodness which ever came to his knowledge; and of course, among the materials of this generalization those instances that were brought to his mind during the impressible years of childhood must have taken a very prominent part. Every story, therefore, which you relate to a child to exemplify the principles of justice or goodness takes its place, or, rather, the impression which it makes takes its place, as one of the elements out of which the ideas that are to govern his future life are formed.

Vast Importance and Influence of this mental Furnishing,

For the ideas and generalizations thus mainly formed from the images and impressions received in childhood become, in later years, the elements of the machinery, so to speak, by which all his mental operations are performed. Thus they seem to constitute more than the mere furniture of the mind; they form, as it were, almost a part of the structure itself. So true, indeed, is this, and so engrossing a part does what remains in the mind of former impressions play in its subsequent action, that some philosophers have maintained that the whole of the actual consciousness of man consists only in the *resultant* of all these impressions preserved more or less imperfectly by the memory, and made to mingle together in one infinitely complicated but harmonious whole. Without going to any such extreme as this, we can easily see, on reflection, how vast an influence on the ideas and conceptions, as well as on the principles of action in mature years, must be exerted by the nature and character of the images which the period of infancy and childhood impresses upon the mind. All parents should, therefore, feel that it is not merely the present welfare and happiness of their child that is concerned in their securing to him a tranquil and happy childhood, but that his capacity for enjoyment through life is greatly dependent upon it. They are, in a very important sense, intrusted with the work of building up the structure of his soul for all time, and it is incumbent upon them, with reference to the future as well as to the present, to be very careful what materials they allow to go into the work, as well as in what manner they lay them.

Among the other bearings of this thought, it gives great weight to the importance of employing gentle measures in the management and training of the young, provided that such measures can be made effectual in the accomplishment of the end. The pain produced by an act of hasty and angry violence to which a father subjects his son may soon pass away, but the memory of it does not pass away with the pain. Even the remembrance of it may at length fade from the mind, but there is still an *effect* which does not pass away with the remembrance. Every strong impression which you make upon his perceptive powers must have a very lasting influence, and even the impression itself may, in some cases, be forever indelible.

Let us, then, take care that these impressions shall be, as far as possible, such as shall be sources of enjoyment for them in future years. It is true that we *must* govern them. They are committed to our charge during the long time which is required for the gradual unfolding of their embryo powers for the express purpose that during that interval they may be guided by our reason, and not by their own. We can not surrender this trust. But there is a way of faithfully fulfilling the duties of it—if we have discernment to see it, and skill to follow it—which will make the years of their childhood years of tranquillity and happiness, both to ourselves and to them.

THE END.